Consumer Culture

Consumer Culture

Celia Lury

Rutgers University Press
New Brunswick, New Jersey

The right of Celia Lury to be identified as author of this work has been asserted in accordance with the Copyright, Designs and Patents Act 1988.

First published in the United Kingdom in 1996 by Polity Press in association with Blackwell Publishers Ltd and in the United States by Rutgers University Press.

ISBN 0-8135-2328-1
ISBN 0-8135-2329-X (pbk.)

A CIP catalogue record for this book is available from the Library of Congress.

Typeset in 10.5 on 12pt Plantin
by Wearset, Boldon, Tyne and Wear
Printed in Great Britain by Hartnolls Ltd, Bodmin, Cornwall

This book is printed on acid-free paper.

Contents

Acknowledgements

I would like to offer my thanks to Nicholas Abercrombie and Brian Longhurst for the thoughtfulness and good humour they showed in the meetings in which we discussed popular music, television and consumer culture, and to Beverley Skeggs for sharing with me her ideas on class and consumer culture. I would also like to thank Stephen Pope for taking many of the photographs that accompany the text – they tell their own story about consumer culture. And of course many other people have shared this project with me – Lisa Adkins, Mary Cutler, Sarah Franklin, Marci Green, Liz Greenhalgh, Scott Lash, Lynne Pearce, Jackie Stacey, John Urry, Alan Warde, Alison Young, and an anonymous reviewer: to them, too, I offer my thanks. But perhaps, a special word of appreciation should go to my family – my brothers, Adam and Giles, who are themselves 'captains of consciousness'; my sister, Karen, a favourite companion in the study of consumer culture; and my mother, who is the sharpest critic of us all. And a big thankyou to Pam Thomas and Lin Lucas at Polity for their hard work and enthusiasm.

The author and publishers wish to thank Stephen Pope for the photographic work he carried out for this book. They also wish to thank the following for permission to use copyright material:

Benetton for permission to reproduce the front cover of the catalogue, Spring/Summer Collection 1993. Citizen UK and DMB&B London for permission to use the advertisements 'Time well spent' for Citizen watches. Douglas Coupland and Little, Brown and Company (UK) for 'Numbers' in *Generation X* by Douglas Coupland, Abacus, 1992. *The Economist* for 'Cher luxury', 24 September 1994. Copyright *The Economist*. *Elle* (UK) for 'Bombay Mix' November 1994 and 'Orient Express' *Elle* November 1994. *Guardian Weekly* for 'Hog for you baby' by Olly Duke; 'Branding iron still hot' by Roger Cowe; 'Close shave cuts dash in condom campaign' by Angella Johnson; 'Compulsive shopping "real illness"' by Chris Mihill and 'No more mail shots in the dark' by Emily Bell. Copyright *Guardian Weekly*. Habitat UK for permission to reproduce illustrations from the Habitat catalogue Autumn/Winter, 1994. *The Independent* for ' "Waste not, want not" is the word' by David Nicholson-Lord, 2.10.94; 'In praise of paper lampshades and jumbo floor cushions' by Jonathan Glancey; 'What should I collect' by John Windsor. Copyright *The Independent. Marie Claire* and David Downton for the 'Making the most of what you've got', October 1994. Copyright for text, Charlotte-Anne Fidler/Marie Claire/Robert Harding Syndication. Copyright for illustration, David Downton. *The Observer* for 'Young grufties find solace in shadow of suicide' by Nick Thorpe, 23.10.94; 'In the pink of plastic health at 35' by Charlotte Eagar, 30.10.94; 'Nike town, Chicago's sporting pantheon' by Ruth Shurman, 10.10.94; and 'Worldly goods' by Elspeth Thompson, 6.11.94. Copyright, *The Observer.* D. Wynne and J. O'Connor to reproduce Figures 4.1–4.5 from 'Tourists, hamburgers and street musicians' in R. Reichardt and G. Muskins, eds, *Post-Communism, the Market and the Arts*, Peter Lang. Open University Press for table of statistics on young people and cultural activities from *Common Culture* by Paul Willis, Open University Press, 1990. Publicis for permission to reproduce the Perrier 'Afreau' advertisement. Routledge and M. Savage *et al.* for permission to reproduce Tables 4.1–4.3 from *Property, Bureaucracy and Culture: Middle-Class Formation in Contemporary Britain*, 1992. Stroh International for permission to reproduce the Schlitz Beer advertisement featuring Lisa Bonet. Trademark, Stroh Brewery Company of Michigan, USA – European Director Patrick Delafield.

Every effort has been made to trace all copyright holders. However, if any have been inadvertently overlooked, the publishers will be pleased to make the necessary arrangements at the first opportunity.

1

Introduction: The Stuff of Material Culture

One of the most important ways in which people relate to each other socially is through the mediation of things. *Material culture* is the name given to the study of these person–thing relationships; it is the study of things- or objects-in-use. The first half of the term points to the significance of the use of physical objects in everyday practices and beliefs, while the second half indicates that this attention to the materials of everyday life is not at the expense of a concern with the meaningful, the symbolic or the moral. The term 'material culture' is useful, then, because it implies that the material and the cultural are always combined in specific relationships and that these relationships can be subjected to study. The thesis that will be put forward here is that consumer culture is a particular form of material culture that has emerged in Euro-American societies during the second half of the twentieth century.

To see consumer culture as a specific form of material culture is helpful because it gives a critical distance from everyday understandings of consumption, shifting attention away from the use of things in the sense of consuming or 'using up', to 'use' in a more general sense. (The *Pocket Oxford Dictionary* defines 'consume' as 'make away with, use up, devour, eat or drink up'; this definition and the use of the word in phrases such as 'being consumed by envy, greed, desire' reveals some of the anxieties that are attached to consumption in Euro-American societies; for a discussion of the etymology of 'consumption' see Williams 1983). As the following chapters will show, the use or appropriation of an object is more often than not both a moment of consumption *and* production, of undoing *and* doing, of destruction *and* construction.

Take the example of the so-called consumption of things in housework. From one point of view, the task of cooking a family meal can be seen as an instance of destruction – the using up of objects and services produced by others for exchange on the market, but from another it is construction – the making of new objects and services for the use of others in the family. So, while the creation and manipulation of things in order that they may be exchanged on

the market is frequently described as production and the activities that follow their purchase are typically described as consumption, the identification of consumer culture as a specific form of material culture helps ensure that it is studied in relation to interlinking *cycles* of production and consumption or reappropriation. The consumption that is referenced via consumer culture can, through the lens of material culture, be seen as *conversion*, or, more precisely, 'the manner in which people convert things to ends of their own' (Strathern 1994: p. x).

This understanding is especially useful since there is a tendency for consumption to be understood as the completion of a process of production for the market, and thus for consumption to be seen as secondary, responsive or derivative. Moreover, the process of production for the market is often taken to be the sole economic system in operation in Euro-American societies, not only in commonsense understandings but also in the social sciences; the significance of other systems of exchange, or cycles of production and consumption, in the state, the family and communities of one kind or another tends to be played down.

This privileging of production for the market typically relies upon a number of unfounded assumptions. There is, for example, the assumption that what distinguishes so-called modern from pre-modern societies is the determining force of the economic – specifically, in the form of production of goods for the market. However, this assumption misrepresents both pre-modern and modern societies: it plays down the significance of economic activities in pre-modern societies and exaggerates their significance in modern societies, marginalizing the importance of other kinds of exchange. In contrast, the use of the term material culture enables possible continuities between (so-called) pre-modern and modern societies to be investigated, without either assuming a radical change or making assumptions about what counts as 'modern'. It thus holds open the question of historical periodization, and invites a flexible approach to the study of social change. It also enables multiple cycles of production and consumption to be investigated, without presuming the dominance of one above others, while recognizing that they will be interrelated in changing ways over time and space.

With these points in mind, the principal concern of this book is to identify what is distinctive about consumer culture as a specific form of material culture in contemporary Euro-American societies. The thesis put forward is that *a process of stylization is what best defines consumer culture*. As chapters 2 and 3 will demonstrate, however, there are a number of different explanations of this process. Reviewing these accounts, it is possible to identify the following four factors as those commonly held to be especially important in shaping the stylization of contemporary consumer culture:

1   The importance of the circulation of *commodities*, that is, things appropriated or produced for exchange on the market within a capitalist division of labour.

2   *Changes in the interrelationship of different systems of production and consumption or regimes of value*, and the multiplication of relatively independent sites for the use of things. These changes are seen to have created a situation in which the activities of the users of commodities and other things are linked through a whole set of inter-related cycles of production and consumption, associated with, but not determined by, the industrial division of labour and economic exchange on the market.

3   The relative *independence of practices of consumption from those of production*, and the growing power and authority that this gives (at least some) consumers.

4   *The special importance given to the consumption or use of cultural objects or goods* in contemporary societies by specific social groups or cultural intermediaries.

Chapters 2 and 3 introduce a number of explanations of the increase in consumer demand and the emergence of contemporary consumer culture, each of which gives a different emphasis to these factors. A comparison will be drawn between *producer-led explanations* (dominated by proponents of 1, although also including some recognitions of 3) and *consumer-led explanations* (typically based on a combination of 2 and 3). In making the comparison (which, somewhat artificially, opposes the two types of explanation), the importance of the use of cultural goods (that is, 4) in both kinds of explanation will be emphasized by drawing attention to the *art-culture system*. This will provide the basis for a more detailed description of the stylization of consumption. In chapters 4–7 the role of different social groups in the emergence of consumer culture will be investigated, with special attention paid to their use of cultural goods. On this basis, the final chapter will explore the implications of consumer culture for contemporary understandings of the self, for people's sense of social belonging and for politics.

It is important to point out here that this book is about consumer culture, not modern consumption as such. Its focus is thus necessarily on the relationship between the material and the cultural, on the culture of things-in-use; it does not seek to offer a review of current debates on the relationship between ownership of material goods or things, economic status and inequality. However, this literature is important in so far as it shows that a significant proportion of the populations of Euro-American societies are *dispossessed*, that is, they are excluded from many forms of consumption as they do not have access to the economic resources necessary for participation. As Zygmunt Bauman points out,

> All commodities have a price-tag attached to them. These tags select the pool of potential customers. They do not directly determine the decisions the consumers will eventually make; those remain free. But they draw the boundary between the realistic and the feasible; the boundary which a given consumer cannot overstep. Behind the ostensible equality of chances the market promotes and advertises hides the practical inequality of consumers – that is, the sharply differentiated degrees of practical freedom of choice. (1990: 211)

Deprivation in contemporary Britain is widespread and institutionalized; it extends throughout the bottom half of society, becoming particularly acute in the bottom 30–40 per cent. A recent study of the extent of poverty in Britain shows that: nearly 3.5 million people do not have consumer durables such as carpets, a washing machine or a fridge because of lack of money; around 3 million people cannot afford celebrations at Christmas or presents for the family once a year; and nearly half a million children do not have three meals a day because their parents are so short of money (Mack and Lansley 1985: 90). Clearly, poverty places severe limits on the ability to exercise choice; as such, it is a fundamental index of the ability to participate in consumption. Is it also an index of the ability to participate in consumer culture?

An interviewee from the study just mentioned asks:

> A standard of living surely should give you the benefit of making a choice of whether you have a piece of beef or a small chop. A piece of beef would last you two or three days where a chop would last you one. Surely living standards should be able to give you the choice of being able to buy a small joint? (Quoted in Mack and Lansley 1985: 132–3)

The study shows that the answer the interviewee gives to her own question – 'You can't do it' – is the only possible answer for those living on the minimum income provided by the state. In this sense, then, it is clear that economic status sets certain limits to an individual's participation in consumption or their practical freedom to exercise choice. However, it is also important not to jump to conclusions about the nature of the relationship between economic status and participation in consumer culture, nor to assume that there is a direct or straightforward relationship between poverty and exclusion from consumer culture or wealth and inclusion.

Studies on poverty have shown that the relationships between economic wealth and participation in material culture are highly complex and historically variable; there are no direct relationships between an individual's economic standing, and their ownership of goods, perception of which goods count as necessities or luxuries, understandings of needs or wants, their tastes, or their sense of style. As Bauman points out, consumer inequality is felt

> as an oppression and a stimulus at the same time. It generates the painful experience of deprivation, with . . . morbid consequences for self-esteem . . . It also triggers off zealous efforts to enhance one's consumer capacity – efforts that secure an unabating demand for market offers. (1990: 211)

While poverty restricts the possibility of participating in consumption, it does not necessarily prevent – indeed, it may incite – participation in consumer culture.

Moreover, as the four factors listed above indicate, while the general increase in the circulation and ownership of commodities is one criterion of the growth of consumer culture, a special importance is also attached to the use (and it is important to note that this may or may not include ownership) of cultural goods in the development of consumer culture. While economic status provides an indicator of likely ownership of goods or possessions in general, it is not as good an indicator of the use of cultural goods. Moreover, as later chapters will show, certain groups have had much greater impact than others in determining the contours of contemporary consumer culture as a consequence of their ability to influence developments in fashion, style, art and culture; these groups – described here as cultural intermediaries – are not necessarily those with economic wealth.

A further point to be noted here is that the dominance of a culture in a society does not require all that society's members to be able to participate in that culture on the same terms. Indeed, a culture may be dominant even if most people can only aspire to participate in it: its dominance is felt to the extent that people's aspirations, their hopes and fears, vocabulary of motives and sense of self are defined in its terms. All these points suggest that while it is important to recognize that the terms of participation in consumer culture are profoundly unequal, these terms are not directly tied (although they may be indirectly related) to economic inequality, but are peculiar to the culture itself. Indeed, a further thesis that this book seeks to address is that one of the distinctive features of consumer culture is the inequality it produces in the individual's relation to his or her self, sense of agency and mode of belonging to social groupings. It further argues that consumer culture emerges in response to 'tournaments of value' (Appadurai 1986) in which the politics of this inequality are contested.

In general terms, modern Euro-American societies are characterized by the strongly rooted belief that *to have is to be* (Dittmar 1992); this is related to the privileging of a relationship between individuals and things in terms of *possession*. The emergence and growth of this preference is tied up with the rise of individualism and mass consumer society, which are seen to have led people to define themselves and others in terms of the things they possess. Indeed, most people describe possessions as aspects of the self, and their loss is experienced as a personal violation and a lessening of the self. It is in this context that possessions have come to serve as key symbols for personal qualities, attachments and interests. Helga Dittmar sums up this view thus:

in Western materialistic societies . . . an individual's identity is influenced by the symbolic meanings of his or her own material possessions, and the way in which s/he relates to those possessions. Material possessions also serve as expressions of group membership and as means of locating others in the social–material environment. Moreover, material possessions provide people with information about other people's identities. (1992: 205)

It will be suggested, in the final chapter of this book, that, in an extension of this way of thinking about identity, consumer culture provides the conditions within which it is not just that self-identity is understood *in relation to* possessions, but that it is itself constituted *as* a possession.

Consumer culture has thus contributed to the development of what is sometimes called the possessive individual (Macpherson 1962; Abercrombie, Hill and Turner 1986; Clifford 1988; Pateman 1988), that is, it has contributed to, and revised, a notion of the ideal individual as an owner, not only of accumulated property and goods, but also of his or her self. More specifically, it will be argued that consumer culture is a source of the contemporary belief that self-identity is a kind of cultural resource, asset or possession. However, given the different position of different social groupings in relation to the emergence of consumer culture, chapter 8 will put forward the view that this resource is not equally available to all. It is in this sense, that consumer culture can be seen to provide the conditions for a politics of identity.

A related theme is that consumer culture has contributed to an increasingly *reflexive* relation to self-identity through its provision of a series of expert knowledges – for example, in relation to lifestyle, taste, health, fashion and beauty – which the individual may use to

enhance his or her self-identity. This reflexive relation to the self can be understood in terms of a reflection upon the process of self-fashioning. This reflection is informed by technical, social and aesthetic knowledges, perhaps especially the latter.

It thus encourages a link between aesthetics and ethics in everyday life.

A number of these expert knowledges – which have grown in importance as the distances from one another of producers, traders and consumers have increased – are to be found in the invitations, prescriptions and advice of popular culture, the media and education. These agencies are often in conflict with one another, as different social groups work through them to define their interests; indeed, a sub-theme of the book is how the advice emanating from these different sources can itself be seen as part of a competitive game between these groups as to how aesthetics, ethics and politics are to be brought together in contemporary society.

This raises an issue about how this book itself and its illustrations and extracts, variously drawn from the media, popular culture and other academic writings, is to be used or consumed. At times, the illustrations may seem to support the argument being developed in the text; at other times, they may contradict it; at others still, they may offer an ironic commentary on either the tone or the substance of the argument that the main text seeks to develop. One of the aims in including extracts and illustrations from the media and advertising is precisely to show the extent to which there is disagreement amongst 'experts' as to what the political or ethical implications of consumer culture may be. If the thesis the book develops is accurate, you, the reader, will be engaged in a process of reflexive self-fashioning in which your self-conscious relation to this expert

knowledge – academic, journalistic, commercial – will both provide you with a way of evaluating objects and offer others a way of evaluating you. At the same time, though, the book is not intended (only) as an advice manual, catalogue or guide to etiquette; it is concerned with knowledge not as 'issue-bound instruction' but as 'illumination' (Bauman 1992b: 22).

2

Material Culture and Consumer Culture

Introduction

It was suggested in chapter 1 that consumer culture can be seen as a specific form of material culture – the culture of things-in-use – in contemporary Euro-American societies. This chapter will start by introducing general accounts of material culture before moving on to identify some of the main features which distinguish consumer culture as a specific form of material culture. The aim is to demonstrate both the general principle that the circulation of things and culture are inextricably interconnected in society, and that the nature of these interconnections is both complex and historically changing.

Social lives have things

An influential example of the anthropological study of material culture is provided by Mary Douglas and Baron Isherwood (1979). For Douglas and Isherwood, an anthropologist and an economist respectively, consumption as it occurs in all societies is 'beyond commerce', that is, it is not restricted to commerce, but is always a cultural as well as an economic phenomenon. It is to do with meaning, value and communication as much as it is to do with exchange, price and economic relations. They suggest that the utility of goods is always framed by a cultural context, that even the use of the most

mundane objects in daily life has cultural meaning. From this perspective, material goods are not only used to do things, but they also have a meaning, and act as meaningful markers of social relations; indeed, part of their usefulness is that they are full of meaning. *It is in acquiring, using and exchanging things that individuals come to have social lives.*

Douglas and Isherwood suggest that it should be standard practice to assume that all material possessions carry meanings and to analyse their use as communicators. This practice, they believe, should apply both to so-called traditional *and* to modern societies. Indeed, Douglas and Isherwood suggest that the application of this approach reveals that there are similarities in the ways in which all societies – traditional and modern – make meaning through the use of material goods. They seek to demonstrate this by showing the significance of goods in ritual.

Rituals, in the anthropological sense, give shape and substance to social relations; they fix or anchor social relationships, making sense of the flux of events and containing the drift of meaning. They are a kind of ballast against cultural drift; as such, they are a fundamental component of all societies. While ritual can take a verbal form, as in greetings or prayers, it is more effective, Douglas and Isherwood argue, when it is tied to material things, for goods 'are the visible part of culture' (1979: 66). From this perspective, the use of material things – consumption – is a key aspect of ritual processes.

Some examples of the use of consumer goods in ritual processes in contemporary society are provided by McCracken (1988). He identifies a number of examples of such rituals, including possession, gift and divestment rituals.

1   'Possession rituals' is the term used by McCracken to refer to rituals involving the collecting, cleaning, comparing, showing off and even photographing of possessions – in, for example, the creation and display of a collection of Elvis memorabilia, or the decoration of a bedroom with posters. These rituals allow the owner to lay claim to a kind of personal possession of the meaning of an object which is beyond simple ownership. They are a way of personalizing the object, a way of transferring meaning from the individual's own world to the newly obtained good, and are the means by which an anonymous object – often the product of a distant, impersonal process of mass manufacture – is turned into a possession that belongs to someone and speaks to and for him or her. Possession, in this view, is not a static state, but an activity. Through possession rit-

uals, individuals create a personal world of goods which reflects their experience, concepts of self and the world. Such rituals help establish an individual's *social identity*. And it is in rituals such as these that the performative capacity of goods is made visible; through performance, objects express certain aspects of a person's identity.

2 Gift rituals, especially those of birthday and Christmas, typically involve the choice and presentation of consumer goods by one person and their receipt by another. This movement of goods is also a movement of meanings. Often the gift-giver chooses a particular gift because its possesses the meaningful properties he or she wishes to see transferred to the gift-receiver. So, for instance, a woman who receives a dress is invited to define herself in terms of its style; the giver of flowers or chocolates may be asking the receiver to show properties of gentleness, or sweetness. In the same way, many of the gifts that are given by parents to children are motivated by a desire to transfer meanings as well as material possessions. From this point of view, the giving of objects on ritual occasions – birthdays, anniversaries, special occasions such as Valentine's Day – can be seen as a powerful means of interpersonal communication or influence.

3 Divestment rituals are employed to empty a good of meaning when it is transferred from one person to another. They are employed for two purposes. When an individual purchases a good that has been previously owned, such as a house or a car, the ritual is used to erase the meaning associated with the previous owner. The cleaning and redecorating of a newly purchased house, for example, may be seen as an attempt to remove the meanings associated with the previous owner. A second kind of divestment ritual takes place when an individual is about to dispense with a good, either by giving it away or selling it. An attempt will be made to erase the meaning that has been invested in the good by association. What such rituals suggest is a concern that the meaning of goods can be transferred, obscured or confused, or even lost when goods change hands. McCracken suggests that the fear of dispossession of personal meaning resembles the fear of 'merging of identities' that sometimes occurs between transplant donors and recipients. In order to counteract this fear, the good is emptied of meaning in a divestment ritual before being passed along. What looks like superstition is an implicit acknowledgement of the *movable* quality of the meaning with which goods are invested, and of their significance in a system of symbolic exchange.

As a consequence of their use in ritual processes, goods are a means of making visible and stable the basic categories by which we classify people in society. Goods thus act as sources of social identity and bearers of social meaning. They are capable of creating or enacting cultural assumptions and beliefs; they give such beliefs a reality, a facticity, what Douglas and Isherwood would call a concreteness, that they would not otherwise have. They have the effect of stabilizing human life.

What this discussion of the use of goods in rituals illustrates is that goods can act as markers or performers of social identity and carriers of interpersonal influence, and that their meaning is movable, that is, that it may be changed as goods circulate. Putting these together suggests that the movement of goods can be seen as part of *a system of symbolic exchange*. A question that arises here, then, is how that system – or systems – of exchange operate.

In general terms, for Douglas and Isherwood, the process of making goods meaningful in ritual is primarily *consensual*. It results from the active participation of everyone in a particular culture in a process of making meaning:

> Goods are endowed with value by the meaning of fellow consumers . . . Each person is a source of judgements and a subject of judgements; each individual is in the classification scheme whose discriminations he is helping to establish. . . . The kind of world they create together is constructed from commodities that are chosen for their fitness to mark the events, such as birthdays, weddings and funerals, in an appropriately graded scale. (1979:75)

Douglas and Isherwood also suggest that individuals will strive to put themselves in a position from which they might gain not just access to but control of cultural meanings, and that individuals will adopt strategies to make sure that they are not marginalized by the system. However, they do not focus on the relationship between symbolic exchange and social inequality, and do not investigate the ways in which material culture may help create or consolidate inequality in any detail. They thus put forward a rather static account of the operation of power and conflict in this system. Others would suggest that there are enormous differences in the way that symbolic exchange and social inequality are related in different societies.

Nor do Douglas and Isherwood really consider how modern systems of production, publicity, and communication, such as television, films, newspapers or advertising, may affect individuals' participation in this process of making judgements and being judged. All goods are simply treated as 'a non-verbal medium for the human creative faculty' (1979: 62). Some would say that in adopting this approach Douglas and Isherwood end up accepting the advertising industry's view of itself as doing no more than help-ing free, creative consumers to make their own meanings, and that they fail to deal adequately with issues of symbolic power and con-trol. As this chapter will go on to suggest, other writers believe that a distinctive feature of contemporary material culture is the extent to which the complex cultural dimensions of the contemporary economy have acquired an autonomy such that they can be distin-guished as a discrete culture with its own rules and practices.

To sum up, Douglas and Isherwood suggest that it is possible to see continuities in the ways in which individuals make social mean-ings through their use of material goods in traditional and modern societies. Indeed, they suggest that there is nothing especially dis-tinctive about the expressive use of material goods in modern soci-eties. This argument is important in so far as it points to continuities between traditional and modern societies; in doing so, it challenges the often exaggerated differences between them. It restores the 'cultural dimension to societies that are often represent-ed simply as economies writ large, and restores the calculative dimension to societies that are too often simply portrayed as solidar-ity writ small' (Appadurai 1986: 12). It points to ways in which what Clifford calls 'some sort of "gathering" around the self and the group – the assemblage of the material world, the marking-off of a subjective domain that is not "other"' is a pervasive feature of most, if not all societies (1988: 218). However, in its emphasis on the often apparently timeless nature of ritual, it ignores contrasts between different worlds of things and the social lives they make possible.

Marshall Sahlins puts forward a similar anthropological approach to material culture, focusing once again on the moment of use, rela-tively isolated from the cycle of production, distribution, use and reproduction. However, where Douglas and Isherwood draw on the concept of ritual, Sahlins (1976) draws on the anthropological con-cept of totemism to develop an analysis of consumption – especially of food and clothing – in modern Western societies.

Totemism is the symbolic association of plants, animals or objects with individuals or groups of people, and is a characteristic feature of traditional societies. In one of the most well known analy-ses of totemism, Lévi-Strauss (1964) argues that it is a common process in which the natural world is divided into different groups of species and things in ways which reflect and create social differ-ences. He argues that the term totemism covers relations, posed ideologically between two series, one *natural* the other *cultural*; that is, a natural object comes to stand for, or be the symbolic representation of, a tribe or a social group. That tribe is recognized by its use of the object and its members' shared appreciation of what the object stands for. The object is thus simultaneously a natural and a cultural object; its meaning is closely tied to the ways in which it acts as a means of communicating the social hierarchies of the group for whom it has cultural significance.

Sahlins extends this argument, applying it to modern societies. He argues that modern societies have substituted manufactured objects for species or natural objects. In other words, manufactured objects act as totems in the modern world; and consumer groups are like tribes in traditional societies. Sahlins shows, for example, how items of clothing can act as totems, communicating distinct social identities and identifying different 'tribes'. He sees our clothing system not simply as a set of material objects to keep its wearers warm, but as a symbolic code by which its wearers communicate their membership of social groups. So, for example, the clothing that shows a distinction between men and women or between upper and lower classes also shows something of the nature of the difference that is supposed to exist between them. It communicates the supposed 'delicacy' of women and the supposed 'strength' of men, the supposed 'refinement' of the upper classes and the supposed 'vulgarity' of the lower classes. Clothing can thus be seen to communicate the properties that are supposed to inhere in each of these categories and that serve as the basis for their discrimination.

Another example of this kind of anthropological analysis is to be found in Paul Willis's study of a motorbike club (1982). In the conclusion to this study, Willis suggests that the motorbike acted as a kind of totem for the group of young men who belonged to the club. Their dress, their appearance and their values were all linked to their use and understanding of the motorbike, and in that way the motorbike marked them out from other groups. The motorbike was not simply appreciated for its ability to get someone from A to B, that is, for its utility as a means of transport, but as a totem of a certain kind of working-class masculinity; it was part of a symbolic code.

> The motorcycle boys accepted the motorbike and allowed it to reverberate right through into the world of human concourse. . . . The lack of the helmet allowed long hair to flow freely back in the wind, and this, with the studded and ornamented jackets, and the aggressive style of riding, gave the motorbike boys a fearsome look which amplified the wildness, noise, surprise and intimidation of the motorbike. . . . The motorbikes themselves were modified to accentuate these features. The high cattle-horn handlebars, the chromium-plated mudguards gave the bikes an exaggerated look of fierce power. . . . The ensemble of bike, noise, rider, clothes, *on the move* gave formidable expression of identity to the culture and powerfully developed many of its central values. (1982: 297–9)

The bikers did not value clothing which protected the wearer from the elements, or deliberately streamlined clothing. Instead, they preferred loose clothing that blew in the wind and allowed them to feel the excitement of travelling, even though this reduced their speed. Similarly, they customized their bikes by giving them high handlebars which meant that they were forced to sit upright. Once again, this restricted the speed they were able to travel at, but gave them a frightening appearance. In other words, the relation of these young men to the motorbike was not a functional or instrumental one, but one which allowed them to display a particular set of values, in this case, those associated with a working-class masculinity.

At the same time, an individual member's relation to the use of the motorbike provided the basis for hierarchies within the group. So, for example, members who, while technically very skilled mechanics, were very cautious riders were placed low on this internal hierarchy, while members who risked life and limb were rated highly by other members irrespective of their mechanical skills. Members who died in accidents were ritually mourned, and were accorded the status of heroes. In this way, members' relations to each other were mediated through a particular understanding of the bike as a totem of working-class masculinity.

This kind of analysis, once again, is drawing parallels between the use of goods in traditional and modern societies. However, while Sahlins, like Douglas and Isherwood, points to similarities in the use of material goods as totems in traditional and modern societies, he also identifies some differences. He writes:

> The object stands as a human concept outside itself, as man speaking to man through the medium of things. And the systematic variation in objective features [in manufactured objects] is capable of serving, even better than the differences between natural species [as the medium of a vast and dynamic system of thought] because in manufactured objects many differences can be varied at once, and by a godlike manipulation. (1976: 43)

The question that arises here is how another moment in the object's circulation, namely its manufacture or 'godlike manipulation' alters the functioning of ritual and the practices of totemism in modern societies. Or perhaps there are also changes in the organization of consumption which transform the use of objects in rituals? This question – how industrialization and other aspects of modernization have transformed material culture – is the focus of the last section of this chapter.

Things have social lives

Before beginning to address this question, however, it is helpful to look at an alternative, complementary, anthropological approach to

the study of material culture. The work considered so far has made the claim that it is through the acquisition, use and exchange of things that individuals come to have social lives, but an alternative way to look at the importance of material culture in societies is to consider *the social life of things*. By explicitly directing their attention to objects and their circulation, by looking at goods as 'objects in motion', Arjun Appadurai and others (Appadurai 1986) take up the classical anthropological themes of culture and economy from a different angle to Douglas and Isherwood and Sahlins.

Through the rather surprising technique of treating objects as living beings leading 'social lives', acquiring and losing value, changing meaning, perhaps becoming non-exchangeable (as they become 'sentimental' items, cult objects, or maybe even sacred icons), only later to sink back into 'mere' exchange objects, Appadurai focuses attention on the changing ways in which goods create social identity, the different ways in which they act as carriers of interpersonal influence, and the movability or transformability of their meanings. He argues that, by following the paths through which objects are exchanged, we open a window offering 'glimpses of the ways in which desire and demand . . . interact to create economic value in specific social situations' (1986: 4). He identifies two kinds of trajectory of things, differentiated by temporality and scale:

1 The life history of a particular object, as it moves through different hands, contexts and uses, leading to the identification of a specific 'cultural biography' of the object.
2 The 'social history' of a particular kind or class of object, as it undergoes long-term historical shifts and large-scale dynamic transformations (Kopytoff 1986).

As Appadurai points out, however, these two types of trajectory are not entirely separate matters: the social history of things constrains the course of more short-term, specific and intimate trajectories, while many small shifts in the cultural biography of things may lead, over time, to shifts in their social history.

The importance of this approach is that it does not focus exclusively on one moment in an object's life: its production for the market, its mediation in, for example, publicity and advertising, or its reception. It is tempting, when thinking about material culture, to run these three moments together or to give undue prominence to one of them so that either production, mediation or reception becomes the 'determining instance' which dictates the meaning of the object in every other context. In each case, the result is more or less the same – a delicately balanced sequence of relationships is obscured to be replaced by a simplistic set of reductions, ignoring the changes in the meanings of objects as they circulate through networks, trajectories, cycles or 'lives' of production, promotion and reception. This problem is obviously exacerbated as the pathways along which objects travel become extended or more complex; this, Appadurai suggests, is what happens in industrialized, market-intensive societies.

For Appadurai, both types of trajectory – the cultural biography and the social history of an object – need to be problematized, and empirically investigated by looking at the 'social lives' of things. The key claim here is not simply that things are *social* or *cultural*, as Douglas and Isherwood and Sahlins make clear, but that they have *lives*. In attributing life to objects, Appadurai points to the weight and authority that objects can exert in our lives, almost as if they were people, with the power to influence our beliefs and direct our actions, able to give performances, extract obligations and give pleasure. Furthermore, studying the social lives of things enables the distinctive organization of different types of material culture to be identified because it draws attention to the different pathways along which objects travel.

Appadurai further suggests that the social dimension of things can be narratively studied, that is, that it can be told as a story, through the device of the 'life history'. This methodological device facilitates the investigation of changes in the meaning and status of objects as they circulate in the everyday world. To map out an object's narrative, the following questions need to be considered (Kopytoff 1986: 66–7):

Where does the object come from and who made it?

What has been its career so far, and what do people consider to be an ideal career for such objects?

What are the recognized 'ages' or periods in the object's 'life', and what are the cultural markers for them?

How does the object's use change with its age and what happens to it when it reaches the end of its usefulness or dies?

The article 'In the pink of plastic health' gives a journalistic life history of the Barbie dolls and Dick Hebdige also provides an example of this kind of approach in his article, 'Object as image: the Italian scooter cycle' (1988). For Hebdige, the central question is:

In the pink of plastic health at 35 as wanna-Barbies fail to break mould

Toyland

Charlotte Eagar
meets the most
popular girl on Earth –
wooed by Warhol and
mauled by millions.

'I HAVE considered having a breast-reduction operation,' said Barbie, smoothing the white grosgrain skirt of her Classique Collection coat dress (£37.50 in Harrods), 'but when they made a doll in America with a more normal figure she didn't sell at all.

'Anyway, life would be very boring if we were all the same shape,' she said with a flick of her ankle-length golden locks (10 million 'Totally Hair' Barbies have been sold since 1992).

Barbie's shape — 39-18-33 — is reclining on a pale pink net-draped bed in the suite she may or may not share with Ken at the Toyland Ritz. Ken, who has not uttered a word in the past 30 years, is fiddling with the Swing/Grill, before heading off in his Island Fun swim trunks (£14.95 for both Ken and Barbie) to take Barbie's little sisters, Stacie and Skipper, to the plastic beach.

'I'm glad he's gone,' Barbie said, leaning forwards on her rotating pelvis. 'He kind of gives me the creeps sometimes. Now we can have a real girls' chat.'

Barbie has come a long way for a girl from Hawthorne, California, who last week celebrated her thirty-fifth birthday. If all the 500 million Barbie dolls ever sold were placed head to toe, they would circle the world more than six times.

Barbie's Californian PR may not have heard of the feminist and academic Camille Paglia, but Paglia has heard of her. 'Barbie is truly one of the dominant sexual personae of our time,' she announced.

In 35 years she has metamorphosed from Career Girl Barbie, aproned Barbie-Q and Doctor Barbie to Astronaut Barbie, while managing to keep her good-time girl image. Sun Jewel Barbie, the new fuschia-bikinied and diamond-necklaced model, is the best-selling Barbie ever. She has also got as politically correct as a 39m-bust blonde can be, with Jamaican Barbie, Hispanic Barbie and Chinese Barbie filling the cultural gaps.

She is the dominant partner in her relationship with genital-less Ken. In recognition of Barbie's hold over three generations of women,

American literary critic M. G. Lord has written *Forever Barbie — the Unauthorised Biography of a Real Doll*, published by William Morrow next month.

'She's a wonderful role model for little girls,' said Michelle Norton, PR person for Mattel, Barbie's creators. 'She does everything they want to do and dream of. She's got lovely fashions, a boyfriend. It's a friendship sort of thing. She moves with the times.'

But Barbie has made her enemies. Until she took the UK market by storm in the Seventies, Sindy (a mere 36-22-36) had ruled supreme since springing forth, fully clothed, in 1962.

For a while things looked bad for the blond former house captain with the boyfriend from Fulham; sales slumped and Mattel sued when Sindy was remodelled after the American superdoll. But Paul (also genital-less), her boyfriend since 1965, stood by her and now Sindy is clawing her way back up the sales.

'Sindy is quintessentially British,' said Sara Howard, who markets Sindy for Hasbro. The difference shows in the clothes. Barbie's evening and formal day wear — Outerwear Fashions — are all very Ivana Trump.

Norton shrugs off Sindy's pretensions: 'Barbie is definitely the market leader. She outsells other dolls by two to one.' Sadly, the interview with Barbie had to be held telepathically, as Teen-Talk Barbie was sold out. Sindy, however, was more forthcoming, as she walked into the suite, dressed in her Surprise Jeans which change pattern when wet.

'Talk with me,' pleaded Talk-With-Me Sindy, when I pressed a button in her back. 'Will you come to my party this evening? That reminds me,' she added, 'have you seen Paul's new haircut?'

I hadn't but I was about to: Paul and Ken walked in hand-in-hand with Action Man silhouetted in the doorway behind them. 'We're leaving,' they mimed. 'After 30 years of playing second fiddle, we've found love. We're setting up with Action Man in a *menage à trois*. He doesn't own a single piece of pink plastic. And we're taking the Porsche.'

'And I'm getting a Blue Beret,' glowered Action Man, 'So I can join the United Nations and do nothing. I need to stop taking these crazy risks and take responsibility for my own life.'

Or perhaps not. Barbie and Sindy may move with the times but not quite so fast as that.

Barbie: Doll to dream about.
The Observer

> How . . . can we hope to provide a comprehensive and unified account of all the multiple values and meanings which accumulate around a single object over time, the different symbolic and instrumental functions it can serve for different groups of users separated by geographical, temporal and cultural location? (1988: 80)

His answer is to investigate what he calls an object's *cultural signifi-cance*. This significance is explored by mapping the paths and diversions through which an object circulates, accumulating a life history of associations and meanings.

Here is what Hebdige has to say about his method for studying the significance of the scooter:

> The sequence of the narrative corresponds loosely to the progression of the object from design/production through mediation into use though there is a good deal of cross-referencing of different 'moments'. Theoretical models have been introduced to frame the material and the narrative at certain points so that sections dealing with larger economic and social developments can be inserted. It is hoped that by presenting the 'history of the motor scooter' in this way, some indication of the extent of variability in its significance can be given as 'echoes' and 'rhymes' build up within the text. The text itself is variable because there is no one 'voice' speaking through it. The same or similar information may be relayed through a different 'voice' in a different section, i.e., its significance may vary according to its placement. In the same way, for the same reason, any 'echoes' which do accumulate cannot be closed off, summed up, reduced to a 'silence' or amplified into a thunderous conclusion. (1988: 83)

Hebdige begins his study of the scooter by noting that it is an object which has seen vast changes in status and meaning since it was first manufactured in Europe in the years immediately after the First World War. He points out that from the outset the word 'scooter' denoted a small, two-wheeled vehicle with a flat, open platform and an engine mounted over the rear wheel. However, its status has fluctuated throughout the twentieth century, veering from its initial lowly status and vulnerability to ridicule because of its visible resemblance to a child's toy scooter, through its elevation to a cult object sought after for its associations with everything that was chic and modern in the early 1960s, to its current status as an item of nostalgia.

When it was first introduced the scooter was clearly located within what Hebdige calls a system of 'mechanical sexism' in which sexual difference is relayed along a chain – man/woman: work/pleasure:

production/consumption: function/form. This chain is secured, more or less firmly, in practices of production, mediation and consumption (and still continues if the newspaper article 'Hog for you baby' is any indication). So, for example, Hebdige draws on documentary evidence to show that the scooter was initially sexed at birth as female by the formula motorcycles: scooters as men: women. This arose because of the way in which the scooter was widely understood as an example of an investment in design and styling that was taken to be indicative of the 'feminization' or 'emasculation' of product design in British manufacturing.

As a female object, the scooter grew up in the expectation of a life of marriage; indeed, Hebdige writes, 'Scooters were . . . wedded to motorcycles in a relation of inferiority and dependence'. He comments:

> British manufacturers were eventually forced into scooter production though the transition from heavy, utilitarian vehicles to light, 'visually attractive' ones was never satisfactorily accomplished. . . . However, the initial response was one of scorn and dismissal. . . . Scooters were defined as 'streamlined' and 'effete'. The original sales line – that this was a form of transport which (even) women could handle – was turned against itself. Scooters were not only physically unsafe, they were morally suspect. They were unmanly. They ran counter to the ethos of hard work, self-sufficiency and amateur mechanics upon which the success of the British motorcycle industry and the prevailing definitions of masculinity – the 'preferred readings' of manhood – were based. (1988: 104)

But the authority of these definitions of masculinity was called into doubt, and the marriage of motorcycle and scooter did not last. Hebdige records how, by the mid-1950s, the Italian scooter was beginning to represent a threat to the British motorcycle industry which until the Second World War had dominated the international market. By the 1955 Earl's Court Motor Cycle Show, three motorcycles were on a display competing against fifty new scooters.

The scooter went on, then, to acquire a new life following its divorce from the motorcycle. A clash of opinion had emerged between, on the one hand, a declining heavy engineering industry with a vested interest in preserving the industry as its stood (with a fixed conception of product and market) and, on the other, a design industry on the point of boom, with a vested interest in transforming the market, in aestheticizing products and 'educating' consumers. The Italian origin of the scooter had very different meanings in these two views. In the first, 'Italianness' defined the scooter as 'foreign' competition and doubled its effeminacy (Italy: the home of 'male narcissism'). In the second, it defined the scooter as 'the look of the future' and doubled its value as a well-designed object (Italy: the home of 'good taste').

● Roadrunner: Olly Duke

Hog for you baby

Harley-Davidson Bad Boy
Price: £11,950

THE IMAGE of the Harley-Davidson is all about freedom: freedom to be an urban cowboy, a weekend warrior, to wear Harley boots and leather fingerless gloves and sleeveless denim jackets; it's about strumming your Harley guitar and sporting your Harley wristwatch ... and, of course, the company who makes the bikes hopes it's about riding its motorcycles.

Hog owners — as those who own and ride Harleys are known — believe they are living the American Dream. Nowhere is that image captured better than with the new 1995 model Bad Boy, a machine that harks back to the real Harley heritage.

The FXSTB Bad Boy is the Brando bike of The Wild One, a throbbing, low-slung custom cruiser with its roots firmly in the Thirties and Forties.

The technology matches the era: the small, chromed headlamp shell was last seen during the Depression, the bike's style of forks went out of production in 1948 and the rigid rear end (on the Bad Boy it's mock) died away at the end of the second world war.

The front wheel is traditionally steel-spoked while the rear is solidly-mounted, the wide handlebars haven't been seen since the Japanese created the modern motorcycle and the engine technology first appeared in 1909.

Harley's Bad Boy may not be fast and it's not very comfortable, but it certainly turns heads. It's beautifully-styled and the lustrous black paint sets off the deep, high-quality chrome.

The American firm's first V-twins were capable of an impressive 60mph. Now, however, the Bad Boy's massive but softly-powered and slow-revving 1,340cc engine will thunder to over 90mph.

It is solidly fixed in the chassis and the whole bike shudders and shakes and vibrates from little over 70mph. Stick to the speed limit and you'll have a far more enjoyable ride.

The five-speed gearbox is slow and clunky — typically Harley-Davidson — but the bike's belt-drive smoothes out the transmission and is maintenance-free.

The rear suspension gives a fairly hard ride, with minimal damping. Two shocks are concealed beneath the frame and control the triangular-shaped swingarm.

Up front, the Springer forks are equally ingenious. They consist basically of parallel rods on each side of the wheel, pivoted at the wheel spindle, which operate two springs and a damping unit placed directly below the headlamp.

Although they are not adjustable, they are very effective and cope well with all but the worst roads.

And the front mudguard is kept at a constant distance from the wheel by a clever arrangement of small torsion bars.

Harley-Davidson has been criticised for its brakes and it has tried to improve things by fitting "floating" discs to the Bad Boy. But in practice they are no better than the usual fixed discs.

Freedom Harley-style costs £11,950. That's pricey, but then Harley-Davidson UK sells every bike it imports. And buyers also know that they'll make money on their machines, even after a year's use.

Also new for next year is the FXD Dyna Super Glide. It is pitched at the lower end of the Harley range and has been designed to encourage a lot of new recruits into the Hog ranks.

Your £8,895 spent on the Super Glide is just the beginning. Hooking in to Harley-Davidson freedom can be an expensive business.

Guardian Weekend,
24 September 1994

But the carefree and newly single life of the scooter could not be secured by designers and publicists alone. Hebdige points to the importance of user clubs and rallies in providing a new environment for the scooter to exercise its new-found freedom:

> As many as 3,000 scooterists would converge on Brighton and Southend for the National Lambretta Club's annual rally where, at the service marquee, set, according to one enthusiast, amidst 'banners and flags, bunting and a carnival atmosphere . . . your Lambretta would be repaired and serviced entirely free of charge'. . . . During the evenings, there would be barbecues, fancy dress competitions and dances . . . One of the records played at the Southend rally dances in the early 1960s was an Italian hit entitled the Lambretta twist. (1988: 107)

The subculture of the mods was especially influential in transforming the scooter's life, especially since Mods' own significance and influence came to stretch beyond the confines of a particular subcultural milieu. At a more general level, mods highlighted the emergence of a new consumer sensibility, a more discriminating 'consumer awareness'.

After all, as Hebdige points out, it was during the late 1950s that the term 'modernist' first came into use, that design departments were set up in all the major art schools, that royal patronage was formally extended to industrial design, that the Design Centre itself opened in the Haymarket in London, and that magazines like *Which?*, *Shopper's Guide*, *Home* and *House Beautiful* began publicizing the ideas of 'consumer satisfaction' and 'tasteful home improvement'. And it was in 1964, when 'mod' became a household word, that Terence Conran opened the first of the Habitat shops which, according to the advertising copy of the day, offered a 'pre-selected shopping programme . . . instant good taste . . . for switched on people'. According to Hebdige, the perfection of surface, form and line evident in the design of the scooter and dramatized by the mods was simply part of a general aestheticization of everyday life.

This was a process which opened multiple new lifelines or pathways, not simply for the scooter, but also for many other mass-produced objects. However, while this process of aestheticization is not only still in evidence but may actually have intensified, the scooter itself seems to have seen its heydey. There have been attempts to bring it out of retirement, but the recession, the appearance of small Japanese motorcycles, and compulsory crash helmets seem to have laid the scooter low, at least for the present.

What is important about this biography of the scooter is that it shows how the methodological 'animation' of objects can reveal new aspects of material culture, aspects which remain hidden if only one moment of an object's life is privileged. As Appadurai writes, 'even though from a *theoretical* point of view human actors encode things with a significance, from a *methodological* point of view it is the things-in-motion that illuminate their human and social context' (1986: 5). Furthermore, as the example from Hebdige suggests, tracing the social and cultural movement of objects leads to a focus on the *dynamic, processual* aspects of material culture, pointing not simply to the small-scale shifts in an object's meaning as it traverses circuits of exchange, but also to broader transformations in the organization of material culture itself.

According to Appadurai, every society lays out culturally and legally approved 'paths' for the circulation of objects; conditions are set about what objects may be exchanged for what, by whom, when and under what conditions. Examples of such paths include both the formal economic and legal rules surrounding the sale of goods, conditions of credit, and guarantees of product quality, and informal norms about whether, for example, second-hand goods can be offered as gifts, or whether unwanted gifts can be returned or passed on by their recipient. But, at the same time, in any such system there are countervailing tendencies for interested parties to engineer 'diversions', to step off the prescribed paths. So, the passage of 'paths and diversions' by objects is always a dynamic, contested, political one, and the value of a given object in a given context is always a political question. However, Appadurai further points to the increasing importance of aesthetic knowledge in the creation of pathways in modern Euro-American societies – supporting Hebdige's finding that an aestheticization of everyday life has provided changed conditions for the organization of material culture.

So far then in this chapter, material culture has been considered from two perspectives: first, the ways in which things are used to enhance the social lives of individuals, and second, how the cultural significance of objects is made visible by animating objects, giving them a life and exploring their cultural biography and social history. While these perspectives require different methodologies, a common question emerges from their application: is there something distinctive about modern consumption, and if so, what is it? Or, to put this another way, how have modern ways of life transformed material culture? What is the 'godlike manipulation' which Sahlins refers to, and is it related to the new 'consumer awareness' that Hebdige discovers?

Cher luxury

CELEBRITY has always sold: ask the constellation of stars, from Cindy Crawford to Angela Lansbury, who have toned-up their bank accounts by flogging fitness videos. Now several of the famous are peddling their own mail-order catalogues. The latest to do so is Cher, an ageless singer and actress who has already marketed her own fitness videos and "Uninhibited" perfume. This autumn, Cher is launching "Sanctuary", a 47-page home-furnishing, clothes and jewellery catalogue (or "a coffee-table book you can order from"). Some 350,000 selected American households will find it in their mailboxes.

Cher joins the cast of a mail-order show that also stars Robert Redford, Spike Lee, the Grateful Dead and, vicariously, Britain's royal family. All are aiming for the upper crust of America's $70 billion-a-year mail-order market, which now accounts for 3% of the country's total retail sales. The keenest buyers are affluent shoppers tired of surly service and crowded malls. In lieu of the instant gratification of shopping, most of the celebrity catalogues offer two-day express delivery. "We sell convenience, lifestyle and uniqueness," says Brad Larschan, president of the House of Windsor collection, which this year launched its catalogue with help from a guest appearance by Prince Michael of Kent.

Snob appeal and "lifestyle" loom large in celebrity catalogues. Cher's wares—which include a chain-mail helmet candlestand ($170) and leather camels ($58)—are strong on medieval gothic (fleur-de-lys is everywhere), together with the odd see-through dress. Spike Lee's "Spike's Joint" (an offshoot of his shops) offers premium-priced street-chic, while Robert Redford's "Sundance" catalogue (a pioneer of the genre) is heavy on ethnic crafts. But for real class it is hard to beat the House of Windsor Collection's week-long, $25,000 holiday in Britain, complete with supper with an unspecified but presumably hungry peer of the realm.

One like that, please

Unsurprisingly, celebrity catalogues tend to appeal to other celebrities: the House of Windsor Collection sold Madonna a $42 goblet—tastefully engraved with "Wine Gives Courage and Makes Men Apt for Passion"—while Cher herself purchased a $58 red linen notepaper box. But the House of Windsor Collection is also being mailed to 2m normal households, and should sell some $7m-worth of goods in America this year. The Sundance catalogue, which will be mailed to 9m homes in 1994, is making a healthy profit.

The next stop may be the ultimate yuppie retail therapy—the virtual shopping mall. Mr Larschan says his company is considering making the House of Windsor collection available on CD-ROM computer discs. Though retail analysts doubt that this technology will reach a mass market, Mr Larschen reckons that interactive "mail order" will be a cost-effective way to reach rich customers: an e-mail address of "gifts@palace.com" would have a suitably regal ring.

The Economist,
24 September 1994

'Waste not, want not' is the word

By David Nicholson-Lord
Consumer Affairs Correspondent

HANGING your tea-bags out to dry is back in fashion. More than half a century after the birth of the throwaway society, a new generation is rediscovering the watchwords of its grandparents: thrift, frugality, resourcefulness.

Over the next six weeks, Channel 4 will devote three hours of prime-time television to making do and mending. Its series, *Scrimpers*, starting at 8pm tomorrow, is devoted to the "new frugalists": people who pillage rubbish skips and refuse tips for mendables, turn old music centres into seed propagators and recycle toilet-roll cores into cheap and cheerful Christmas decorations.

The series symbolises a new economic consciousness. Its roots are financial: recession, unemployment; uncertainty; and psychological: growing environmental awareness, resistance to consumerism and the global cash economy. It has surfaced, statistically, in the rise of the black economy: last year, after a long period of decline, the number of hard-cash transactions went up.

David Collison, its producer, describes scrimping as "a serious public statement that resourcefulness is a deep-seated and valuable activity – a reaction against the supermarket culture where all you do is jump in a car, drive off and buy stuff, then throw away what you don't use. The scrimpers represent something very widespread."

They include a London man who is collecting and selling aluminium drinks cans, at 40p a kilogram, to try to save his £70,000 house from repossession; the villagers of South Molton, Devon, where rubbish-scavenging has created thriving community businesses; and a Brighton single mother who collects old bricks from skips and sell them as hard-core.

Scrimpers also offers tips, from "green burials" – in biodegradable, cardboard caskets costing £49.50 – to treading on toilet rolls before you put them on the holder: a sharp pull will pull off only one or two sheets.

Scrimping is part of Britain's informal economy – the fastest-growing part of the economy, where the most radical changes in attitude are occurring and people are experimenting with new types of organisation. Other examples of this new consciousness include:

■ The mushrooming of Local Exchange and Trading Systems (Lets). In effect a reinvention of the barter economy, these create local currencies that enable people to swap skills and services without using cash. More than 200 schemes and 20,000 people are involved in the UK, with similar networks in nine European countries, the US and Australia. Advocates of Lets argue that eschewing cash creates genuinely local economies insulated from the global economy.

■ The growth of car-boot sales. In the UK, these date from the early Eighties and combine two of the most popular British pastimes: shopping and recycling. They are a response to the switch from public to private consumption in the Eighties and the "waste mountain" this generated. A million people are estimated to visit car-boot sales every weekend.

■ A new "proud to be poor" mentality. In Japan last year, *The Concept of Honest Poverty*, a book by Koji Nakano, sold 700,000. New magazines devoted to saving money include, in the US, *The Tightwad Gazette* and *The Cheapskate Monthly*,

and in the UK, *The Scrimpers*, set up by a couple featured in the Channel 4 series.

■ A local economic renaissance. As banks, high-street chains and superstores have deserted deprived areas, the vacuum is being filled by charity and second-hand clothing shops, community businesses and co-operatives. There are now more than 400 credit unions, for example: small-scale co-operative banking organisations.

The idea for *Scrimpers* came from Ian Davidson, a former *Monty Python* scriptwriter, after he had made a garden table out of bits of old wood. Making the programme, according to Third Eye, the production company, was like "joining a resistance movement ... there was the feeling that by refusing to be a conspicuous consumer, our scrimpers were getting back at 'them'".

According to Ed Mayo, director of the New Economics Foundation, a green think tank, the informal economy is undergoing "incredible ferment – partly because it provides an easy way into work and also a means of surviving. But there is an element of rediscovering the joys of self-reliance, autonomy and community".

Car-boot sales pull an estimated million people each weekend

Independent on Sunday
12 October 1994

(handwritten note in margin: – buying things can get in the way of you)

Production, consumption and consumer culture

If the first half of this chapter has introduced the idea of material culture in general, the second half will begin to consider the special or distinctive characteristics of contemporary material culture. One way to do this is to identify some of the features which characterize modern consumption. This section lists some of these features, culled from a variety of sources.

1   The availability of a large (and constantly increasing) number and range of types of consumer goods.

2   The tendency for more and more aspects of human exchange and interaction to be made available through the market. One instance of this is the contemporary shift away from state or publicly provided services to their marketization. Examples include housing and education – so, for example, it is often said that Britain is now a home-owning nation and that students are consumers of education.

3   The expansion of shopping as a leisure pursuit. In the United States, shopping is the second most popular leisure pursuit – six hours per person a week – after watching television (Nicholson-Lord, 1992).

4   The increasing visibility of different forms of shopping, from mail order (see 'Cher luxury') to shopping malls to car boot sales and second-hand shops (see "Waste not, want not" is the word').

5   The political organization by and of consumers. Examples include so-called green consumption (*The Green Consumer's Supermarket Shopping Guide* sold 75,000 copies in its first week of publication (Simmons 1994)) and the use of consumer boycotts, as well as the growth and popularity of consumer organizations such as the Consumers Association (see Winward 1994). A key issue in consumer politics is who benefits from these political actions – are consumers being mobilized by producers for their own benefit or are consumers able to create their own political interests? (See *'The Earth Pledge'*).

6   A growth in the visibility of the consumption of sport and leisure practices. This involves not simply the broadcasting of sports events, including snooker, cricket and football competitions and the Olympics, but their reorganization (one-day Test matches) to suit the requirements of commercial sponsors.

THE EARTH PLEDGE
Recognizing that people's actions towards nature and each other are the source of growing damage to the environment and resources needed to meet human needs and to ensure survival and development,
I PLEDGE to act to the best of my ability to help make the Earth a secure and hospitable home for present and future generations.

HELPING SAFEGUARD OUR FUTURE

Time to move is the name of this UN Special Swatch Automatic. And as we are all aware, it is time to move – and fast – if we wish to leave a planet worth living on to our children and grandchildren. By purchasing this Swatch Automatic you have made a personal contribution towards the financing of Earth Summit 1992, a meeting of all 166 UN member states in Rio de Janeiro. And we would like to thank you for your support. Together we are helping ensure that representatives of virtually every country in the world will be at the summit in Rio de Janeiro to join forces against a common threat. Only if the world stands shoulder to shoulder now can we make any meaningful and lasting improvement. The burning issue at Earth Summit 1992 is the future of our planet. And that affects us all.
Today, we can all play a central role in helping save the world of tomorrow. If we want our world to survive, we must act now: there is no time to lose.
You can signify your commitment through the above Pledge, of which this Swatch Automatic will be a constant reminder.

Maurice F. Strong
Secretary General of the
United Nations
Conference
on Environment and
Development

Nicolas G. Hayek
Chairman of the Board
and CEO of SMH/Swatch

IN OUR HANDS
EARTH SUMMIT '92
UNITED NATIONS CONFERENCE ON
ENVIRONMENT AND DEVELOPMENT

Swatch Time to move

Consumer credit has been growing in Britain by at least 10 per cent in real terms nearly every year since 1977. In 1988, 15.3 million people had a Visa card and 12.2 million had an Access card, numbers which have increased over four-fold since the mid-1970s. Two-thirds of all adults now possess some kind of plastic money card. (Lunt and Livingstone 1992: 27)

7   The lifting of restrictions on borrowing money and the associated change in meaning of being in debt. During this century, for example, there has been a shift from the dubious respectability of the 'never-never', through the anxieties of hire purchase, to the competitive display of credit cards – to a situation now in which an Access card is your 'flexible friend' and a gold American Express card is a symbol of elite exclusivity.

8   An increase in sites for purchase and consumption, such as the spread of shopping malls (between 1986 and 1990 almost 30 million square feet of shopping centre space was opened (Cowe 1994)), the growth of retail parks (250 were opened in the 1980s (Cowe 1994)) and leisure complexes and their stylization, from the increase in 'themed' pubs to the building of Disneyworlds.

Specifications of the MetroCentre, 'Europe's largest shopping mall'.

- 135 acres
- 360 stores and shops
- a themed 'Mediterranean village'
- a 'Roman' forum
- an 'Antique Village'
- a £20 m. indoor amusement park with white-knuckle ride
- more than 50 cafes, restaurants and fast-food joints
- a 28-lane bowling alley
- video games arcades
- multi-screen cinema
- 26 million visitors in 1991

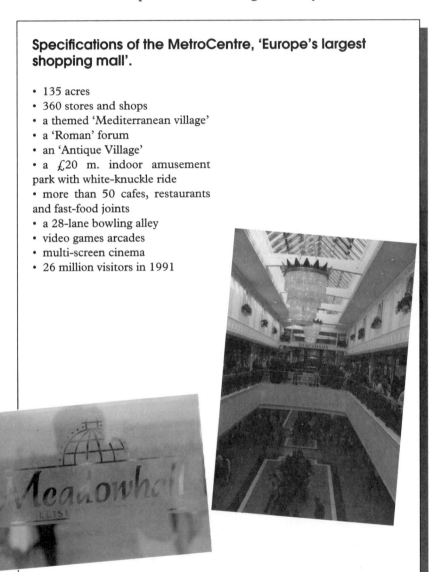

9 The growing importance of packaging and promotion in the manufacture, display and purchase of consumer goods.

10 The pervasiveness of advertising in everyday life (see 'No more mail shots in the dark').

11 The increasing emphasis on the style, design and appearance of goods.

In Swatch's hands, the traditional wristwatch was transformed beyond recognition. It ceased to be a nagging timekeeper, a dowdy gift presented to mark a 12th birthday or retirement. The old-style wrist shackle, intimating sobriety and punctuality, was reborn as a Gherkin, Jellyfish or Chandelier; an ephemeral thing, stripped of numerals and gravitas, bought for £23.50 and strapped three to each available limb, or dangled from the earlobes as a disposable fashion accessory. . . .

At 9 o'clock this morning, a crowd of more than 2,000 will 'stampede through the doors of The Rock Shop in Piccadilly Circus for the release of the Tresor Magique, the first non-plastic Swatch. Within two hours, the UK ration of 800 Tresors, limited to 12,999 worldwide, will have sold out, and the platinum self-winder, priced £1,000, will have at least doubled its value on the black market. . . .

The Havana Puff, its face surrounded by acrylic fur which has to be blown out the way before you can read the time, sold for £45 in 1988. Today, collectors will pay up to £100,000 for a mint set of six puffs in the six original colours.

Swatch releases 70 new designs each year in two seasonal fashion ranges. Production has consistently fallen short of demand and as models priced at £23.50 sell out, they automatically become limited editions. The company's Milan-based design team have commissioned artists such as the late Keith Haring and Sam Francis and designer Vivienne Westwood to devise Specials priced at £45 and issued in smaller runs which have further fuelled the collecting mania. (Brooker 1993: 37)

12 The manipulation of time and space in the simulation of 'elsewheres' and 'elsewhens' to promote products, as in the case of, for example, the company 'Past Times' which sells 'fine and unusual gifts inspired by the past' including a 'Roman fresco silk scarf', 'Anglo-Saxon Christmas music' and 'Henry VIII mint chocolates'.

No more mail shots in the dark

DIRECT marketing was once associated with irritating methods such as junk mail and those leaflets which flop out of magazines. But new technology has transformed advertising's poor relation into marketing's potentially most useful tool.

Colin Lloyd, chief executive of the Direct Marketing Association, will explain at the CIM conference just how close technology can take a company to its customers. The much-discussed fragmentation of media audiences means many companies are looking at the merits of direct marketing, compared with the traditionally-favoured brand advertising. New techniques in information gathering and dissemination mean that direct marketing is no longer a mail-shot in the dark, but an increasingly secure way of selling.

"What we now have is an unprecedented depth of understanding of customers," says Lloyd. "If you count knowing a customer's name as one attribute and address as another attribute, there are now databases which can instantly provide you with 100 attributes for just one person." So where you work, where you shop, where you holiday and what you do in your leisure are all being logged on sophisticated databases which are then used by companies to hit you with a selling proposition at exactly the right time.

"It might sound a bit Big Brother-ish to consumers who don't even know it's out there, but there are a whole host of checks and balances to protect privacy — and of course it means the end of junk mail," claims Lloyd.

What lies behind this accurate profiling system is what Lloyd calls "neural network technology", or massive databases which process customer information in order to target very specifically. The technology is "self-correcting", which means that every time a marketing company sends out a mail shot which misses, or places an interactive television commercial which elicits no response, it adjusts itself not to do it again.

Experiments by some companies with neural network technology suggests that the system can be as accurate in practice as it sounds in theory. For instance one company found that it elicited 55 per cent of the responses it would expect from a full list of customers by using only a fifth of the database.

Tracing a customer who is willing and able to respond to a marketing message cuts out the waste and irritation of untargeted solicitation, but it also to some

---

'There are a whole host of checks and balances to protect privacy' — Colin Lloyd

---

extent robs the marketeer of the fame which big brand advertising delivers. "Nobody has all the answers, but we will see above-the-line advertising [TV, newspapers, posters] increasingly paired with below-the-line marketing [direct mail, promotions]," says Lloyd. A recent joint survey produced by the DMA and the Henley Centre for Forecasting estimates that in 1994 £4.5 billion was spent on direct marketing — about half the amount spent on all advertising — which includes an estimated £1.5 billion on direct response press, and a further £1 billion on tele-marketing. Even the relatively new direct response television attracted an estimated £237 million.

During the latest recession, direct marketing has gained the competitive advantage over the more expensive and less quantifiable advertising, as marketeers realise the increasing importance and efficiency of one-to-one selling. Direct marketing in Britain is growing at three times the speed of above-the-line advertising.

In America the direct marketing industry has gone one step further, and estimating how much trade was stimulated through direct marketing, with the pleasing if spurious result that it amounts to 5 per cent of the gross domestic product — about the same as the arms trade contributes.

All this has been achieved without the impact of the Internet and interactive television being included. These have the advantage of providing an instant two-way path between advertiser and consumer, offering the opportunity for an even more detailed dialogue between customer and advertiser. "We are seeing a move from mass marketing to micro marketing which will produce a new order in the industry," says Lloyd.

Guardian, 1 May 1995

Companies like Crabtree and Evelyn, Laura Ashley and Ralph Lauren employ a successful generic nostalgia in their identities, and what has become known as 'retro' is an indeterminate style which can veer from the 20s to the 50s in one stylistic leap, catering non-specifically for past hankerings. American marketing has already spoken of Nostalgia Exploitation Potential (NEP), and Marshall McLuhan's trope of the media's 'rear-view mirror' ushered in the post-modern obsession with quoting past styles. (Bennett 1991: 56)

13 The emergence of a range of so-called consumer crimes – credit card fraud, shoplifting and ram-raiding – and consumer surveillance technologies – the remote video camera and the itemized financial records of banks, telephone and telecommunications companies.

14 The impossibility of avoiding making choices in relation to consumer goods, and the associated celebration of self-fashioning or self-transformation in the promotion of lifestyle as a way of life.

15 The increasing visibility of so-called consumer illnesses linked to what have been called 'maladies of agency' (Seltzer 1993) and pathologies or 'maladies of the will' (Sedgwick 1994) such as addiction, whether it be addiction to alcohol, food or shopping (see 'Compulsive shopping "real illness" ').

16 The interest in the personal and collective collection, cataloguing and display of material goods, whether these be artworks, stamps, antiques, music tapes or photographs (see 'What should I collect?').

These characteristics are obviously very diverse, and are not all equally important features of modern life. However, all of them are related to the rapid increase in consumer demand associated with modern industrial societies. How, then, is the increased scale of consumption to be explained? To some extent, explanations can be divided into two types: production-led and consumption-led. The first sees the increase in demand as a response to changes in production, while the second identifies independent causes for the growth in demand. This next section outlines the most influential examples of each type of explanation.

Compulsive shopping 'real illness'

Psychologists blame mental stress for "addiction," says Chris Mihill

A STUDY into "shopping addiction" was launched by psychologists yesterday because they believe it can amount to a form of illness on a par with compulsive gambling and alcoholism.

Richard Elliott, specialising in marketing and consumer affairs at Lancaster University, who wants compulsive shoppers and health professionals to contact him, said yesterday: "There is a syndrome of behaviour involving loss of control over shopping and consumption which is very similar to other forms of addiction. It is largely, overwhelmingly, seen in women, and it is usually carried out in secret."

Some studies in the US had suggested that 6 per cent of shoppers could be addictive.

One of the purposes of the two-year British study being funded by a £55,000 grant from the Economic and Social Research Council, is to establish if there is a "continuum" of shopping, running from normal purchasing, through impulse buys or binge shopping, into full-scale addictive behaviour.

Dr Elliott, who is working with Professor Kevin Gournay, head of mental health studies at Middlesex University, said the behaviour in 61 patients in a smallscale study was triggered by stress, anxiety, or depression and usually hinged on personal relationships.

"A key issue is that there is little pleasure or use from the goods which are bought. Some people are spending vast amounts of money two or three times a week, usually on credit cards. They buy multiples — six of the same skirt or blouse in different colours — and very often do not wear them.

"They take them straight home and put them in a cupboard and never take them out, because, having spent the money, they are consumed by guilt."

One in his smallscale study told him: "I am risking everything, my children and my marriage, just for goods I do not event want. I feel awful so guilty."

Another confessed: "I spent all the mortgage money, the rates money, the gas and phone bill money and we very nearly had our house repossessed. How could I do this to my husband? I do not know if he will ever really forgive me."

Guardian, 6 October 1994

TVs and fishing reels are in, teddy bears and Dinky toys out. **John Windsor** offers tips on what to buy and when

What should I collect?

Perched on park benches, their bicycles propped beside them, young Chinese haggle over old coins gleaned from rummage boxes in dealers' shops around Tottenham Court Road in London. No Dinky toys or vintage radios for them: they are convinced that, by the end of the decade, coin and stamp prices will have rocketed worldwide and rummage boxes will be but a memory.

Industrialisation is tilting the world's economic axis towards South-east Asia. British auctioneers predict that in China alone the demand for coins (and telephone cards) will rise 20-fold in the next 15 years. In the past five years, the number of Chinese stamp collectors has soared to 30 million.

For investors seeking new collectables, the first question must now be: how much will they pay in South-east Asia? The region is dictating taste and forcing up prices.

Those young Chinese on London's park benches rummage not only for Chinese coins but for big and grand coins of any nation. Britain's coin market has been moribund since collapsing in 1982. For them, it is time to buy.

Meanwhile, back home, even tradition-conscious Chinese, for whom collecting meant nothing beyond blue-and-white Chinese porcelain, (sometimes more than £1m a piece), are now looking abroad. Some want banknotes that were printed for China-based Dutch, German or French banks or by the American Banknote Company and Britain's Bradbury Wilkinson, supplier of Hong Kong's paper money. Their spending power will soon extend to stamps and coins of all nations. So do not mind if dealers scoff at your humble collection. Sit on it.

Sotheby's expects China's most expensive stamp, an 1897 overprint, to double in value before the end of the century. It was worth only £1,200–£1,500 20 years ago. But in May, Sotheby's sold one for £143,965 at its first Hong Kong stamp sale. Even in the West, where the stamp market has been bumping the bottom since a speculative bust in 1979, a stamp can fetch £1m. Sotheby's expects that South-east Asia stamp prices will soon catch up. So sit on your stamps, too.

Western dealers hoping to become rich in South-east Asia are having to come to terms with the region's varying tastes. The Chinese are reluctant to buy excavated antiquities, second-hand jewellery or sapphires – blue is the colour of death. Unlike the Chinese, the Taiwanese buy Western-style art, much of it their own.

For the Western speculator, fine Western watches are one of a number of possible gambles. As collectables, they have found favour in Malaysia, Indonesia and Singapore – while in Britain they have been cheap since easy City money boosted then bust the market for them in 1989–90. In 1989 Patek Philippe's 150th anniversary watch retailed for £4,950, rocketed to £25,000 at London auctions then plummeted to £6,000. Current value: £7,500 and rising.

It is still possible for a single enthusiast to create a sustainable market for a new collectable by writing the first textbook. Michael Bennett-Levy did it for pre-war televisions and Graham Turner did it with his *Fishing Tackle: A Collector's Guide*, published five years ago. He is now selling his collection. The first of four auctions in London last month sold out. A Hardy Zane Grey Big Game reel fetched £6,270.

Has Mr Turner's home-made market peaked? Not at all, he says. He reckons that fishing tackle, like golfing tackle, should be classified as a sporting collectable, and that fishing prices are on their way towards the record £92,400 paid for an old golf club.

The Independent Weekend

The growth in consumer demand

In his discussions of material culture, presented in the first half of this chapter, Sahlins suggests that one of the key differences between material culture in traditional and modern societies is that it is manufactured goods or artefacts which act as totems in the latter rather than natural objects. The factor which distinguishes the manufactured good or artefact from the natural object is that it is the product of human labour. But why should this alter the capacity of an object to act as a totem?

In fact, it is not simply that an artefact is the product of human labour in and of itself that affects its capacity to act as a totem, but the way in which this appropriation is socially organized; or at least this is the view put forward in one of the most influential interpretations of what is distinctive about modern material culture. This interpretation draws on the work of Karl Marx and his analysis of appropriation as it is organized in what he calls the capitalist mode of production. Put simply, this interpretation suggests that it is the changes in the mode of appropriation associated with the development of capitalism that have led to the emergence of a distinctive consumer culture in modern societies.

For Marx, the mode of appropriation is the critical site where human societies develop their distinctive characters. It is through the activity of labour, the use and adaptation of natural resources, that human consciousness comes to be what it is. This means that human consciousness is realized or objectified in the material products of labour. This is why the product of labour – the material artefact or good – is so central for the self-understandings of individuals and society generally. Material culture, for Marx, is the objectification of social consciousness. Under a capitalist mode of production, however, this objectification is turned against people.

This line of argument starts from the distinction that Marx made between appropriating or producing something for one's own direct or immediate use and producing something within an alienating division of labour that is created solely to be exchanged on the market. This latter process is the production of goods as *commodities* (although there is some debate about the nature of the link between the production of goods within a specific system of division of labour and their production for exchange on the market; see Appadurai 1986). It is the special features of objects as commodities which, it is believed, explain the distinctiveness of consumer culture as a type of material culture.

Marx himself did not live to see modern material culture emerge, but he did notice certain features of the good as commodity that others have gone on to suggest are responsible for the distinctive character of consumer culture. These features include the commodity's 'enigmatic' or 'mysterious' quality. This is said to arise, on the one hand, from the commodity's combination of features that we can see, touch and smell, and, on the other, from the hidden social relations involved in its production. Leiss et al. describe this mysterious quality well:

> Commodities are . . . a unity of what is revealed and what is concealed in the processes of production and consumption. Goods reveal or 'show' to our senses their capacities to be satisfiers or stimulators of particular wants and communicators of behavioural codes. At the same time, they draw a veil across their own origins: products appear and disappear before consumers' eyes as if by spontaneous generation, and it is an astute shopper indeed who has much idea about what most things are composed of and what kinds of people made them. (1986: 274)

Marx used the term *fetishism of commodities* to describe the disguising or masking of commodities whereby the appearance of goods hides the story of those who made them and how they made them.

But, you may ask, do consumers need to hear this story? In being deprived of it, are they experiencing a systematic distortion of communication within the world of goods itself? Marx suggests that they are. He argues that in market societies, commodities not only hide but come to *stand in for* or *replace* relationships between people. The (presumed) unity between production and consumption is broken. People's thinking about themselves and others is distorted by a fetishism, in which beliefs about the material products of labour – artefacts – are a substitute for an understanding of the social relations which made the production of the goods possible. Marx writes: 'The object that labour produces, its product, stands opposed to it as *something alien, as a power independent* of the producer' (quoted in Lee 1993: 7). A related term to describe this process is *reification*, which means a process of making a product or object thing-like. As a result of this process, the social relations represented in an object come to appear absolutely fixed or given, beyond human control.

The suggestion here is that the modern fetish does not serve us in the same way as the totem in traditional societies served its members, as a result of consensual agreement amongst the members of a particular culture. This is because the use of the good as a means of communication is said to be systematically distorted by the capitalist search for profit. The need for profit has led, it is argued, to the production of an ever-expanding range of products which can only be sold as a result of increasing control over and manipulation of the consumer. This is hidden by *the mask* of the commodity, and it is this mask which is held responsible for a stylization of consumption. This is thus a view which attributes the stylization of consumer culture to changes in the organization of production in modern societies, specifically the increasing production of objects for exchange on the market.

A related point made by many Marxists is that the fetishism of the commodity in modern society is strategically manipulated in the practices of packaging, promotion and advertising. Through packaging, promotion and advertising, goods are said to be fitted with masks expressly designed to manipulate the possible relations between things on the one hand and human wants, needs and emotions on the other. Adorno (1974), for example, speaks of how, once the dominance of exchange-value has managed to obliterate the memory of the original use-value of goods, the commodity becomes available to take up a secondary or ersatz use-value. Commodities become free to take on a wide range of cultural associations and illusions; this is the basis for what has been called *commodity aesthetics*. Advertising in particular is said to be able to exploit this freedom to attach images of romance, exotica, fulfilment, or the good life to mundane consumer goods such as soap, washing machines, cars and alcoholic drinks. These images or masks fix the ways material objects are able to act as carriers of meaning in social interaction. They encipher goods in symbolic codes that consumers cannot resist. This is the 'godlike manipulation' that Sahlins identifies, and is seen to be responsible for the rapid and apparently insatiable increase in consumer demand. The next chapter will discuss this view in more detail, but in the mean time it is important to note that other commentators on consumer culture have questioned the effectiveness of such masks to promote consumer demand. Indeed, it has been argued that, in relation to some goods at least, the so-called godlike manipulation of the producers is by no means infallible, and that the power of consumers *vis-à-vis* producers has been radically understated.

Moreover, the increase in consumer demand in modern Western societies should be understood not simply in relation to the activities of the market and the dominance of exchange-value, but also in relation to the state. One of the most influential writers here is

Castells (1977), who has mapped the history of what he calls 'collective consumption', by which he means the consumption of services and goods provided by the state for consumers as a public collective. This currently includes the provision of some housing, health care, transport and education in Britain, although the question of whether such services should continue to be provided by the state or the market is a subject of much contemporary political debate.

Central questions in this debate are: what conditions give consumers power, relative to producers, and under what conditions can consumers obtain what will give them satisfaction and pleasure? But there are also other questions here: do different groups have different (more or less, better or worse) access to services and goods according to whether they are provided through the market or through the state – that is, does the medium of distribution contribute to social differentiation? Are differences in modes of access to goods the source of differences between different groups of people? This idea has been explored through the investigation of what are sometimes called 'consumption sector cleavages', that is, the differential social advantages to be derived from having access to private as opposed to state provision of services (Saunders and Harris 1994).

Alternatively, Zygmunt Bauman (1987) has argued that it is possible to identify two broad social groupings – the seduced and the repressed – on the basis of whether people's needs are satisfied by the market or the state. The seduced, he believes, are free to make decisions in the market arena and are incorporated into consumer culture; their lives are in large part devoted to the acquisition and display of commodities. The repressed are those who, lacking economic and cultural resources, are excluded from the market – they are not full members of the club of consumers; instead their lives are intricately entangled with the bureaucracy of the state. We live, then, Bauman argues, in a society of two nations, not of exploiter and exploited, or even of the haves and the have-nots, but of the seduced and the repressed, those free to follow their desires and those subject to surveillance and control through the bureaucratic regulations organizing state provision of services. (For a critique of this view, in which it is suggested that the category that Bauman describes as repressed is more adequately described as the poor, see Warde 1994.) This is an analysis which suggests that while not everyone participates in consumer society on the same terms, it can be said to be characterized or dominated by a consumer culture or consumer attitude (Bauman 1990; see below) in so far as it is the individual's relation to consumption – which he or she cannot control – that defines his or her social position.

It has also been pointed out that many of the goods and services provided, whether through the market or the state, are the subject of further work before they are finally consumed, and thus that increasing consumer demand is likely to be linked to changes in other systems of exchange. Feminist writers have pointed out that this work is typically part of housework, and is usually done by women (Delphy and Leonard 1992). The point being made here is that while it may be the woman in a household who actually purchases many goods, and in that sense is identified as the primary consumer, it will also typically be the woman who goes on to do further work on the goods bought before they are finally consumed by the other members of the household. She is thus also a producer. This point indicates the importance of looking at *cycles* of production and consumption, and the relations of power at work within these cycles, rather than simply positing some general increase in consumer demand. There are usually a number of different cycles of production and consumption before the final enjoyment of a good, service or experience. As Alan Warde notes,

> frequently in the making of something that is 'finally consumed', several different cycles of production and consumption occur one after the other. This can be seen from considering the food chain as a whole. What we eat off our plates typically passes through a number of production processes (the growing, wholesaling, processing, retailing and domestic preparation) and several exchange transactions (some of which are often [misleadingly] called consumption) before final enjoyment as a meal. . . . Analytically, it is worth recognising the existence of sequential episodes of production and consumption, and to notice that episodes are not necessarily identical, and may involve specifically different kinds of social relationships. (1992: 18–19)

Consumer demand can thus be seen to be mediated by multiple circuits of exchange, only some of which are directly linked to the production of commodities, and others of which are mediated by the state and/or the social relations of the household or domestic mode of production.

Nevertheless, most of the accounts presented so far in the second half of this chapter have located the growth in consumer demand characteristic of contemporary material culture in the particular kinds of production and distribution and the associated divisions of labour that characterize modern societies. These arguments identify production, most commonly, the process of commodification, as responsible for the distinctively 'enigmatic' or 'mysterious' character of consumer culture. They can thus be described as *producer-led* explanations, that is, they assume the importance of the organization of appropriation in relation to the capitalist and/or domestic mode(s) of production, and establish a largely one-way relationship between production and consumption (of commodities), with production determining or shaping both consumption itself and thus, by implication, the distinctive organization of consumer culture. However, this view can be criticized for assuming the passivity of the consumer and failing to consider whether or how consumers are active in the process of consumption.

Other approaches have been developed to explore this possibility. These can be grouped together as examples of a *consumption-led* explanation of the distinctiveness of modern consumer culture. This type of explanation is summed up by Paul Willis, who claims that he wants to 'rehabilitate consumption, creative consumption, to see creative potentials in it for itself, rather than see it as the dying fall of the usual triplet: production, reproduction, reception' (1990: 20), although, as noted above, Willis's approach can be criticized for not addressing the question of whether or not this creativity takes new forms in consumer culture. Yet consumption, or demand, cannot be taken for granted, but is itself a socially organized set of practices. As Appadurai writes:

> Demand emerges as a function of a variety of social practices and classifi-
> cations, rather than a mysterious emanation of human needs, a mechani-
> cal response to social manipulation (as in one model of the effects of
> advertising in our own society), or the narrowing down of a universal and
> voracious desire for objects to whatever happens to be available. (1986:
> 29)

One example of an explanation that begins to move beyond these assumptions is that which develops the view that the character and pattern of the consumption of commodities is related to their use as positional goods. The suggestion here is that the patterns of use of consumer goods and the satisfaction that people derive from their use depends upon and is shaped by the consumption choices of other people. So, for example, with what are sometimes called luxury objects, it is the fact that such goods are only affordable by an elite group of consumers which gives them their value. In the case of so-called cult objects it is not the limited availability arising as a result of economic cost that is the source of value, but the fact that certain items have limited appeal. In both cases, acts of consumption are actively carried out by consumers to indicate social status, good taste or simply being 'in the know' – that is, commodities are actively used as markers of social position and cultural style by consumers who seek to define their position *vis-à-vis* other consumers.

A number of writers suggest that the use of goods in positional consumption has a new significance in modern societies because it is tied in with the emergence of a new social group, what Thorstein Veblen famously called the leisure class (1925). This class, Veblen claims, sought to demonstrate its status publicly through the use of consumer goods in leisure practices; its characteristic feature was 'a conspicuous abstention from all useful employment'. This abstention was made visible or conspicuous by a spectacular display of consumption. Good taste became associated with the expression of distance from the world of work, the practical or the natural world, was termed 'refined' or 'cultivated', and was dissociated from that which could be regarded as 'cheap'. In short, this class – the so-called *nouveaux riches* – made use of material goods to assert their social pretensions. Other writers suggest that it is not just this class of consumers that has developed its own autonomous consumption practices, made visible through spectacular display, but that so too have more and more members of society, in part through a process of emulation by which lower groups in the hierarchy have sought to imitate higher groups. However, it has also been argued that consumption is not just motivated by a desire for status, that the impulse to emulate is not the only engine of consumer demand, but is also driven by hedonism, escapism, fantasy and the desire for novelty (Campbell 1989) or 'identity-value' (Featherstone 1991; but see Warde 1992; and see chapter 3).

One important example of this approach is the work of Daniel Miller, an anthropologist who is specifically concerned with material culture in the context of what he calls mass consumption (1987). As he points out, there is often a view that modern material culture is either trivial or degraded. He suggests that this 'anti-materialism' often stems from the belief that members of pre-industrial societies, free of the burden of artefacts, lived in more immediate, natural relationships with each other. He argues that this view is mistaken, and has obscured the activities which comprise contemporary material culture. In his own studies, he attempts to adopt what he calls a non-dualistic model of the relations between people and things.

This is an approach which brings together the two techniques outlined above, studying neither people nor things in isolation from one another.

Miller argues that such an approach reveals the positive appropriation of goods by, and at the level of, the pluralistic, small-scale communities which he believes make up the population of contemporary society. He argues that it is inappropriate to understand mass consumption in modern societies as one thing, that is, in relation to the workings of a single, central hierarchical principle, whether it be the division of labour or the practice of emulation. He writes:

> As mass consumption, a particular array of objects may be found to represent and assist in the construction of perspectives relating to control over production or rivalry between consumers, but also to wider issues concerning morality and social ideals. (1987: 158)

He thus argues for the necessity of analysing mass consumption in relation to 'a wide range of agents and relevant factors', including,

> forms of production and commerce and the demands of profit, the interests and constraints on manufacture, design, marketing and advertising, whose role it is to create the images of industrial goods in relation to specified target populations, and the interests and constraints on the consumer population, who use and in their turn manipulate the meaning of these forms through differential selection, placement, use and association. (1987: 158-9)

For Miller, mass consumption is the site at which a whole range of often self-contradictory and unbalanced desires, constraints and possibilities come together in a very incoherent process – what he describes as a kind of *practical kitsch*.

Despite this incoherence, he believes that mass consumption has at least the potential to produce what he calls an *inalienable culture*, that is, a culture invested by its users through a process of recontextualization of objects in specific sites with meanings that 'negate the abstraction of commodification'. He writes: 'Mass consumption may also be seen as . . . the creation of an inalienable world in which objects are so firmly integrated in the development of particular social relations and group identity as to be clearly generative of society' (1987: 204). So, for example, he argues that the sheer profusion of fashion, rather than overwhelming us with its diversity, facilitates the building up of multiple social groups who define themselves through the assertion of a specific style. He also points out that

> Small sections of the population become immersed to an extraordinary degree in the enormous profusion of hobbies, sports, clubs, fringe activities, and the nationwide organizations devoted to interests as diverse as medieval music, swimming, ballroom dancing, steel bands and fan clubs. The building of social networks and leisure activities around these highly particular pursuits is one of the strangest and most exotic features of contemporary industrial society, and one which is for ever increasing. There is no more eloquent confrontation with the abstraction of money, the state and modernity than a life devoted to racing pigeons, or medieval fantasies played out on a microcomputer. (1987: 209–10)

Furthermore, he argues that the self created in these processes may keep afloat several possible characters for him or herself, aided by a range of goods which externalize these multiple personalities. For Miller, this is a positive response to a necessarily contradictory world. He writes:

> It may not be desirable to act in relation to a work situation in the same way that one interacts with a family at home, not because of some fault in either situation, or the greater authenticity of one, but because the possibilities of modern life have developed from such divisions and frames. (1987: 209)

He can thus be seen as a representative of the view that increased consumer demand is a consequence of the activities of consumers at least as much as a consequence of the activities of producers.

Consumer demand and consumer culture

The previous section showed that there is some disagreement about the reasons for the growth in consumer demand, a factor that is often identified as a fundamental condition for the development of consumer culture. However, these explanations are not necessarily exclusive. It seems likely that large-scale changes in consumer demand are associated with various sequences and conjunctures of factors. It may be misleading to search for a single, overarching sequence of change, axiomatically defined as constitutive of the consumer revolution. Certainly there are significantly different national histories of consumption in different parts of the world suggesting that there are multiple processual flows underpinning changes in consumption, each of which is likely to have its own periodicity and rhythms, and none of which is solely responsible for the complex patterns of contemporary consumer demand. It is perhaps for this reason that Jonathan Friedman claims that

> No theory of consumption is feasible because consumption is not a socially autonomous phenomenon. The best we can do is supply a framework of analysis. This framework must connect the macro processes of social reproduction with the formation of social projects of consumption as well as the interaction between them. (1994: 17)

In the chapters that follow, a combination of the processes outlined in the explanations above will be identified as responsible for the particular patterns of consumer demand that have developed in Euro-American societies. However, it is important to recognize that the growth of consumer demand is not in and of itself responsible for the emergence of the features listed above. They indicate that it is not just that demand has increased, but that it has increased in specific kinds of ways. There are a complex set of intermediary processes involved here, and they have been described in a number of ways, including not only the development of consumer culture but also consumer logic (Leiss 1976) and consumer attitude (Bauman 1990).

In relation to the first of these, Leiss (1976) argues that modern Euro-American societies are characterized by what he calls a high-intensity market setting in which individuals are trained to act as consumers. This change is seen to have two key features: the number and complexity of available goods in the market-place grows enormously and individuals tend to interpret feelings of well-being more and more exclusively in terms of their relative success in gaining access to high levels of consumption. However, he suggests that the intensification of commodity circulation has a number of negative effects in relation to the ethics of the good life or well-being as a result of the fact that the 'direct interaction between impulses and sources of satisfaction is broken; impulses are controlled and consciously directed towards an enlarged field of satisfaction' (1976: 61). The negative effects include a fragmentation and destabilization of the categories of needing; the difficulty of matching the qualities of needs with the characteristics of goods; a growing indifference to the qualities of needs or wants; and an increasing environmental risk for individuals and for society as a whole. Together, these comprise what he calls a logic or ethic of consumption. Leiss does not think that there is anything 'inherently evil' in commodities and market exchange, but suggests that there is 'cause for concern' when commodity exchange becomes the exclusive mode for the satisfaction of human needs, displacing friendships and family relationships, engagement in political or community activities and so on.

Bauman (1990) shares similar concerns. He describes what he calls the consumer attitude as a way of life in which the market is the principal reference-point:

> What does it mean to have and to display a consumer attitude? It means, first perceiving life as a series of problems, which can be specified, more or less clearly defined, singled out and dealt with. It means, secondly, believing that dealing with such problems, solving them, is one's duty, which one cannot neglect without incurring guilt or shame. It means, thirdly, trusting that for every problem, already known or as may still arise in the future, there is a solution – a special object or recipe, prepared by specialists, by people with superior know-how, and one's task is to find it. It means, fourthly, assuming that such objects or recipes are essentially available; they may be obtained in exchange for money, and shopping is the way of obtaining them. It means, fifthly, translating the task of learning the art of living as the effort to acquire the skill of finding such objects and recipes, and gaining the power to possess them once found: shopping skills and purchasing power. (Bauman 1990: 204)

For Bauman, the widespread adoption of the consumer attitude means, on the one hand, that life is turned into an individual affair, that public issues are individualized, and, on the other, that what it is to be an individual is defined by consumer activity. This is seen to have transformed the basis of modern politics, which is now concerned with the self-making of individuals (see chapter 8 for a more detailed discussion of this politics).

Both the notion of a consumer logic or ethic and that of a consumer attitude offer useful ways of thinking about the implications of the escalation of consumer demand in modern societies, showing how its effects are not straightforward, but involve complex processes of interpretation, evaluation and struggle. The notion of consumer culture also does this, but it does so by suggesting that the cultural dimensions of the increase in consumer demand have come to take on a distinctive form and a special importance. As a term, it thus highlights what might be described as *the stylization of consumption*. But what is this process of stylization, and how is it to be explained? These questions are the focus of the next chapter.

Conclusion

This chapter has introduced the idea that consumer culture can be seen as one example or one type of material culture. The anthropological literature on material cultures discussed in the first part of the chapter showed that *consumption is always a cultural as well as an economic process*. It can be explored by looking at how the use of things is a means of creating a social identity and/or by looking at how things come to have social lives. The second part of the chapter identified some of the key features of consumer culture and introduced two contrasting sets of explanations of one especially important feature, increasing consumer demand. These were called *producer- and consumer-led perspectives* (additional differences between these approaches will be discussed in more detail in the next chapter). However, this chapter has also emphasized the necessity of looking at *cycles* of production and consumption. It is in the context of these multiple cycles that the development of consumer culture must be situated.

3

The Stylization of Consumption

Introduction

A number of writers argue that contemporary consumption is largely about meaning, that it is 'culturally drenched' (Featherstone
1991), that 'Modern consumption is not only about images, it is
also about play, especially play with meaning' (Abercrombie 1994:
51) and that culture is 'the very element of consumer society itself;
no society has ever been saturated with signs and images like this
one' (Jameson 1991: 131). This saturation is the basis of the claim
that we live in a society which is not just infused with a consumer
ethos or consumer attitude, but one which is dominated by a consumer culture.

   Arjun Appadurai (1986) provides one way of exploring this
claim. In general terms, he suggests that the movements of goods
within and across societies is shaped by the distribution of a combination of technical, social and aesthetic knowledge in the pathways
through which they flow. This distribution of knowledge is a key
determinant of the kinds of value attributed to objects as they circulate through these pathways. Appadurai further argues that, with the
mass production of objects, there has been a fundamental shift in
the regime of value associated with many kinds of exchange: from a
regime structured in terms of exclusivity, where the value of goods
was indirectly regulated by the costs of acquisition, to one which is
structured in terms of authenticity. This is seen to be a consequence
of the increasing importance of aesthetic knowledge in the pathways
along which objects flow.

However, Appadurai also argues that aesthetic and other knowledge is very unevenly distributed in these pathways, and points out that 'Problems involving knowledge, information, and ignorance are not restricted to the production and consumption poles of the careers of commodities, but characterize the process of circulation and exchange as well' (1986: 43). This is a point of view that suggests that the cultural drenching said to be characteristic of modern consumption does not make us all equally wet. Different interpretations of the causes of the uneven distribution of aesthetic knowledge and the problems it produces underpin rival accounts of the development and political implications of consumer culture. As Nicholas Abercrombie notes,

> if images are at the centre of modern consumption and of the producer–consumer relationship, then the control of their *meaning* is similarly central to the distribution of authority in that relationship. . . . Producers try to commodify meaning, that is try to make images and symbols into things which can be sold or bought. Consumers, on the other hand, try to give their own, new, meanings to the commodities and services that they buy. (1994: 51)

In the second half of this chapter three different accounts of the development of consumer culture will be put forward, each identifying different moments in the cycle of production and consumption as determinant of the uneven distribution of aesthetic knowledge. All three, however, acknowledge the growing importance of what is sometimes called the art-culture system (Clifford 1988) for the development of consumer culture, so it is to this system that the chapter will turn shortly. But, first, a note of caution.

It is widely argued that the art-culture system, a system made up of the set of institutions, practices and beliefs which, historically, has organized the production and consumption of cultural goods (such as visual art, literature, music, radio, film and television), has influenced the development of consumer culture in a number of ways, particularly following the rapid growth in the so-called culture industry in the twentieth century (Adorno and Horkheimer 1979). It is argued, for example, that the history of art and the development of popular culture have shaped the production and display of consumer goods. This argument is substantiated by pointing to the pervasive and taken-for-granted use of high art in advertising (Berger 1972); the ubiquity of commercial design, packaging and display in everyday life (Forty 1986); the increasing importance attached to imagery in the production and consumption of all material goods and services (Jameson 1991); and the growth of sectors of the economy concerned with some kind of cultural production (Lash and Urry 1994). It is also argued that the art-culture system has provided a context within which an aestheticized mode of involvement with objects has been adopted by many consumers, a mode within which the objects of material culture are related not simply to social relationships but also to specifically symbolic or cultural values, especially authenticity (Bowlby 1985; Featherstone 1991; Campbell 1989).

However, despite the apparent certainty of the claims noted above concerning the drenching of consumption in culture, the impact of the art-culture system on consumption as a whole has, rather surprisingly, not been subject to systematic empirical investigation. As a result, it is not clear to what extent the art-culture system has shaped consumption of *all* objects. As the studies discussed in the following chapters indicate, the consumption of cultural goods is frequently taken to be typical or symptomatic of consumption more generally, as if the consumption of cultural goods in some way exemplifies the changes in consumption of all goods, but this is by no means established. Abercrombie, for example, simply states that 'the *best* examples' of the struggles over meaning which shape consumption 'come from cultural commodities' (1994: 51, emphasis added). A number of writers are thus sceptical of generalizing about consumption *per se* on the evidence provided by studies of the consumption of cultural goods. So, for example, Alan Warde suggests that the result of studying the more spectacular instances of consumption leads to an underestimation of purely routine consumption:

> Although some people may attempt to create total life-styles as expressions of personal identity, most, despite the intentions of advertising agencies, probably see choices between soaps or soups as not seriously prejudicial to their self-image. (1992: 25)

Nevertheless, although Warde may be right to express a note of scepticism about the extent to which the consumption of cultural goods is typical of consumption more generally, it has clearly been given a special significance in the activities of many social groups who have sought to redefine their identity and the meaning of consumption for themselves through their use of cultural goods, such as literature, music and art. So, while the consumption of cultural goods may be neither *representative* nor *typical* of consumption more generally, it may be especially important in understanding consumer culture in so far as it operates as an *exemplary* mode of consumption. However, it is important to bear in mind that the extent to which the consumption of non-cultural goods is organized in ways which are parallel to or diverge from the patterns of use established in relation to cultural goods is a matter of considerable dispute.

The organization of the art-culture system

If it is accepted that the consumption of cultural goods has a special significance in the development of consumer culture, then as well as looking at the use of material goods as a communicator it is also necessary to look at the social organization of the cultural field and the market principles of supply, demand, accumulation, competition and monopolization which operate within the sphere of lifestyles, cultural goods and commodities (Featherstone 1991). This can be done by looking at the historical organization of the art-culture system in modern Euro-American societies.

James Clifford employs the term art-culture system to mean 'the general system of objects within which [aesthetically] valued objects circulate and make sense'; it is the outcome of 'powerful discriminations made at particular moments' (1988: 221). By virtue of this system, he argues, a world of aesthetic value is created and a meaningful deployment and circulation of artefacts maintained. However, a crucial aspect of this system, as its name implies, is the alliance between 'culture' and 'art'. Historically, the operation of this alliance has meant that while the term 'culture' in principle includes all learned human behaviour, in practice it privileges, through its connection with 'art', the coherent, balanced and 'authentic' aspects of the life of a community or society above the contradictory, incoherent and disruptive aspects.

Clifford provides a diagram (see Figure 3.1) to illustrate the workings of the modern art-culture system. His special interest is in the role of the discipline of anthropology in the operation of this system, and this interest means that he is particularly sensitive to the significance of circuits of valuation *across* national boundaries, and, in particular between 'the West and the rest'. However, it is impor-

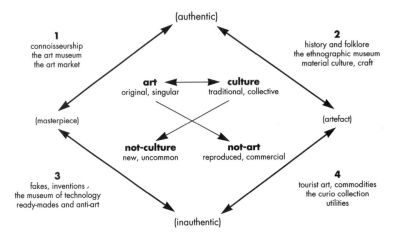

(authentic)

1
connoisseurship
the art museum
the art market

2
history and folklore
the ethnographic museum
material culture, craft

art ◄——► **culture**
original, singular   traditional, collective

(masterpiece)   (artefact)

not-culture   **not-art**
new, uncommon   reproduced, commercial

3
fakes, inventions ⁄
the museum of technology
ready-mades and anti-art

4
tourist art, commodities
the curio collection
utilities

(inauthentic)

Figure 3.1   The art-culture system: A machine for making authenticity
Source: Clifford 1988.

tant to bear in mind that the processes that create authenticity operate within as well as across national boundaries.

According to Clifford, the system classifies objects and assigns them value relative to one another; it also establishes the contexts in which they properly belong and between which they circulate – such as museums, art galleries and libraries – and marginalizes other sites. Clifford calls it a machine for *making authenticity*. This helps explain its special significance for the development of modern consumer culture, since, according to Appadurai, authenticity has become an especially important value in contemporary Euro-American societies. Movements towards positive value, or authenticity, proceed from bottom to top and from right to left, and result in the creation of pathways of authentification according to particular (historically changing) criteria.

During the nineteenth and early twentieth centuries, the dominant criteria employed in the creation of these pathways in Euro-American societies were those associated with the complex of ideas relating to originality, aesthetic form and social distinction. These were ideas deriving from a particular conception of artistic *production*, in which the author or artist was elevated as the principal source of meaning. So, for example, the 'artist' was set apart from, often against, society, and his (or, more rarely, her) genius was recognized in terms of the artwork's transcendence of everyday life.

The legitimation of this transcendence was secured through practices such as collecting, connoisseurship and the creation of artificial scarcity. They, in turn, contributed to the development of a notion of *the possessive self* as an ideal. This is a self who is judged in terms of the accumulation of possessions, and for whom identity itself is a kind of wealth (of objects, knowledge, memories and experience).

More generally, the consequence of the application of these criteria, Clifford argues, has been the creation of hierarchies of value in the art-culture system. One especially important instance of this was the creation of the hierarchy of culture, from 'high' to 'popular', within European nations during the course of the second half of the nineteenth and the first half of the twentieth century. This distinction, sometimes perceived to be at its most acute in the separation between *modernism* in the fine arts and popular or mass culture emerged in the course of the nineteenth century in association with a tangle of other social and political processes, including industrialization, urbanization, imperialism, the development of mass technologies of cultural production and the differentiation and institutionalization of distinct domains of knowledge and expertise. Importantly for the arguments to be presented here, while it is almost impossible to establish an objective aesthetic basis for this distinction, one of the ways in which popular culture was subordinated to high culture was through its association with (a particular understanding of) mass *consumption*. Consumption was understood to be a thoughtless, trivial, or passive activity in which the author-derived criteria for valuing artworks – including originality and individual genius – were lost; through the association of their meaning with this negative conception of consumption, the objects of popular culture were excluded from the preferred movements of authentification.

During the second half of the twentieth century, however, the validity of the distinction between high and popular culture has been called into doubt, especially in certain understandings of contemporary culture as *postmodern*. This is seen to be, in part, a consequence of a re-evaluation of the significance of the activity of consumption itself. This re-evaluation is, in turn, a consequence of the challenge to the opposition between the notion of 'the original', which has historically been so central to the Western valuation of art, and the notion of 'the reproduction' or 'the copy' (historically held to be definitive of mass or popular culture). This challenge is linked to the development of technologies of mass communication which have contributed to an ever-greater separation between the relations of production of an artwork from those of its consumption. This has opened up the possibility that independent definitions of value, including competing definitions of authenticity, may arise in the consumption of mass-reproduced works (Thompson 1990; Lury 1993). It is this possibility that has thus provided the conditions in which consumers of cultural goods are able to play a greater part in the attribution of aesthetic value, challenging the authority of the producer and complicating the criteria of authenticity (Appadurai 1986; Abercrombie 1991).

However, it is not clear whether this challenge to the distinction between high and popular culture will merely result in a redrawing of the cultural map or whether it will erase the distinction altogether, resulting in what has, somewhat ironically, been described as a de-aestheticization of art (Whiteley 1994). In this respect, it is important to remember that the art-culture system is itself a contested field, and not all individuals or social groups have historically had the same relationship to either high or popular culture. Indeed, relations of class, gender, race and age were deeply involved in the processes by which high culture was historically elevated above popular culture, as is clear from the implicity derogatory use of terms associated with subordinated groups, such as 'vulgar', 'feminine', 'primitive' or 'juvenile', to describe popular culture. It is not yet clear how these subordinated groups will fare in relation to postmodernism and its re-articulation of the processes of making authenticity. However, the political struggles of these groups are widely seen to have contributed to the undermining of the hierarchical distinction between high and popular culture.

Moreover, the organization of the art-culture system is affected not only by challenges to the distinction between high and popular culture as a consequence of changes in the mass reproduction of cultural objects, but also by challenges to the distinction between high and *folk* or *primitive* culture. So, for example, according to Clifford, both art and culture emerged after 1800 as mutually reinforcing domains of human value – as strategies for gathering, marking off and preserving what were seen as the best and most interesting creations of 'man'. In practice, they were terms of approbation reserved for the creations of elites in Europe and North America. However, in the twentieth century, the domains of both art and culture have undergone a series of developments. A plural definition of culture – cultures – emerged as a liberal alternative to the previously dominant evolutionary classification of (a singular) human culture. Clifford writes that this pluralization was a sensitive means for understanding different and dispersed 'whole ways of life' in a high colonial context of global interconnection. *Culture* in its full evolutionary richness and authenticity, formerly reserved for the best creations of modern Europe, could now be extended to all the world's populations. (1988: 234)

However, as he goes on to argue, while this new pluralism challenged the assumption of the superiority of European high culture, it did not entirely erase it; rather, it transformed the terms of its operation.

He argues that in the early twentieth century, as *culture* was being extended to all the world's societies, an increasing number of 'exotic', 'primitive' or 'archaic' objects came to be seen as *art*. This happened in a number of ways, both through the influence that such objects acquired in the practices of European modernism, including, for example, in the influence they exerted on individual artists such as Gaugin or Picasso, the vogue for *l'art négre* in elite circles, and the institutional reclassification of primitive objects as art and their acquisition and display in the fine arts museums of the West. In many ways, the immediate effect of this was to intensify the distinction between high and both folk and popular culture. However, as Clifford and others have argued (see chapter 6), the implications of the growing interconnectedness of the world's populations is now coming to destabilize the distinctions between high and folk culture. This destabilization is often connected to the contemporary processes of time–space distantiation (Giddens 1991) or time–space compression (Harvey 1989) in which, so it is argued, previously existing conceptions of time and space as homogeneous, uniform axes of social life are being internally ruptured. Objects now circulate not only across extended global pathways; their movement is also determined according to multiple, cross-cutting indices of time and space, connecting people in various relations of immersion and distance, distraction and contemplation.

This account of the organization of the art-culture system has, necessarily, been very schematic. However, it offers an indication of some broad historical transformations in the making of authenticity, while suggesting that there is some debate about how best to characterize these changes, and emphasizing that different social groups are very differently positioned in relation to them. In any case, the significance of these changes for the development of consumer culture cannot be established without considering how they interact with historical developments in other kinds of production and consumption. For this reason, the rest of this chapter outlines three models of the development of consumer culture, focusing on their descriptions of the interaction between the art-culture system and production and consumption more generally.

Captains of consciousness and commodity aesthetics

In very general terms, from what has been called a production-led perspective, the emergence of consumer culture is tied to the way in which the production of commodities has come to be dominated by 'culturally standardised recipes for fabrication' (Appadurai 1986). This perspective suggests that, while the production of goods always involves knowledge, the production of goods as commodities for exchange on the market involves an elaborate standardization in the knowledge used, including the aesthetic knowledge. This is what is seen to have produced the conditions for the emergence of consumer culture or what is alternately called *commodity aesthetics* (Haug 1986).

Such arguments identify the expansion of markets and the growth of consumption as a consequence of the *expansion of capital*. Historically this expansion is linked to the processes of imperialism and colonization in complex ways, incorporating specific forms of specialized knowledge. McClintock (1994), for example, argues that what she calls commodity racism – a specific type of commodity fetishism – in the Victorian forms of advertising and commodity spectacle, the imperial expositions and the museum movement, was used not only to market products but also promoted evolutionary racism and imperial power. According to McClintock, the commodity, abstracted from its social context and the human labour that produced it, was attributed with the civilizing work of empire (for further discussion of the relationship between race and consumer culture see chapter 6).

Over the course of the nineteenth and twentieth centuries, the expansion of capital has continued on a macro- and a micro-level; new markets have been created and existing ones extended. These currently range from the intensified export of consumer capitalism to ex-colonies and the many regions of the Third World whose peoples were the object of imperial commodity spectacle a century ago, to the intensification of internal markets through the commodification of the individual's relation to the body, self and identity in the form of health and diet foods, and expanded sport, leisure, fashion and cosmetic markets. But consumption has not only been extended geographically, growing in *space*; it has also been extended or, perhaps better, intensified, *temporally*.

This, it is suggested, was achieved, from the eighteenth century onwards, through the introduction of the principles of fashion to an ever-wider range of products, often following the model developed for the product category of clothing (Fine and Leopold 1993). These principles led to dramatic changes in the relationship between production, merchandizing and consumption, including the rapid introduction of new products, the attempt to introduce a deliberately rapid obsolescence of style in products, the speedier diffusion of knowledge of specific fashions through catalogues, promotion and advertising, and the use of a wide range of marketing techniques. (For a contrasting view of the emergence of fashion, see McKendrick et al. (1982: 9–34 *passim*) where it is argued that the spread of fashion was dependent upon a new consumer sensibility, a kind of progressive emulation among the lower middle classes and a new fondness for novelty. According to McKendrick, once the pursuit of luxury 'was made possible for an ever-widening proportion of the population, then its potential was released and it became an engine for growth, a motive power for mass production' (1982: 66).

However, a number of writers argue that it is not simply the expansion of markets in space and time which has changed the scale and nature of consumption in recent years, but *the intensification and reorganization of the labour process*, through new flexible technologies, redesigned working practices, new methods of stock and inventory control and the like. Martyn Lee, for example, suggests:

> Qualitative changes to the intensity and structure of labour and means of production tend to be reflected in changes to the commodity-form. This in turn implies some form of change to the composition of needs and to the structure of consumption itself. (1993: 133)

While this is a long-term process, Lee gives examples of a number of new or more marked characteristics of commodities which he suggests are definitive of the changed commodity-form in the 1980s. These include miniaturization – the reduction of the size of commodities in order to create new physical space, especially within the domestic environment, which may then make room for new commodities. Obvious examples here are music systems, television sets, radios and video recorders. Another development is the growth of what Lee calls 'compound commodities', that is, the compression or unification of previously discrete commodities, such as complete prepared meals, combined shampoos and conditioners, washing powders and fabric softeners, and alcoholic spirits and mixers. In these examples he points to the importance of the use of specialized technical and social knowledges in the production process.

However, Lee also suggests that one of the most significant developments in the commodity-form over recent years is the transition in production from *material* to *experiential* commodities. By this, he means that there has been a transition from production organized for the manufacture of durable and material commodities (washing machines, vacuum cleaners, cars, etc.) to the production of non-durable and, in particular, experiential commodities which are either used up during the act of consumption or, alternatively, based upon the consumption of a given period of time, such as leisure or holiday activities. He writes: 'Effectively, there has been a marked "de-materialisation" of the commodity-form where the act of exchange centres upon those commodities which are time rather than substance based' (1993: 135). This process clearly involves an increase in the use of aesthetic knowledge in production, requiring judgements of taste and aesthetic value in the design, development and production of such commodities. Lee further acknowledges that there has been an intensification of aesthetic obsolescence, that is, a more rapid turnover of styling changes. He argues that this is linked to the small-batch commodity production that has been made possible by more flexible working practices, new technologies and improvements in the means of distribution. All these changes, he argues, have resulted in what he calls the *fluidization* of consumption: the freeing-up of the previously static and relatively fixed spatial and temporal dimensions of social life. These changes can be seen to have contributed to what I have here called the stylization of consumption, linking this stylization back to production.

In addition, advertising is identified as an important part of the process of stylization. So, for example, Sut Jhally writes:

> in non-market societies there is a unity between people and goods, but in capitalism there is a separation between object and producer. The world of goods in industrial society offers no meaning, its meaning having been 'emptied' out of them. The function of advertising is to refill the emptied commodity with meaning. Indeed the meaning of advertising would make no sense if objects already had an established meaning. The power of advertising *depends* upon the initial emptying out. Only then can advertising refill this empty void with its own meaning. Its power comes from the fact that it works its magic on a blank slate. (1989: 221)

The suggestion here is that advertising is a tool whereby consumers are controlled and manipulated by the producers of goods, who deliver things for which consumers have no real needs, through the in use of specialist types of aesthetic knowledge in the production and distribution of products. Raymond Williams writes:

> If we are sensibly materialist, in that part of our living in which we use things, we should find most advertising to be of insane irrelevance. Beer would be enough for us, without the additional promise that in drinking it we would show ourselves to be manly, young at heart or neighbourly. A washing machine would be a useful machine to wash clothes, rather than an indication that we are forward looking or an object of envy to our neighbours. (1980: 172)

The imperative for the creation of these artificial needs is seen to come from the ever-increasing number of goods that capitalism must produce in order to survive. To avoid stagnation and the ultimate end of capitalism, manufacturers have to ensure that what is produced is also consumed, and they do so by the manipulation of the meaning of goods.

The dancing raisins that advertise California Raisins have little to do with the properties of the raisins. The creators didn't emphasize their wrinkles, or their small size, or their health properties. A greater leap was made. Seth Werner, who created the California Raisins, explains the beginning of that idea:

'The client said to us, "I'd like a celebrity campaign because I'd like my campaign to be bigger than just raisins. I figure a celebrity will give it personality and give it bigger presence than we can give with our product alone." We said we thought we could make a celebrity out of the raisins themselves by giving them a personality. Our original idea . . . was to have a bunch of raisins dance to "I Heard It Through The Grapevine." And then we started to think about what the raisins would look like. We decided that we wanted the raisins to be cool and a bit intimidating. In contrast, other snack foods would be less cool, less hip. We began creating a relationship between the raisins and other characters – such as the potato chips that wilt, the candy bars that melt, or gum that gets his shoe stuck to the table. And while the raisins were dressed in high-top sneakers with the laces untied and sunglasses, looking cool, the pretzels had wing-tipped shoes, a candy bar had desert boots – anything that would look less hip by comparison.' (Seger 1990: 180–1)

This line of argument is developed further in the study by Leiss, Kline and Jhally (1986), which looks at changes in advertising style and content alongside changes in the organization of production, thus enabling them to focus on the aesthetic knowledges embedded in goods by producers and advertisers. This study identifies a number of different stages in American advertising during the course of the twentieth century, and suggests that these changes have implications for how commodities come to acquire meaning in social life. It suggests that the formerly artistic countercultural notion that life should be a work of art has been taken up and promoted in marketing and advertising as a way of selling the ever-increasing number of goods being produced.

I 1890–1925: The Product-Oriented Approach

The central feature of ads during this period is the product itself – its function, features, price and the quality of its construction. The question for the consumer is assumed to be, what does this product do? – that is, what is its functional or practical utility? Written text explains the 'reason why' a particular product should be used. Although new printing techniques allowed the increasing use of illustrations and design elements, in general the written text explained the reasons for consuming the product, the identity of the user, the appropriate context for use, and provided the key to the meaning of any illustration.

II 1925–45: Product Symbols

During this period there was a shift in the focus of ads from the features of a product to its benefits for the consumer. The product was now presented in terms of its uses for the individual. The ads began to explore the non-practical aspects of use – there was an increasing emphasis on what the product could mean for consumers. The product itself became more abstract, representing a value achieved in use rather than a thing valued in its own right. This period also saw technical advances in the visual presentation of products.

III 1945–65: Personalization

Ads in this period were characterized not so much by representations of the product-in-use as by images of the consumer or user. Various motivations for consuming were represented, including the desire for social approval, pride in ownership, guilt and anxiety. Social interaction was shown to flow through the products people have, and the product itself might be personified, taking on human characteristics. So, for example, an ad from Chrevolet in this period claimed that the vehicle was 'More than a car – a member of the family'. Sometimes the product itself was represented as speaking, as if it were a person. The visual image increasingly came to stand on its own, unexplained by any written text. What written text there was employed a very condensed style – sometimes conversational, sometimes allusive, sometimes poetic.

IV 1965–85: Market Segmentation

This phase was characterized by the joint appearance of lifestyle ads and market segmentation. The focus of most ads shifted to the stylized identification of the consumer and the meaning of the act of consumption in a social situation. The product was displayed in a social context; the people who were displayed in the scene were not clearly defined by social role – instead they were situated within a particular consumption lifestyle. Consumption was represented in terms of the imaginary pleasures of certain settings and occasions – that is, in terms of a fantasy lifestyle – rather than in terms of satisfaction. Sometimes the product was absent altogether, as in the well-known Benson and Hedges cigarette series of advertisements.

This analysis suggests not only that advertising has become more important in contemporary economies, but that changes in the style of advertising – and in particular a shift away from product features to the look of the product and its use in particular settings or lifestyles – have contributed to changes in how consumption is organized. Contemporary consumers are not invited to be rational or instrumental in their use of products, but instead to employ products in an expressive display of lifestyle. This change is attributed to the work of advertisers, marketers and publicists who seek to persuade the consumer to adopt a new role in the cycle of capitalist production and consumption. They do this by highlighting and standardizing the aesthetic knowledge involved in the production of the product, inviting the consumer to see and use the product in these terms.

Similarly, in the work of Stuart Ewen and Elizabeth Ewen (1976; 1982) great attention is paid to the role of 'the captains of consciousness' in marketing and advertising in the shaping of American consumer culture. In *Channels of Desire*, they report on an oral history study they carried out to show how what they call 'mass images', including those taken from cinema and advertising, played a role in the shaping of American consciousness in the early twentieth century. They thus point to the contributory role of the mass media and popular culture in providing a context within which advertising and promotional images could circulate. These images are seen to have created a vision of America which drew immigrants to 'the promised land', and American-ized immigrants on their arrival.

In one example, the Ewens tell how a firm's logo on a cotton bale evoked a utopian image of America in the mind of a young Czech working girl. They argue that this logo produced an image for her of America as a land of abundance. The young woman came to see consumer products as magical objects, and the brand names and images of products became 'channels for her desires', emblems of wishes unfulfilled. She eventually emigrated to the USA, having, as it were, already been introduced to the American way of life. Advertising is thus deemed central by the Ewens to the creation of what they call the 'mass individual'. A more contemporary example of this process is the way in which consumer goods – whose existence was broadcast in the media – are said to have represented Western concepts of freedom, democracy and choice to those living in eastern Europe before the collapse of communism.

However, the Ewens acknowledge that the development of modern consumer society is a contradictory and complex process. They suggest that it is important to consider the historical context in which the manipulation of needs by producers and their agents not only occurs but is effective. They identify what they describe as the disruptive nature of the experience of the processes of modernization as the context in which commodity aesthetics is able to take root. They suggest that the processes of urbanization and migration uprooted many people from familiar patterns of work, family and community, and from customary or traditional ways of understanding the world.

They point to the ways in which people began to learn not only that 'others' were strangers, but that they themselves were strangers to others. This, the Ewens argue, led to a sense of self as strange or alien. It was in this context, they argue, that people became responsive to advertising and commodity aesthetics, since these discourses provided a common vocabulary and a shared way of relating to self and others. The use of a shared commercial vocabulary of image, appearance and style contributed to a shift away from a sense of self-identity understood in terms of internal or subjective moral and ethical values – that is, in terms of character, or of attributes such as goodness or evil. This was increasingly replaced by a sense of self-identity defined in terms of external, presentational, often visual characteristics – that is, in terms of personality, appearance, demeanour and, most importantly, style. The Ewens thus suggest that advertising was effective because it was able to respond to the often disorienting changes associated with modernization, and presented commodities as magical solutions to the problems of alienation and disorientation raised by modern life. Or, as Sahlins puts it, goods allowed Western society to turn 'the basic contradiction of its construction into a miracle of existence, a cohesive society of perfect strangers' (1976: 203).

In sum, this line of argument suggests that Euro-American societies have seen the development of what can be called commodity aesthetics. This is a consequence of a mode of production, and is of profound importance in setting the conditions for a whole way of life. It is the basis of a form of material culture in which

> aesthetic innovation, as the functionary for regenerating demand, is . . . transformed into a moment of direct anthropological power and influence, in that it continually changes humankind as a species in their sensual organization, in their real orientation and material lifestyle, as much as in their perception, satisfaction and structure of their needs. (Haug 1986: 44)

This restructuring of human needs is seen to have had harmful effects. In a much quoted passage, Herbert Marcuse claims:

> People recognize themselves in their commodities; they find their soul in their automobile, hi-fi set, split-level home . . . social control is anchored in the new needs which [the consumer society] has produced. (1968: 24)

John Berger also supports this view:

> Capitalism survives by forcing the majority whom it exploits, to define their own interests as narrowly as possible. This was once achieved by extensive deprivation. Today in the developed countries it is being achieved by imposing a false standard of what is and what is not desirable. (1972: 154)

These arguments about the effect of advertising and commodity aesthetics have been very influential in sociological understandings of consumer culture. However, they have been criticized on a number of grounds. The centrality of production relative to the rest of social life – and in particular the importance of the aesthetic knowledges adopted by producers in shaping its meaning for consumers – has been challenged, and the implicit assertion that production or work is the only true means of human self-creation is called into doubt. A further problem with production-led explanations is that it is not clear how changes in the mode of producing goods have such a powerful or direct influence on other moments in the cycle of product appropriation or use. It is also argued that the Marxist-inspired critique of advertising radically overstates the significance and effectiveness of advertising in contemporary culture, and implies that consumers are passive, suggestible and easily duped. Other critics point out that another problem with this kind of explanation is that it tends to play down the importance of the art-culture system in the development of consumer culture, presenting a rather reductive account of the increasing stylization of consumption, and ignoring the significance of the creative use of cultural goods by consumers in the development of consumer culture.

From Production to Signification: The Logic of the Code

As noted above, many writers have challenged the centrality of work in production-led explanations. One of the most important writers here has been the French philosopher Jean Baudrillard. He calls into doubt the importance Marx and his followers attach to the concept of use-value. The term use-value is used by Marx, or so Baudrillard argues, to refer to the value pertaining to goods by virtue of the 'genuine' human needs to which they relate. (For the argument that Baudrillard misrepresents Marx in this respect see Preteceille and Terrail 1985; Jhally 1987; and Kellner 1983.) The products of labour are assumed to be aimed at the fulfilment of fundamental, often biological, needs, which are the essence of humanity. It is in opposition to these genuine or real needs that the emphasis on exchange-value is seen to lead to the creation of false needs. However, Baudrillard argues, it is impossible to establish what these 'real' needs are; indeed, he suggests that there are no given, essential or real needs for humans, and that the distinction between 'true' and 'false' needs is impossible to sustain. Rather, all needs are always socially created. Baudrillard believes that the Marxist-derived argument that commodities ought to relate to 'real' values is a consequence of an over-emphasis on production as the source of value and prevents any understanding of how commodities actually circulate and acquire meaning in late capitalist societies.

Baudrillard argues that Marx developed his analysis of the commodity and commodity fetishism in relation to a now long-disappeared stage in the development of capitalism. According to Baudrillard, we now live in a society in which the logic of production is no longer paramount; instead the logic of signification is all-important. This latest stage in the development of capitalism is not just an extension of earlier stages, but represents a radical rupture with them, and thus requires new analytical concepts. We have moved, Baudrillard asserts, from a phase in the development of capitalism where the commodity-form was dominant to one where the sign-form prevails. Consumption, then, must not be understood in relation to use-values, as material utility, but primarily in relation to *sign-values*, as *signification*.

Baudrillard suggests that it is through the operation of a symbolic code or the logic of signs that commodities are given meaning. The phenomenon of branding in advertising, whereby an aura of associations is attached to a product – for instance, sexuality to Levi jeans, rugged masculinity to Marlboro cigarettes, and a 'hip' lifestyle to raisins, is identified as an important site of the operation of this code. The meaning of goods created in a brand is understood by Baudrillard to be separate from the social relations of both production and consumption: it is not to be understood in relation to their intrinsic qualities or use, but neither is it to be understood in terms of their economic exchange. Rather, their meaning arises from their position in a continuing process of signification and resignification. In Appadurai's term, it as if the system of aesthetic knowledge has entirely displaced the significance of other forms of knowledge, and is not simply the principal but the sole determinant of the movement of goods between people.

According to Baudrillard, the game of sign consumption is an integral part of the 'society of the spectacle' (Debord 1977), and represents a new historical stage in the process of signification. Instead of reporting on events, the media, including advertising, brings into being events – political demonstrations, sports fixtures, scandal, even products – which would not otherwise have happened. These are simulated events or products; that is, they have no fixed origins: they do not refer to a prior reality, they have no known sources of authority. As a consequence, for Baudrillard, we live in what he calls a *hyper-reality*. Everything is a copy, or a copy of a copy, and what is fake seems more real than the real. Reality has devoured everything, and everything can claim reality with the same (in)justice. Advertising too operates in this mode. But since the audience is increasingly made up of a media-literate generation, its members, rather than seeking the truth, in turn self-consciously mimic the media – they adopt the persona of fictional characters as a way of expressing themselves, they discuss their personal lives via analogies with the story-lines of soap-operas, and talk in the catch-phrases of celebrities and the slogans of advertising campaigns. They are reflexively aware that advertising is trying to persuade them to buy particular products. They know when they've been tango-ed!

What I [a partner in an advertising agency] have found is that the consumer is no longer the 'tabula rasa' that she/he once was. People are no longer passive data bases revealing 'pure' or straightforward feelings about advertising . . .

There are a number of reasons for this, including the marketing of advertising itself, evident in newspaper coverage and TV programmes, the widespread experience of the research process and, not least, the experience of thirty years of TV advertising. . . . when you access today's consumer – *what they think, and what they think you want them to think, are often one and the same.* If you ask people what makes a 'good' financial services advertisement, for example, they will tell you that it is an advertisement that tells you that the organization doing the advertising is 'big, warm, friendly and careful with your money'.

Why is this? Is it because people want financial institutions to project an image of being big, warm, friendly and caring or is it because financial institutions have spent the last ten years telling people that they are big, warm, friendly and caring? The answer is both. Ten years down the line it is impossible to say which came first – the chicken or the egg. (Lury 1994: 96)

According to Baudrillard, the political system no longer needs universal participation in production to enforce order; instead it requires only that everyone play the game of signification. As more and more needs, wants and desires are brought into the realm of signification, individuals lose autonomous control and surrender to the code. A potentially infinite play of signs orders society while providing the individual with an illusory sense of freedom and self-determination. What Baudrillard is arguing here is that there have been historical changes in the ways in which material goods acquire and convey meanings in modern societies. Objects are no longer related to in terms of their practical utility, but instead have become empty signifiers of an increasing number of constantly changing meanings. There is an over-production of signs and a loss of referents.

Clearly the rise of the mass media is central to this account. In contrast to Williams, Baudrillard suggests that it no longer makes sense to criticize people for being insufficiently materialistic; instead, we should submit to the magic of advertising as a playful code:

> In [the] field of connotations the object takes on the value of a sign. In this way a washing machine *serves* as an equipment and *plays* as an element of comfort, or of prestige, etc. It is the field of play that is specifically the field of consumption. Here all sorts of objects can be substituted for the washing machine as a signifying element. In the logic of signs . . . objects are no longer tied to a function or to a *defined* need. This is precisely because objects respond to something different, either to a social logic, or to a logic of desire, where they serve as a fluid and unconscious field of signification. (1988a: 44)

Although in this extract Baudrillard appears to be suggesting that the logic of signification is tied to other processes, such as 'the social logic' or 'the logic of desire', in his later work he goes so far as to suggest that objects not only do not signify use value but do not signify *anything* outside of themselves. Rather than people using objects to express differences between themselves (as Sahlins suggests), for Baudrillard people have become merely the vehicles for expressing the differences between objects.

The logic of sign-value represents the final triumph of capitalism through the imposition of a cultural order compatible with the demands of large-scale commodity production. It results in a depthless world, in which meaning is a sham. Baudrillard comments that reality flickers like a television screen: there is a new flimsiness to reality. This is sometimes described as *the implosion of the social*, its internal dissolution as a consequence of its own contradictions.

This has been a very influential argument, especially in so far as it opens up a way of exploring the organization of the distinctively stylized nature of consumer culture, but many commentators are critical of what they see as the sweeping generalizations which Baudrillard proposes. He is widely seen to have adopted an overly pessimistic interpretation of contemporary society, in which both producers and consumers are caught up in the endless reproduction of signs with no escape possible, for he claims we live 'everywhere already in an "aesthetic" hallucination of reality' (1983 in

Featherstone 1991: 148). For some commentators, however, this is a misleading claim, which overstates the significance of signification and ignores the activities of consumers.

Romanticism and the daydreaming consumer

In explicit contrast to the two preceding types of explanation, Colin Campbell (1989) develops an alternative view of consumption. He argues that it is not an automatic response to either production or signification, but should, rather, be seen as springing from autonomous, independent sources. Central to this argument is Campbell's belief that people have independent desires to pursue pleasures; this is not a desire that has to be manipulated into being. However, he also suggests that there have been changes in the social organization and expression of the pursuit of this desire for pleasure, or hedonism. He thus sees consumption as a voluntaristic, self-directed and creative process that involves shared cultural values and ideals, but one which has undergone a process of historical change.

Traditional hedonism, he suggests, was characterized by a concern with sensations, and pleasing the senses. Each pleasure was relatively finite or discrete and was associated with specific activities, such as eating. In this sense, it was standardized. There was a more or less direct connection between pleasure and satisfaction. However, a distinctively modern form of hedonism emerges from the late eighteenth century onwards in Western societies. This new form of hedonism is tied by Campbell to the emergence of the Romantic ethic of the late eighteenth and early nineteenth centuries, which in turn is related to the Protestant ethic of the seventeenth and eighteenth centuries. (The Protestant ethic was argued to be an important contributing factor in the emergence of capitalism by Max Weber (1930).) Campbell notes that, while the Protestant ethic is commonly understood in terms of asceticism or puritanism (and thus might be seen to be hostile to the emergence of consumer culture), some strands within the ethic associated virtue with the charitable feelings of pity and sympathy. This, argues Campbell, was the basis of the growth of an emotionalist way of life in which the good man or woman could display his or her virtue through the expression of emotions, especially those of pity and melancholy. In time, this expression came to bring its own pleasure, rather than simply being a means of displaying virtue.

This way of life took on a wider cultural significance through the influence of the work of the Romantics, a group of writers, poets and artists, including Keats, Wordsworth and Shelley, whose work displayed a sometimes sentimental, nostalgic form of Romanticism in which the individual longs to experience in reality those pleasures which can only be imagined. It is this Romantic ethic, Campbell suggests, which provides the conditions for the emergence of a distinctively modern form of hedonism, in which pleasure is separated from physical satisfaction, but pursued in the art of daydreaming.

Pleasure is no longer given by specific activities, or associated with particular sensations; indeed, it is no longer localized or focused, but instead is a potential aspect or dimension of all experiences. This potential is to be found in the imagination; the individual learns to substitute imaginary for real stimuli, and by self-consciously creating and manipulating illusions or imaginary experiences or emotions in daydreams and fantasies constructs his or her own pleasurable environment. Campbell argues that modern hedonism is characterized by a longing to experience in reality those pleasures created or enjoyed in imagination, a longing which results in the ceaseless consumption of novelty. Pleasure, once detached from specific activities, has the potential to be never-ending. Moreover, once the direct link between objects and sensations is broken, once it is mediated by daydreaming and fantasy, then images, as the vehicles of the imagination, become more and more important in modern forms of pleasure.

Consumption expresses the romantic longing to become an *other*; however, whatever one becomes is never what one wants to be. This is because the actual consumption or use of goods becomes a disillusioning experience. The actuality of consumption fails to live up to the dream or the fantasy. This persistent cycle of pleasurable expectation and disappointment explains the never-ending, insatiable character of modern consumption, why people continue to shop until they drop. Campbell thus explains what he sees as the inherent dynamism of modern consumption – the endless quest for novelty – in terms of the ever-changing, never satisfiable hedonistic desires of modern consumers, what might be called the Walter Mitty imperative. (See Campbell 1994 for a description of contemporary types of what he calls neophiliacs, lovers of novelty).

Campbell's account of the emergence of modern consumption goes some way to explain a number of the characteristics of contemporary consumer culture that other commentators have noted. These include many of those that Mike Featherstone describes in terms of the aestheticization of everyday life (1991). He suggests that aestheticization is a consequence of 'the desire to be continuously learning and enriching oneself, to pursue ever new values and vocabularies . . . [and an] unending curiosity in which the artist and the intellectual are heroes' (1991: 48). A key characteristic of the individual pursuing these heroes through the imitation of the lifestyles of artistic subcultures is what Featherstone calls a calculated hedonism, the calculated decontrol of emotions (1991: 71–2; see below in this chapter and, for more discussion of this idea, chapters 4, 5 and 8).

Featherstone suggests that there are a number of historical precedents for this attitude or mode of consuming. One is to be found in certain artistic movements, including (as Campbell also suggests) Romanticism, but also the artistic avant-garde at the turn of the nineteenth century. Amongst the latter – especially the Surrealist movement, whose members included writers (Jean Cocteau, Louis Aragon), playwrights (Eugene Ionesco and other so-called dramatists of the absurd), film-makers (Luis Buñuel), photographers (Man Ray and a host of others) and painters (René Magritte, Max Ernst, Marcel Duchamp, Joan Miró and Salvador Dali), there was an impetus to collapse the boundary between art and everyday life, to show that the most banal consumer objects and the kitsch and detritus of mass culture could be aestheticized and introduced as the subject of art.

Indeed, in his two *Manifestos of Surrealism*, André Breton described Surrealism in terms of 'the crisis of the object'. One of the ways in which this crisis was provoked was by pluralizing the contexts in which the object was perceived, specifically by removing it from the contexts where we conventionally perceive it and placing it in surprising ones (thus disturbing the operation of the art-culture system). As it appeared simultaneously in multiple contexts, 'the object' was put in crisis because its solid identity could no longer be established. Another technique adopted by the Surrealists was to distort the scale of objects *vis-à-vis* one another. Both techniques had the effect of revealing the constructedness of objects, their dependence for meaning on context and conventional norms of perception. In the 1960s postmodern art, reacting against what was seen as the institutionalization of modernism and the avant-garde in the museum and the academy, revived and built on these strategies. In postmodern artistic practice, aesthetic value was to be found in the anti-work, in the 'happening', in 'performance art', in the creation of artworks that cannot be catalogued and preserved in the museum, and which thus resist the operation of the art-culture system. Such art practices thus helped to bring art into everyday life.

A second precedent for modern consuming habits is found by Featherstone in the modernist notion of the artist as hero, as the advocate of radical values, challenging the consensus of public life and disturbing the complacency of domestic life. A complementary figure amongst elite groups was that of the dandy, the man (historically, dandyism was a role available more or less exclusively to (middle class) men) who made his body, his behaviour, his feelings and passions, a work of art. This figure was the subject of much philosophical and literary writing at the turn of the century, and was related to a particular understanding of pleasure, which 'was to be experience itself, and not the fruits of experience, sweet or bitter as they may be' (Oscar Wilde, quoted in Bowlby 1993: 15). The dandy is *against* pleasure in the 'fruit' and *for* pleasure in the experience of tasting it, and celebrates an experiential-experimental openness to what is 'new' or 'exotic'. As Rachel Bowlby suggests, Wilde's *The Picture of Dorian Gray* – in which the hero and his portrait swap places and Gray adopts as his own identity an artistic image, a portrait that does not age – can be seen as an investigation of the pleasures and costs of the lifestyle of a dandy:

> [Dorian] exchanges a moral self for the unfettered freedom of the new hedonist, for whom 'insincerity' is 'merely a method by which we can multiply our personalities': 'Eternal youth, infinite passion, pleasures subtle and secret, wild joy and wilder sins – he was to have all these things'. There is no limit to what Dorian can have, to the number of 'personalities' he can adopt, to the experiences he can sample. All poses, all personalities, are equal, circumscribed by neither moral nor numerical boundaries, and referrable to no state of authenticity from which they differ: 'Being natural', too, 'is simply a pose'. (Bowlby 1993: 16, references omitted)

This is a description of the dandy as the ideal modern consumer: 'a receptacle and bearer of sensations, poser and posed, with no consistent identity, no moral self' (Bowlby 1993: 23).

What Featherstone suggests is new today is that the practices of dandyism are no longer confined to artistic or elite enclaves, but are increasingly widespread (but see chapter 8 for a consideration of the view that these practices are restricted). This is the project of turning one's life into a work of art. It is as if, Featherstone suggests, aesthetics has become the basis of decision-making in everyday life: put simply, the question is no longer 'is this a good thing to do?' but 'does it look good?' (For a contrasting view on the relative importance of ethics and aesthetics in contemporary society see the discussion of Lamont 1992 in Chapter 4.)

'I just love shoes. Tina Chow was the first person I saw in Manolo Blahnik shoes, and I had to have some.' She [Veronica Webb] has dozens – striped plastic mules, red perspex-heeled stilettos, dominatrix heels in black. It's a fetishist's heaven. 'My first Manolo's were these.' She takes out a pair of blue pumps in hairy goatskin with little bows on the front. 'They reminded me of Marcel Duchamp's [Surrealist] fur cup and saucer'. (Muir 1995: 70)

A further condition for the development of consumer culture identified by Featherstone is the rapid flow of signs and images which pervades everyday life in contemporary society. He suggests that the widespread availability of images, in conjunction with the heroization of the artist's way of life, has provided a context for the development of mass consumer culture dream-worlds. Within these dream-worlds, the individual is said to be developing a capacity to decontrol the emotions, to open him or herself up to an extended range of sensations, and is gaining the ability to enjoy the swing between the pleasures of immersion in objects and detachment from them. This can be seen in the development of an aestheticized relation of the individual to his (and perhaps her) self-presentation. Featherstone writes that this controlled decontrol of the emotions is brought about through

techniques of the self which will permit the development of sensibilities which can allow us to enjoy the swing between the extremes of aesthetic involvement and detachment so that the pleasures of immersion and detached distantiation can both be enjoyed. (1991: 81)

An important part of this calculating hedonism is an emotional and cognitive distancing on the part of the individual since it is this distance which introduces the possibility of reflection on consumption and facilitates the adoption of playful and ironic ways of consuming. It can also be seen to have contributed to a *reflexive* attitude on the part of the individual to his or her identity, appearance and self-presentation.

Market researchers themselves discuss the experience of consuming in similar ways:

> Normal consumers . . . phenomenologically experience moderate swings from being in control to being out of control and back again. These swings, because they can be appropriately monitored and responded to, create a feeling of diversity-within-sameness that is comfortable and comforting to most people. Their lives are balanced between feelings of completeness and incompleteness – the warp and woof of the life experience. (Hirschman 1992: 175)

This interpretation of consumption as comforting and comfortable is somewhat ironic in the context of Campbell and Featherstone's analysis of the radical bohemian roots of contempary consumption. It suggests that the expansion of the aesthetic values into the field of consumption is not straightforward, and that the project of self-transformation may not be as radical as some of its proponents imply. There are other questions to be addressed too. Can consumers really monitor and respond to their feelings of being in or out of control? Is this oscillation really typical for most people? Is aesthetic knowledge accessible in the same way by all individuals? Many critics would suggest that this is an unrealistic analysis of the experience of consumption, and that it ignores the dependence of consumers on what is produced.

Conclusion

This chapter has introduced the notion of the stylization of consumption and put forward the view that this stylization, or aestheticization, is what defines consumer culture as a contemporary form of material culture. It refers to the production, design, making and use of goods, that is, their design, making and use as if they were works of art, images or signs and as part of the self-conscious creation of lifestyle. It therefore includes the design emphasis on the surface appearance of goods themselves, the importance of images in related packaging, marketing and advertising, and the thematization of their context of presentation and display in specialized sites of purchase and consumption. Importantly, however, it also includes an increasingly aestheticized mode of use of goods, that is, their use as if they were works of art, images or signs, to be engaged with via processes of fantasy, play, daydreaming and image-making. In some of the accounts above, this has significant implications for the processes of identity-creation and transformation, in so far as it is seen to encourage a reflexive relation to the self.

This chapter has also put forward an outline of three different explanations of the emergence and development of this process of stylization. Each provides an interpretation of why consumption has been stylized, although, significantly, they differ in where, in cycles of production and consumption, they locate the principal source of meaning-making or stylization – with 'captains of consciousness', the logic of the code or the daydreaming consumer. They also place different emphases on the significance of the art-culture system in the development of a stylized consumer culture. The chapters that follow will suggest that the relative importance of the art-culture system in the experience of consumer culture may well depend upon the social position of the consumer, and that each of these explanations is more or less accurate for different social groups.

4

Habitat and Habitus

Introduction

In the last chapter, the distinctively stylized character of modern consumer culture was attributed to the increasing importance of aesthetic knowledge in the creation of value. However, it was also pointed out that this aesthetic knowledge is unevenly distributed. Three accounts of the causes of the unevenness of the distribution of this knowledge were put forward: the structuring effects of either production or signification (specifically, in terms of either the production of commodity aesthetics or the logic of the code), or the activities of the user or the consumer. Each of these accounts, although in different ways, also saw the uneven distribution of aesthetic knowledge to be, in part, a consequence of the operation of the art-culture system. However, the special character of contemporary consumer culture is not typically presented in such starkly exclusive terms – that is, *either* productionist *or* consumerist; there is, more commonly, an attempt to look at the interrelationship of changes in production, signification and the activities of users in relation to struggles over meaning and the distribution of aesthetic knowledge.

There are different ways of doing this, one of which focuses on the role of specific social groups as the carriers of aesthetic knowledge or as *cultural intermediaries.* In this chapter, work which foregrounds *class* groups as the key social carriers of aesthetic knowledge will be introduced. This work is often associated with a broader analysis of social change within contemporary Euro-American societies, namely what is sometimes described as a shift from fordist to post-fordist society.

Lifestyle and positional consumption

The last chapter argued that the emergence of consumer culture is characterized by its increasing stylization, and that the production, exchange and use of consumer goods is increasingly structured by the perceived expressive or symbolic aspects of those goods. This thesis suggests that there has been an increase in the relative importance of the expressive rather than the functional or instrumental uses of goods. It is summed up by the view that we are approaching that 'great day when cutlery and furniture swing like the Supremes' (Hebdige 1988), and is closely related to the emergence of lifestyle as the definitive mode of consumption.

'Lifestyle' is a term which is used to refer to the new consumer sensibility that Hebdige (1988) identifies as characteristic of modern consumption; through lifestyle, consumers are seen to bring a more stylized awareness or sensitivity to the processes of consumption. As a mode of consumption, or attitude to consuming, it refers to the ways in which people seek to display their individuality and their sense of style through the choice of a particular range of goods and their subsequent customizing or personalizing of these goods. This activity is seen to be a central life project for the individual. As a member of a particular lifestyle grouping, the individual actively uses consumer goods – clothes, the home, furnishings, interior decor, car, holidays, food and drink, as well as cultural goods such as music, film and art – in ways which indicate that grouping's taste or sense of style. In this sense, lifestyle is thus an instance of the tendency for groups of individuals to use goods to make distinctions between themselves and other groups of individuals, and thus supports the view that consumption practices can be understood in terms of a struggle over social positioning. (This view was referred to in chapter 2 as positional consumption.) However, the notion of lifestyle emphasizes the symbolic or aesthetic dimension of this struggle.

As discussed earlier, it has been argued – by anthropologists in particular – that the use of goods has always been partly structured in terms of their symbolic dimensions. However, what is being argued here is that this aspect of consumption is becoming increas-

ingly important in modern Euro-American societies as a consequence of the activities of particular class groups. The emergence
and success of mass design-oriented furniture and interior decor
retail outlets such as Habitat is an everyday example of this (see 'In
praise of paper lampshades and jumbo floor cushions').

One line of argument, proposed by Fred Hirsch (1977) among
others, is that historically only a small aristocratic elite engaged in
positional consumption, while the mass of individuals in the society
consumed goods more or less wholly on the basis of their functional
or practical characteristics. Hirsch argues that it has only been more
recently that the people who make up the mass of the population
have come to engage in positional consumption. So one characteristic of modern consumption, according to Hirsch, is that it shows a
democratization of positional or competitive consumption. The
newspaper feature on the fortunes of Habitat suggests that this is
not always a straightforward process: 'something went wrong when
Habitat got too big for its salad bowls'. Indeed, Hirsch suggests that
increasing consumption – in so far as what is bought thereby is relative position – becomes a zero-sum game. Furthermore, he suggests
that the expansion of the use of consumer goods as positional goods
creates an overload of demands, which cannot be met, and, in turn,
is leading to economic instability. The point being made here is that
if goods function primarily as symbols, and all groups of individuals
use them to establish distinctions between themselves and other
groups of individuals, then there are, in principle, no limits to consumer demand. In other words, mass competitive consumption will
have disorganizing effects on modern economies rather than, as is
often claimed, being functional for the capitalist economy.

Habitus and struggles over taste

However, other writers suggest that mass competitive consumption
has its own rules, and is not necessarily disorganizing; rather, it is
seen to be subject to cycles of *dis*organization and *re*organization. A
particularly influential analysis of these rules understands their operation in terms of the dynamics of taste. This line of analysis is most
often identified with Pierre Bourdieu, and his study of taste in
French society in the late 1960s, *Distinction* (not published in
English until 1984). Bourdieu provides a critique of, and an alterna-

In praise of paper lampshades and jumbo floor cushions

HEY man, just look at those happening guys and chicks crashing out on their big, bean-bag chairs. What kind of event is this? A photo-shoot from the 1971 Habitat catalogue? Wow.

Hard to remember it now, perhaps, but Habitat was once the most fashionable "lifestyle" shop in London. This is where, in the mid-Sixties, John Lennon and George Harrison, Lord Snowdon and Stanley Kubrick did their shopping. Three decades and many lifestyles later, the ghost of Terence Conran's Habitat has yet to be laid to rest.

Conran lost control two years ago of the famous chain store he created in 1964. Last week, the cut-price Swedish furnishing giant IKEA bought Habitat from Storehouse plc. Even so, the Habitat of 20 years ago still exists for a generation for whom its name really did mean "home".

It is still hard to escape those Japanese paper lampshades that now hang – somewhat wrinkled and fly-blown – from thousands of ceiling roses up and down the country. Twenty-one years ago, Japanese paper lampshades were as fashionable as char-grilled polenta is today. In 1971, Habitat was still at its peak and setting the tone for a generation of youthful, middle-class, university educated home-owners.

If those time-worn Japanese paper lamps yell Habitat at you, what about those other crucial items that were inextricably linked with Conran's chainstore? Leafing through early Habitat catalogues, familiar items ambush the design-conscious memory. Here is a set of that ubiquitous Blue Denmark patterned china, a nicely turned French wooden salad bowl, a white plastic Proform occasional table (available at £9 10s and £11 10s) and those red and orange French peasant enamel coffee pots ... Who remembers listening to *Imagine* lying on an Indian dhurrie (from £3 15s) or draping their flares across a shag-pile bedspread?

Without Habitat, there would have been no IKEA in Britain.

Habitat set a style for the modernistic homes of the Sixties and Seventies, before *Brideshead Revisited*, *The World of Interiors* and Thatcher's credit boom ushered in an ersatz country-house style that held sway (especially among the young and well-heeled) until two or three years ago. At its most inspirational, Habitat offered a home that was a fusion of the white-hot technological revolution, pop culture and sophisticated peasant design. Old Habitat catalogues reveal room-sets that mix white plastic furniture, white stereo-systems and white plastic tables with French country kitchen gadgets and Indian rugs. Walls are decorated with posters – rather than framed prints – showing the Earth as seen from the Moon, racing cars and rock stars. The models are young people in headbands and dungarees, smiling and generally having a good time. This was anathema to the super-cool furnishing and lifestyle catalogues of the Eighties, in which snappy suits and pouting sneers had replaced smiles.

Something went wrong when Habitat got too big for its salad bowls. The first shop – in London's Fulham Road – had been as delightful as it was revolutionary. At the opening, the knowledgeable and glamorous staff wore butcher's aprons over outfits designed by Mary Quant; their hair was cut by Vidal Sassoon (who else?). The shops that followed were inevitably housed in interesting buildings – a redundant cinema in King's Road, Chelsea and a former Spitfire factory in Manchester. So when Habitat began to see warehouse outfits like MFI as serious rivals, something was wrong, and the chain declined. In 1990 it recorded a crippling loss of £11.9m. The dream was over. Over the last two years, Habitat's management has made the shop more fashionable again, but it is a far cry from its stylish, modern-age heyday. (IKEA promises not to take Habitat further down-market.)

The Independent
Jonathan Glancey

tive to, traditional or commonsense understandings of taste as something which is so intangible, fluid and subjective that it cannot be analysed. He argues, instead, for a view of taste as a social phenomenon, suggesting that taste is not the result of individualistic choices, but is socially patterned.

Bourdieu's work is centrally concerned with social reproduction, that is, with how societies reproduce or maintain themselves over time, not simply as a set of individuals, but as individuals in certain groupings in certain relations of power to each other. As part of this general project, he argues that the resources or assets of different social classes are as much symbolic as economic, political or organizational. For Bourdieu, taste is a key mechanism for organizing the distribution of symbolic resources; as such it is an important part of social reproduction. He describes how individuals struggle to improve their social position by manipulating the cultural representation of their situation in the social field. They accomplish this, in part, by affirming the superiority of their taste and lifestyle with a view to legitimizing their own identity as best representing what it means to be 'what it is right to be'. Disputes about taste are not trivial from Bourdieu's point of view, but are tied into social reproduction in general and the reproduction of class relations in particular. The reproduction of shared cultural style contributes to class reproduction.

One of the most important terms in Bourdieu's analysis is that of *habitus*. This is defined as a system of dispositions, a system which organizes the individual's capacity to act. Bourdieu writes that habitus is

> a system of lasting, transposable dispositions, which, integrating past experiences, functions at every moment as a matrix of perceptions, appreciations and actions and makes possible the achievement of infinitely diversified tasks, thanks to analogical transformations of schemes permitting the solution of similarly shaped problems. (1977: 83)

The habitus is evident in the individual's taken-for-granted preferences about the appropriateness and validity of his or her taste in art, food, holidays, hobbies, etc. It is shaped primarily in childhood, within the family and through schooling, by the internalization of a given set of material conditions. In this way, an individual's habitus is shaped by, or linked to, his or her family, group and, perhaps most importantly for Bourdieu, the individual's class position.

The supermarket chains are in a sense 'classless' but it would be more accurate to call them 'multi-class'. We cannot resist allocating virtually everything we do to a specific place in our still class-bound lives.

We start by grading in our heads, the supermarket chains themselves. Waitrose is executive class, Sainsbury covers a wider span with its centre somewhere in the lower-middle-class to respectable working-class range.

Safeway is rather less securely near there. Tesco is trying to get rid of its 'pile 'em high, sell 'em cheap' image. Presto is deliberately down market. And so on . . .

In the big supermarkets, class dividing is easy; you can classify by day and time of day, by aisles and by the goods on each aisle. Middle-class housewives tend to come in early, in the second car. They tend to do their shopping mid-week, especially on Thursdays, thus leaving the week-

ends freer. Working-class people, usually by necessity, favour Saturday. Husband and wife then shop together and may have tea in town afterwards. That is more of an occasion.

The newest pattern is Sunday morning shopping, which has been hugely taken to, particularly by working-class customers – wife, husband and the children, often with a 'breakfast platter' afterwards. (Hoggart 1994: 21)

Habitus does not simply refer to knowledge, or even competence or sense of style, but is also embodied, literally. That is, it is inscribed in the individual's body, in body size, shape, posture, way of walking, sitting, gestures, facial expression, sense of ease with one's body, ways of eating, drinking, amount of social space and time that an individual feels entitled to occupy; even the pitch and tone of voice, accent and complexity of speech patterns are part of an individual's habitus. All these things, according to Bourdieu, are bodily manifestations of your habitus of origin.

The habitus is not just a random series of dispositions, but operates according to a relatively coherent logic, what Bourdieu calls the *logic of practice* and this is organized by a system of classification. The habitus, which operates below the level of individual consciousness, is what will shape an individual's apparently personal taste through the way in which the individual applies the system of classification. The system of classification operates with dichotomous distinctions like high/low, masculine/feminine, white/black, distinguished/vulgar and good/bad. These principles of categorization are initially developed in specific situations, but can subsequently be applied across a wide range of situations as unconscious regulating principles.

Habitus is thus a relatively flexible framework for making sense of social experience: a stable, although never static, set of classifying principles. It is the application of these principles as a distinctive mode of cultural consumption which is recognized as taste, or lack of it. It is in operation, for example, in the particular way in which domestic goods are assembled for display in a Habitat catalogue – a book of poems by Ezra Pound casually laid on the arm of a chair, or the selection of a large leaf and a single stem of flowers rather than a bunch of flowers to show off a jug, for example. According to Bourdieu, what seems like an individual practice – taste – is regulated by the logic of practice and is always a variant of class practice.

Indeed, the source for the basic divide in taste in contemporary society is attributed by Bourdieu to the different experiences of class in the modern world. The immediacy of working people's tastes derives from the immediacy of their work experience, and the pressure imposed by their needs. A person who carries out manual labour, and whose access to the basics of sustenance and comfort is not guaranteed, has a respect and a desire for the sensual, physical and immediate. An individual who has been brought up in the abstractions of education and mental labour and who is certain of obtaining daily necessities cultivates a distance from these needs, and affects a taste based in respect and desire for the abstract, distanced and formal. These objective conditions are interiorized through habitus as desire expressed in taste.

This notion of habitus can thus be seen as an attempt by Bourdieu to develop a *social* analysis of taste; it acknowledges the social conditions for the acquisition of taste, but also allows some space for human agency. Bourdieu suggests that, although the logic of practice which structures the habitus and thus an individual's taste is determined by a particular material set of conditions, the individual's practice is also always a strategy in situations of which the outcome is uncertain, not least because these strategies are opposed by the strategies of other individuals. So, although the habitus provides a framework for action, it is not static, and can be shaped by the outcome of the interaction of the strategies adopted by different social groups.

Sienna armchair from £399.00
As shown **custom made** in Linette Atlantic £419.00
H80 x W69 x D86 cms
Garrick large sofa from £999.00
As shown **custom made** in Lisbon Saffron £1089.00
H83 x W208 x D103 cms
Also available as armchair and medium sofa
Stripe cotton durry 170 x 260 cm £199.00
Throws from £39.00
White porcelain jug £20.00
Gloucester mug blue £5.75
Kew box file £12.50

An extensive range of styles and size options and a choice of over 100 fabrics, are available in Habitat's **custom made** service. Specialist staff help complete your order, advising on the options available - some ranges have armchair, two sizes of sofa and sofabed. Delivery of **custom made** upholstery is free within mainland UK, and is normally completed within 4-6 weeks.

Moreover, according to Bourdieu, as part of the process of social reproduction, classes in competition with each other attempt to impose their own habitus or system of classification on other classes, as part of their more general struggle to become dominant. What has been described here as the art-culture system is central to this competition, and its organization can itself be seen to be the cumulative result of these struggles. Education has been a central institution in the development of this system in so far as it provides a key route to the appreciation of high culture which historically has been defined by its abstraction from everyday life. It produces specialized groups of users or consumers of art, who then may form the basis of new cultural markets.

Bourdieu himself adopts the term *cultural field* to describe what has been called here the art-culture system, and conceptualizes it as if it were an economy. He argues that the cultural economy is characterized by cultural markets, competition, inflation, and attempts at monopolization. As part of this understanding of the operation of the art-culture system as an economy, a key concept for Bourdieu is 'cultural capital', the sedimented knowledge and competence required to make distinctions or value judgements, such as those between works of 'art' and 'non-art'. Bourdieu suggests that different classes and different class fractions are engaged in a series of struggles with each other to increase the volume of the cultural capital they possess, and to increase the valuation placed on the particular forms of this capital.

In exploring the significance of taste for social reproduction, Bourdieu looks at the interplay between cultural and economic capital; he believes that people actively invest cultural capital to realize economic capital. An example of this exchange is provided in 'Digital Design', a review of a book which maps out the changing fortunes of the graphic designer Neville Brody. The review gives several examples of what Bourdieu would see as the complex, unstable relationship between cultural and economic capital; for example, it suggests that an exhibition of Brody's work at the Victoria and Albert Museum, which, one might have thought, would have increased his cultural capital enormously, did not lead, in the short term at least, to an increased ability to acquire economic capital, but rather the reverse. The review claims 'Brody was so over-exposed that potential clients figured he would be too expensive to use and hired cheap designers to rip him off.'

In general terms, Bourdieu argues that questions of cultural capital have become increasingly important in recent years, as, in many

print

edited by steve beard and kodwo eshun

digital design

The Neville Brody story is a familiar one. How he enrolled on a Fine Art foundation course at Hornsey College Of Art in 1975, but switched to graphic design because he thought it was more open to experimentation. How he went on to do a three year course at the London College of Printing, but was failed for producing 'uncommercial' work. How he got caught up in the whole punk ethos of assertive pop modernism, and began turning out distinctive record sleeves for the likes of 23 Skidoo, Clock DVA, The Bongos and Cabaret Voltaire ("the record shop was just as valid a showcase as the framed environment of art galleries", he said at the time). How he became Art Director for *The Face*, and turned the magazine into a style bible which became synonymous with the design revolution of the '80s. How shop fronts, TV logos, British Rail stations all began to look as if they had been designed by some distant Brody clones. How the V&A gave the man the seal of professional approval by staging an exhibition of his work in 1989, and how design pundit Jon Wozencroft published a scholarly tome – *The Graphic Language Of Neville Brody* – to go with it.

Most readers of *i-D* will know all this. Well, five years have passed since then. All of which is a way of saying welcome to *The Graphic Language Of Neville Brody 2* (Thames & Hudson). Wozencrofts's sequel to his first book wastes little time recapitulating the familiar story. Instead, it picks up where things left off. Whereas the first book ended on a note of triumph with Brody seemingly poised to redesign the world, *2* is more circumspect. It tells how the success of the V&A exhibition was a disaster in commercial terms. Brody was so over-exposed that potential clients figured he would be too expensive to use and hired cheaper designers to rip him off. Brody nearly went bankrupt in 1990. What saved him was the move into digital design. He was commissioned by the Body Shop to design their annual report, which led to an introduction to the photographer Ian McKinnell who rented studio space above one of the stores being used in a spread. McKinnell had one of the first Macs in the country, and encouraged an initially sceptical Brody to play around with it. Since then, he has rarely ventured out from behind his screen.

2 showcases a range of Brody's computerised design work in different media – from magazines and newspapers (*Arena*, *The Guardian*) to shops (Christopher New, Bloomingdales), political organisations (Rio Earth Summit, Amnesty International) and corporations (Nike, Parco) – and demonstrates how design is not a buzzword confined to the '80s. Wozencroft makes large claims for the value of digital design – that it is returning us from the alphabet to the pictogram, that it is rewiring our nervous systems McLuhan-wise. What is incontestable is the way Brody's design in the '90s has become more fluid, more sampladelic, more clearly driven by an internal evolutionary code. Whether this makes it any harder for the big corporations to co-opt is another story entirely. **SB**

Euro-American societies, the economic differences by which class distinctions have traditionally been signalled have become less clear-cut (although, as noted in chapter 1, there still remain deep and enduring economic inequalities). He argues that the increasingly important relationship between economic and cultural capital gives rise to a number of competing groups within the middle classes in particular. He identifies three principal groups in French society. A dominant group comprises senior industrial managers who have a great deal of economic capital but relatively little cultural capital. A second group is clustered in a rapidly growing set of occupations including the media, the so-called caring professions and marketing. These have less economic and more cultural capital. A final group is low in economic but high in cultural capital; it includes teachers, artists and the like. For Bourdieu, these groups, and others in other class formations, are engaged in a constant struggle with one another to improve their social position, by using and enhancing their possession of the different types of cultural and economic capital.

An example of these struggles in British society was the attempt by literary critics such as F. R. Leavis and Denys Thompson in the early and mid-twentieth century to build up English literature as a discipline in British universities (Mulhern 1974). This was achieved through the elevation of particular principles of reading as the preferred techniques of literary criticism, and by establishing what has come to be called the literary canon, that is, a selection of writings which are held to be the best of English literature. These strategies contributed to the formation of an educated public for certain kinds of fiction – particularly novels. It helped consolidate the development of two levels of literacy – being able to read and being well read, and also trained certain groups in a literary mode of appropriation (Abercrombie 1996), including the skills of intense contemplation of a text; following its narrative from beginnng to end; and interpreting the text in relation to an individual author's *oeuvre* of work. It can thus be seen to have contributed to the creation of the distinction between high and popular culture in the art-culture system by institutionalizing particular techniques for the appreciation of authenticity in terms of originality and uniqueness.

In Bourdieu's terms, this skill is not a neutral set of techniques for identifying the inherent value of literature, but, rather, is a set of techniques for legitimating the values of what was an emerging fraction of the middle classes and their preferred mode of consumption. In Bourdieu's terms, differential access to literary consumption is a crucial aspect of the reproduction of class and class conflict – being able to show that you are well read is an important aspect of class domination, and the success of Leavis and his colleagues was to set the terms of judgement according to the values of an emerging professional fraction of the middle classes. It could also be pointed out, however, that this type of literary criticism also represents the judgements not simply of a particular class but also a particular gender and a particular ethnicity (the literary canon excludes many women and non-white writers from consideration), and is associated with white understandings of Englishness. The practice of literary criticism is thus also an aspect of gender and race or ethnic domination. Bourdieu's analysis is not especially concerned with these aspects of taste, but they will be considered in chapters 5 and 6 (see Moi 1991, for a discussion of the relevance of Bourdieu for feminism).

More generally, the expansion in higher education in Euro-American societies during the second half of the twentieth century is seen by Bourdieu as having very important implications for cultural consumption. While education was closely associated with high culture in the first half of this century, as we approach its end, education is increasingly linked to the study of popular culture through the growth of courses in media and communication, cultural studies, film and television studies, and the publication of textbooks in popular music, television – even consumer culture! Featherstone summarizes this shift:

> One of the subversive strategies of outsider intellectuals and the new culture entrepreneurs is to seek to legitimate new fields to stand alongside and undermine the traditional restricted definitions of taste provided by the established intellectuals and embodied into a high culture. Rock music, fashion, the cinema become canonized as legitimate intellectual arenas for critics, interpreters and popularizers. (1991: 93)

Through the legitimacy given by educational institutions to the study of cinema and popular music, the literary mode of appropriation is being extended beyond the confines of literature. So, for example, Bourdieu notes:

> Where some only see 'a Western starring Burt Lancaster', others discover 'an early John Sturgess' or the 'latest Sam Peckinpah'. In identifying what is worthy of being seen and the right way to see it, they are aided by their whole social group . . . and by the whole corporation of critics mandated by the group to produce legitimate classifications and the discourse necessarily accompanying any artistic enjoyment worthy of the name. (1984: 28)

The authority of the academy in these areas is not without challenge. Bourdieu himself tends to focus on the role of educational institutions, rather underplaying the role of commercial organizations and the media. However, it is not clear who the new intellectuals or cultural intermediaries of popular culture are. Given that reflexivity about taste itself is considered essential by both circles, this is a question which the adversaries themselves have necessarily considered.

In 'Pearls and Swine: The Intellectuals and the Mass Media' Jon Savage and Simon Frith attack the legitimacy of their commercial rivals, describing *Modern Review*, 'a magazine dedicated to taking popular culture seriously by defining itself *against* academic cultural studies', as the dominant voice of 'lay cultural populism'. They recognize that 'for both academics arguing about the curriculum and journalists arguing about the arts pages, what's at issue is "popular culture" – how we should think it, how we should study it, how we should value it' (1993: 1). They believe that there is a 'crisis of critical language' (p. 2), since as 'any pop critic knows, for all our good intentions our prime task is as consumer guides' (p. 12). They argue that the authority of the teacher and the critic to assert that his or her reading of a popular work or artist – *Jurassic Park*, *Unforgiven* or Take That – is more important than anyone else's has been called into doubt. Indeed, they suggest that there has been a subtle shift in what is meant by knowledge as a result of the elevation in the media of 'the authority of experience' over 'the authority of the intellect':

> A reportorial tradition of outsiders like Angela Carter and Colin McInnes trying to make sense of social phenomena collapsed into first hand reports from people presumed by insecure editors to *be* the phenomena – Julie Burchill was there puking in the Roxy. (1993: 11)

In this way Savage and Frith contrast the values of professional intellectuals to those of commercial intellectuals, and the claims of competing class fractions to act as cultural intermediaries, as arbiters of taste, especially authenticity, is weighed up.

At the heart of this dispute between different groups of cultural intermediaries, Savage and Frith argue, is the relationship between the intermediary and their audience. They assert: 'If the academic's task is to tell people what they don't already know, the journalist's is to tell them what they do' (1993: 6). The difference in their relationship, obviously itself debatable, is ascribed by Savage and Frith to the journalist's dependence on the market (that is, the magazine's sales to the audience or consumers, rather than the state, that is, education and the judgements of peers), and, following from this, the advocacy of a particular kind of cultural populism – that of 'the positive power of market forces', and 'the creativity of the consumer'. It seems, then, that the nature of a group's relationship to the market and consumer culture is at the heart of contemporary struggles over taste between different fractions of the middle classes. In other words, a group's relationship to and sympathy with the market and consumer culture itself, and not just the state and education, has come to be a key indicator of the legitimacy of its taste.

This dispute over how popular culture should be evaluated and who should set the standards of evaluation is an example of how, in Bourdieu's terms, differential cultural consumption, or taste, both results from the class system and is a mechanism by which classes seek to establish their dominance within a society. Taste is thus shown here to be a process of differentiation, but it leads not only to the creation of distinctions between different categories of goods, but also to the creation of distinctions between social groups. So, for example, Savage and Frith make a distinction between those who subscribe to 'the culture of self-satisfaction' (presumably the readers and writers of *Modern Review*) and those who believe in 'the culture of the dissatisfied' (with whom they identify). Taste not only provides a means of defining why some goods are better than others but also a means of defining the people who use such definitions, and why they are better or worse than others.

The new middle classes

These struggles over taste are held to be highly significant for social reproduction; indeed, it has been argued that they have contributed to what has been described as *a transition from a fordist to a post-fordist society*. The extent and political significance of this transition is much disputed, but it is generally accepted that there have been a number of changes in the nature of production and consumption which are outlined in the box below. It is important to remember here, however, that this use of the terms production and consumption (in the singular) is to be understood in relation to a cycle of appropriation dominated by commodification. Other cycles of production and consumption are not discussed here since Bourdieu and the other writers introduced assume that capitalism is the principal determinant of consumer culture through its organization of commodity production. (The following chapters will introduce alternative or supplementary explanations.)

Fordism

Production

Economy dominated by mass production, with centralized management and wage bargaining, and extensive state welfare.

Workforce primarily composed of semi-skilled workers, with a strong sense of collective solidarity and class identity, expressed in labour movement organization and politics.

Commodities

Most commodities are little differentiated from each other by fashion, season or by specific target markets, but there is a steady production of new commodities.

Consumption

Consumption is mass in nature, uniform and standardized. Consumer demands are regulated via the reorganization of daily life, through, for example, so-called labour-saving goods. There is a high and growing rate of expenditure on consumer goods, but the producer is dominant rather than the consumer. There is relatively little consumer choice, and what there is reflects producer interests rather than consumer needs.

Post-fordism

Production

Production is increasingly organized in terms of what is called 'flexible specialization', that is, it is flexibly organized for specialized rather than mass production via the use of technology and multi-skilling and decentralized through the use of communication media. There is an expansion of production globally. The service sector is increasingly important.

There is a core of multi-skilled workers and a periphery of semi- and unskilled workers. Collective organization and consciousness has been eroded and a plurality of social movements acquire importance. Consumption practices are a significant aspect of these new identities.

Commodities

A greater range of products is available, each of which has a shorter life because of changes in fashion and much greater differentiation of commodities by market segment.

Consumption

Consumption is increasingly specialized, with individualized and hybrid consumption patterns.

Consumers are more volatile; their preferences change more often and are more unpredictable. There is a 'fluidization' of consumption, with a diversification of individual consumption times and spaces.

What these changes add up to is a matter of some debate, and there is certainly dispute about the extent and political implications of the change (Piore and Sabel 1984; Lash and Urry 1987 and 1994; Harvey 1989). However, what is important is that it is the distinctive uses of consumer goods by the developing middle classes that is seen to play some part in the shift from fordism to post-fordism. There is a complex interplay at work here, which can be represented in terms of a *cycle* of processes, feeding into and reinforcing each other.

This cycle can be described in the following way, although this is a very simplified account which artificially takes one moment – production – as the starting point. It is important to remember that these processes should be seen to reinforce one another cyclically. In this analysis, post-fordist production contributes to the expansion and consolidation of the so-called new middle classes, who are to be found in those service and white-collar occupations that are concerned with the production of symbolic goods and services. So, for example, Bourdieu suggests that these new class fragments find 'ardent spokesmen in . . . the directors and executives of firms in tourism and journalism, publishing and the cinema, fashion and advertising, decoration and property development' (1984: 310–11).

In this area of production, members of the new middle classes are typically involved in work that combines adherence to bureaucratized rules with notions of professional autonomy and an effective, if often unstructured, responsiveness to peer group pressure, producing what Pfiel describes as 'an almost guild like sense of individual autonomy and ability within the more or less horizontally perceived company of one's peers' (quoted in King 1989: 133). An example of the work ethos these conditions produce is provided by *Campaign*, an advertising industry magazine in which advertisers take it in turns to evaluate each other's compaigns, and gossip and rumour about changes in staffing in agencies is given a public airing. This mode of working is said to encourage innovation within a quasi-professional ethos, thus not only providing jobs for the new middle classes, but also a distinctive space within which a shared culture, or way of life, can be sustained.

Through the development of this shared culture, the new middle classes seek to assert a distinctive identity *vis-à-vis* other class fragments. As noted above, this is, in part, achieved in their work lives, a self-promotion which is most clearly visible amongst the members of occupations in the media, design and fashion worlds themselves (consider for example, a recent article in the up-market women's

CITIZEN TIME

A time to work. A time to play • Citizen Chronograph gives you both. • Two world time zones. Two alarms. One 24 hour. One for appointments. A calendar that adjusts itself every month. • Altogether much more than a precision stopwatch that is accurate to 1/20 of a second. • After all, if you're going to achieve your goals in life, it requires split second timing and pinpoint accuracy. • Attention to detail and an affordable price are time honoured Japanese traditions. • Which is why every Citizen watch represents time well spent.

Citizen Chronograph, £185. One of a range of Citizen watches from E40–E350.

TIME WELL SPENT

magazine *Elle* about a new shop opened by three of the women 'behind the latest counter culture', one of whom is quoted as saying ' "We know what we like. We're not interested in producing anything we wouldn't wear ourselves"' (Scott 1995: 27)). However, this distinctive class identity is also developed and promoted through the adoption of a highly visible lifestyle. Indeed, Bourdieu and others suggest that lifestyle embodies the ideal manifestation of a new social consciousness, in which the very distinction between work and leisure is problematized.

One symbol of this is the personal organizer – commonly used as a fashion accessory as well as a working tool. In recognition of this, organizers now come in several sizes; possible inserts include not only diaries in various formats, but also planning charts, expense claim forms, maps, computer software guides, crib-sheets for exams, entertainment guides to various cities, lists of wine vintages, and even novels.

> The Filofax looked like an idea whose time and had come – and perhaps it had. There is a certain pretentiousness about owning a PO. It suggests that one's life is too full and varied to be confined within the leatherette bindings of a Letts pocket diary, that one's address book is extensive and expanding, that one's finances and expenses are of such complexity that special proforma stationery is required to keep track of them. In the Sixties and Seventies such pretensions were seen as vaguely absurd – the province of nerds, Americans and graduates in business administration. The Eighties were different . . . We are all personally organized now. (Naughton 1992: 69)

More generally, Bourdieu writes that the new bourgeoisie is

> the initiator of the ethical retooling required by the new economy from which it draws its power and profits, whose functioning depends as much on the production of needs and consumers as on the production of goods. The new logic of the economy rejects the ascetic ethic of production and accumulation, based upon abstinence, sobriety, saving and calculation, in favour of a hedonistic morality of consumption, based on credit, spending and enjoyment. This economy demands a social world which judges people by their capacity for consumption, their 'standard of living', their lifestyle, as much as by their capacity for production. (1984:310)

The increasing importance of this kind of hedonistic consumption is, in turn, seen to require changes in production, enforcing a greater flexibility in the types and speed of production processes. These new class fractions are thus held to have been created by, and to contribute to, the development of the capitalist economy in the contemporary post-fordist era.

So what is the taste that underpins this transformation? According to Mike Featherstone, the new middle classes are distinguished by their pursuit of expressive and liberated lifestyles. He claims:

> Rather than unreflexively adopting a lifestyle, through tradition or habit, the new heroes of consumer culture make lifestyle a life project and display their individuality and sense of style in the particularity of the assemblage of goods, clothes, practices, experiences, appearance and bodily dispositions they design together into a lifestyle. (1991: 86)

They have a very strong commitment to fashion, that is, to rapid and playful transformation of style. So much so, Featherstone suggests, that the alertness of the new middle classes to new popular styles and the marketability of the new creates conditions in which styles travel faster, from the popular to the avant-garde and vice versa. This is seen to have contributed towards the break down of previous distinctions between high culture and popular culture, the old and the new, of the nostalgic and the futuristic, of the natural and the artificial, a set of break downs which, as noted earlier, is said to characterize postmodern culture.

Bourdieu also suggests that these groups have a novel approach to pleasure. The old bourgeoisie is argued to have based its life on a morality of duty, with a fear of pleasure a relation to the body made up of reserve, modesty and restraint, and to have associated every satisfaction of forbidden impulses with guilt. In contrast, the new middle-class groups urge a morality of pleasure as a duty. This doctrine makes it a failure, a threat to self-esteem, *not* to 'have fun'. Pleasure is not only permitted but demanded, so that the individual is encouraged to work at pleasure. This has contributed to what Featherstone calls a *calculating hedonism*, a hedonism in which the individual strategically moves into and out of control, enjoying the thrill of the controlled suspension of constraints. As was noted in chapter 3, this hedonism is sometimes understood by Featherstone in relation to a process of *heroization* of the consumer, who is prepared to experiment with his or her self-identity, strategically to calculate the risks involved in the temporary abandonment of restraint involved in excessive consumption.

The growth of the so-called new middle classes has, however, seen its own internal struggles. Featherstone believes the growth of new media-related professions and marginal service industries such as restaurants, craft shops and therapy clinics is related to the need, because of the relative democratization of education, to create jobs and provide services for members of the old bourgeoisie. These are occupations where inherited as opposed to acquired cultural capital can be put to most profitable use. At the same time, however, members of this old bourgeoisie are likely to display an aesthetic asceticism in contrast to a traditional or commercial bourgeois preference for sumptuousness. Featherstone describes the symbolic subversion of the rituals of bourgeois order demonstrated by, for example, intellectuals in the display of so-called ostentatious poverty. This is evident in the tendency to dress casually even when at work, to favour bare wood interiors – stripped pine is the obvious example here (remember the floor in the Habitat image discussed earlier), and the preference for out door solitary activities like mountaineering, rambling and fell-walking.

In contrast, the new petty bourgeoisie – who make up the lower echelons of the service class – are seen to be developing a lifestyle in which they actively struggle for self-improvement and self-expression. Featherstone offers particular examples of this: for example, he holds that the petty-bourgeois class fraction are uneasy in their own bodies, constantly self-consciously checking, watching and correcting themselves. This, he suggests, explains the current popularity of body maintenance techniques, sports and forms of exercise such as aerobics, and health products – vitamins, ginseng and royal jelly – for this group of consumers. This anxiety is related by Featherstone to the relatively insecure position of the new petty bourgeoisie.

This group is the class fraction which, perhaps more than any other, was the chief recipient and beneficiary of the expansion in the higher educational sector that took place within most Euro-American societies following the Second World War. The expansion was directed towards the relatively direct and immediate needs of occupational vocation, and its focus on training and the acquisition of discrete occupational skills contrasted with the cultivation of abstract cultural competences that had previously monopolized higher education. Consequently, Featherstone suggests, this expansion provides an uncertain basis for the realization of cultural capital, and it is this germinal or not fully formed relationship to the educational field which is said to explain the anxious lifestyle of the new petty bourgeoisie. Featherstone writes:

> The new petit bourgeois is a pretender, aspiring to more than he is, who adopts an investment orientation to life; he possesses little economic or cultural capital and therefore must acquire it. The acquisition of the latter makes him open to being perceived as an autodidact, the product of the education system, who betrays an anxiety about using the right classification, who is always in danger of knowing too much or too little . . . The new petit bourgeois therefore adopts a learning mode to life; he is consciously educating himself in the field of taste, style and lifestyle. (1991: 90–1)

This generation of the middle classes is the first to have experienced the full force of what Raymond Williams (1974) calls *mobile privatization* – the reorganization of domestic life so that, via the television and other forms of consumption, it offers a safe space of almost unlimited access to other places and times, 'elsewheres' and 'elsewhens'. Television can thus be seen as an alternative or complementary medium of education for this generation. And, since the post-war generation has witnessed the evolution of television from a period in which it was highly dependent on the radio for its mode of address and programming style towards self-referential forms that exploit and play upon the evolved forms of television itself, it is familiar with strategies for discovering new significance in the already well known, and establishing a playful distance from established styles (King 1989). Thus, according to Featherstone, the media, together with the (relatively) democratized institutions of higher education, have trained the new middle classes in ways of making meaning which encourage the development of lifestyle as a heroic project, so accelerating the shift towards a post-fordist society.

However, Featherstone's account is highly speculative, and seems to be based on presumed parallels between the class formation in France (where Bourdieu's study was carried out) and Britain. Moreover, there is, as yet, relatively little empirical evidence to support his interpretation of the importance of lifestyle in contributing to the transition from a fordist to a post-fordist economy. Some evidence is analysed in a study of the British middle classes by Savage and others (1992). This study explores the changing structure of the middle classes in relation to their ability to mobilize three kinds of assets – organization, property and cultural assets. They argue that, historically, the three types of asset have given rise to three distinct groupings within the middle classes, with the distinction between the professions on the one hand and the managerial and propertied sectors on the other being particularly strong. However, they also point to the need to recognize the importance of 'organization man', that is, those employed in organizations – including managers – who are dependent on organizational assets, a group which Bourdieu neglects in his own study.

Using data from the British Market Research Bureau's Target Group Index (TGI is an annual survey of 24,000 adults, with respondents asked to give details of a wide range of consumption habits), Savage et al. suggest that there is a strong association between high income, educational attainment and a new culture of

£40,000 to £99,999	£10,000 to £39,999	less than £10,000

371 champagne-drinking
309 (tennis clubs)

─ 300

skiing

skiing holidays

leisure centre city; foreign holidays; mineral waters; health clubs.

─250

(Volvos); French restaurants; tennis; (Japanese restaurants); port-drinking.

restaurants (evenings)

(malt whisky drinking); 'rest of world' holidays; holidays in Italy.

(horse riding)

─200

opera; (ballet); car-tour foreign holidays.   foreign holidays: coach tours

(squash clubs); (vodka drinking); champagne-style wine drinking; drinking wine in box; liqueurs.

holidays in France; (jazz concerts); gin drinking; gym clubs; Italian and Greek/Turkish restaurants.

pub evening meals

─150

bridge playing; (sailing); Volkswagens; tennis.

Chinese evening meals; musicals; Indian restaurants; classical concerts; plays; squash.   foreign holidays: lakes

leisure centre countryside; foreign holidays keep fit/dancing; (brandy drinking).   bowls; classical concerts (outside London).

art galleries/exhibitions; (golf clubs); jogging; beach for holidays; mainland Spain holidays; swimming; golf; pop/rock concerts; holidays in 'rest of Europe'.   football; rugby union; athletics; athletics clubs; badminton; cricket; squash.   no sports clubs visited; champagne; theatres outside London.

information for TGI values from 80 to 120 has been omitted

(vodka); plays; holidays: foreign leisure centre, rest of world, fishing, rest of Europe; keep fit/dancing; jazz concerts; holidays in USA;

sherry drinking; (holidays in USA).   horse racing   brandy; classical concerts (London); gin. hols. in mainland Spain; (malt whisky); golf clubs; yoga; foreign holidays: car-touring; rock concerts

(badminton); ('other sports clubs').   (not London); steak restaurants; beach resort holidays; London museums; holidays in France. weight training; plays; Ford cars; (gym clubs);

─50

(camping)   swimming; (chess); (table tennis); camping; snooker; restaurants (evening). Chinese restaurants; golf; (London theatres); Italian restaurants; tennis. pub meals (evenings); badminton; jogging/training; Vauxhall cars. (squash)

─0

Figure 4.1 Consumption by income group, 1987–8

Note: Uses AB Survey as a base. Vertical axis = Target Group Index (TGI) where the value for Great Britain = 100. Brackets are used when cell counts are too low to produce reliable data.

Source: British Market Research Bureau; figure taken from Savage et al. 1992.

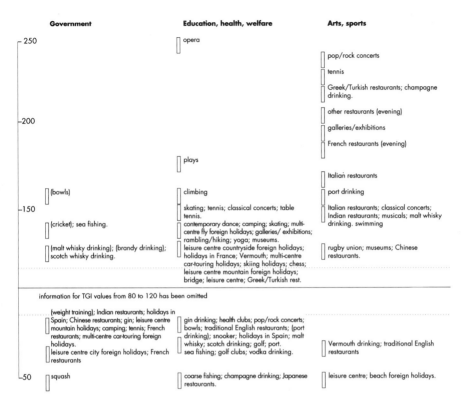

Figure 4.2   Consumption by type of employment 1987–8

Note: Uses AB Survey as a base. Vertical axis = Target Group Index (TGI) where the value for Great Britain = 100. Brackets are used when cell counts are too low to produce reliable data.

Source: British Market Research Bureau; figure taken from Savage et al. 1992.

health and body maintenance (see Figures 4.1–4.3). More particularly, they believe that all three of the groupings mentioned earlier can be identified as having a specific set of tastes.

Members of the first group, primarily located in the public sector professions, display an ascetic style, using their leisure time to exercise and take part in sporting activities as well as having high-culture pursuits. Managers and public sector bureaucrats, on the other hand, have an unremarkable culture; there are no pastimes or pursuits that particularly single them out. In contrast, private sector professionals and specialists adopt a so-called postmodern lifestyle.

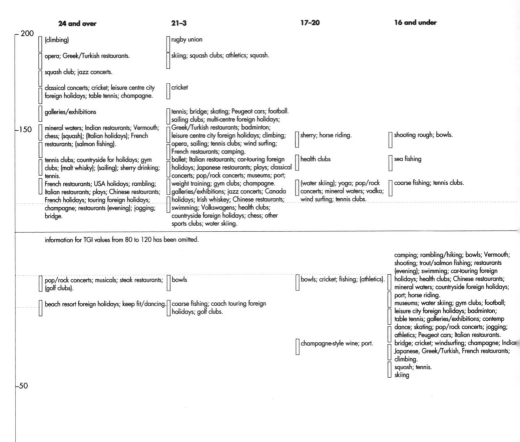

Figure 4.3 Consumption by age of completion of education 1987–8

Note: Uses AB Survey as a base. Vertical axis = Target Group Index (TGI) where the value for Great Britain = 100. Brackets are used when cell counts are too low to produce reliable data.

Source: British Market Research Bureau; figure taken from Savage et al. 1992.

This lifestyle is paradoxical in that it brings together apparently contrasting activities and interests; its advocates showing an interest in health, exercise, sport and fitness, but they are also fond of the good life, as manifested in champagne-drinking and gourmet food. Savage et al. write: 'high extravagance goes along with a culture of the body: appreciation of high cultural forms of art such as opera and classical music exists cheek by jowl with an interest in disco dancing or stock car racing' (1992: 108). The combination of these three lifestyles seems to be the force behind the emergence of the consumer culture identified by Featherstone as responsible for precipitating a shift towards postmodernism in British society.

The contrasting distinctions *within* the middle classes identified by Featherstone and Savage et al. arise because of their different approaches: Featherstone defines groups more or less exclusively in terms of cultural assets, while Savage et al. identify groups in relation to a complex of property, organizational and cultural assets. Nevertheless, while Featherstone's emphasis on cultural assets means that he may overestimate the importance of lifestyle in the creation of class identity, Savage's findings offer some support for the view that cultural assets are increasing in importance in contemporary British society.

Savage et al. identify a number of intersecting processes which give rise to this view. First, they find that organizational assets are of declining importance as companies are becoming less reliant on organizational hierarchies in which managers have clear positions of authority. At the same time, companies have increasingly come to need the skills and knowledge of professionally trained people who can move between companies. In response to this, managers try to convert organizational assets into other forms; for example, they may seek property assets by becoming entrepreneurs, or cultural assets by acquiring professional qualifications. At the same time, Savage et al. suggest that what were once the practices of an 'alternative' middle-class minority, who opposed the values of materialism, have now been adopted on a large scale by those with much greater economic resources. However, in the process, this set of values has been positioned as one of a number of lifestyles from which this group can 'sample', and as a consequence, 'A 1960s-style counter-culture has been transformed into a 1990s-style post-modern cultural conformity' (Savage et al. 1992: 113). Putting these processes together, Savage et al. believe, shows how cultural assets, as mobilized by some fragments of the service class, are becoming increasingly influential in determining not only class formation, but also, indirectly, the organization of production as the economy responds to the shifting patterns of consumer demand.

However, a study by Michele Lamont (1992) comparing how members of the French and the American upper-middle class define what it means to be a 'worthy person' identifies a number of problems with the Bourdieu framework (and thus, by analogy, with Featherstone's analysis). Her data suggests that Bourdieu greatly underestimates the importance of moral preferences while he exaggerates the importance of cultural and socio-economic resources. This may also be the case with the study by Savage et al., since they make use of market research data which does not allow them to explore questions of morality in as great a depth as it does questions of taste. It also means, as Savage et al. themselves note, that the social groups identified in the market research data are not defined in exactly the same way as the fractions of class they believe are salient.

Lamont also suggests that Bourdieu neglects the importance of distinctive national cultures or art-culture systems in providing and organizing a cultural repertoire which provides a backdrop for struggles over taste. She writes:

> individuals do not exclusively draw boundaries out of their own experience: they borrow from the general cultural repertoires supplied to them by the society in which they live, relying on general definitions of valued traits that take on a rule-like status. (1992: 7)

Comparing the French and American cases, Lamont shows that cultural boundaries, that is, boundaries between groups drawn on the basis of education, refinement and cosmopolitanism, are much weaker and more loosely defined in the United States than in France. This is ascribed to the relatively greater importance of high culture and materialism in France and in America respectively. She suggests that while cultural egalitarianism reinforces anti-intellectualism in the United States and generates a more open culture, materialism in France is weakened by the low level of geographic mobility characteristic of this society. One consequence of the relative looseness in drawing cultural boundaries in the United States is that cultural boundaries are less likely to lead to socio-economic boundaries being drawn, and thus less likely to contribute to socio-economic inequality, than in France.

The state and the market

So far in this chapter, then, certain fractions of the middle class have been identified as the bearers of social change, the agents of a complex interrelationship of changes in production and the activities of consumers, culminating in the creation of a postmodern culture in which cultural distinctions are continually displaced. However, it has also been noted that this account focuses too exclusively on the significance of class groups as the agents of change, and ignores the interacting effects of other kinds of social groups, those defined by gender, race and age, for example. The role of these groups in the emergence and development of consumer culture will be the subject of the following chapters.

A further problem with the approach outlined here is that the processes by which cultural capital are transformed into economic capital are not clearly identified. One of the most obvious ways in which this is done is through attendance at educational institutions to acquire qualifications. Such qualifications, legitimated by the state and professional associations, may then provide an entrée into occupations, and a route for the transformation of an individual's cultural capital into economic capital. However, other techniques of transformation are not clearly identified in the studies discussed so far; in particular, it is not clear how taste in the sense of a set of cultural preferences or a lifestyle (rather than educational attainment) may be converted into economic capital. (Indeed, the question of transformation may be the issue that is being played out in the debates between academic and commercial critics discussed earlier.) Bourdieu suggests that the distinctive tastes of members of the dominant class act as status markers and facilitate integration into this group, and that outsiders who have not been socialized into these aesthetic dispositions at an early stage cannot easily become integrated into high-status groups, but this is a difficult claim to substantiate.

As Michele Lamont notes (1992: 182–3), Bourdieu assumes that *differentiation* – the marking of difference – leads directly to *hierarchalization* – the ranking of difference. This is a view of the expression of taste as a form of one-upmanship. But, Lamont argues, it is not necessarily so. Bourdieu's assumption is a consequence of his view that meanings and values are defined relationally – or structurally in relation to each other – within a closed or stable power field. A field is defined here as a competitive system of social relations which functions according to its own specific logic or rules: 'A field is a space in which a game takes place, a field of objective relations between individuals and institutions who are competing for the same stake' (Bourdieu, quoted in Moi 1991: 1021). Lamont stresses that contemporary societies are dynamic, that is, that fields are neither stable nor closed; this reinforces Clifford's point that the art-culture system is open, fluid and subject to rapid movements.

Lamont also argues that contemporary societies are made up of a number of partly overlapping spheres of competition and comparison, each with its own logic and criteria of evaluation. This is well illustrated when the competing claims of different (cross-cutting) social groups, and not just those of class, are considered; these will be discussed in later chapters.

Following this line of argument, it seems as if the writers discussed so far have tended to neglect the ways in which the development of the market and consumer culture have contributed to the emergence and consolidation of new kinds of cultural capital. This may be a consequence of their tendency, not surprising in light of their own position in the academy, to take as legitimate the role of the state, educational institutions and the professions in defining cultural capital, but it may mean that they ignore other logics operating in the social field.

However, a recent study in Manchester by Wynne and O'Connor (1992) documents some of the ways in which not only high culture, education and the professions but also popular culture, market networks and the media have been mobilized as resources in processes of urban regeneration, thus showing some of the ways in which cultural capital is being converted, via the logic of consumer culture, into economic capital.

Drawing on the work of Sharon Zukin (1988; 1991), Wynne and O'Connor point to the history of the ways in which state cultural policy has been linked to urban regeneration. One type of policy has aimed to redevelop areas of urban dereliction or redundant spaces (such as old docks) through investment in artistic activity, with the aim, in part, of setting in motion an interaction between cultural and economic capital. This is also the aim of a second type of policy. This seeks to revitalize specific areas in a city – create a 'buzz' – through the development of what are sometimes called 'cultural quarters' or 'cultural districts':

> The idea here is that if certain areas of a city are associated with a high
> degree of cultural activity – theatre, cinema, concert hall, etc. – then peo-
> ple will . . . be drawn here in search of activity and atmosphere regardless
> of whether they are high users of these areas. Given the right policies,
> cafes, restaurants, small 'culturally orientated' shops, street musicians
> and entertainers – all these will grow as the atmosphere of the quarter
> does. (Wynne and O'Connor 1992: 107)

However, Wynne and O'Connor suggest that both types of policy, although still in operation, are being superseded. They argue that

Table 4.1 Size of organization measured by number of employees

No. of individuals	%
1	31.7
2–4	19.2
5–10	19.7
11–50	21.6
50+	7.7

Source: Wynne and O'Connor 1992.

they are dependent upon a historically specific understanding of cultural policy as a civilizing mission, as education for the masses, a notion which emerged in parallel with the nation-state and an abstract conception of culture as art. In contrast to this, they identify what has been called the 'cultural industries' approach. While this is still, in part, a state-led policy, it works in and through market mechanisms, by encouraging the development of small business in the arts and cultural industries, such as fashion, design, music and film and video.

It is the effects of the operation of this policy in Manchester that is the basis of their study. They found that the organizations in the cultural industries sector, many of which are best described as micro-businesses employing a few people (table 4.1), have a complex relationship to both the market and the state (tables 4.2 and 4.3), and derive their income from a variety of sources (table 4.4). They found that personal and informal contacts were the principal *modus operandi* of these organisations (table 4.5), suggesting that informal networks provide the basis for the collective conversion of cultural capital into economic capital. Wynne and O'Connor conclude that this group of cultural intermediaries is located in 'a series of overlapping and interacting markets according to the activities

Table 4.2 Categories of employment in arts organizations

Type of employment	%
Permanent full-time	35.6
Permanent part-time	14.9
Freelance/short-term contracts	35.6
Voluntary	10.6
Other	3.3

Source: Wynne and O'Connor 1992.

Table 4.3   The legal/statutory forms of arts organizations

Form	%
Limited company (private or public)	20.2
Partnership	9.6
Self-employed or sole trader	8.1
Voluntary association, community group	37.4
Co-operative	2.0
Local authority department(s)	15.2
Government or national organization	1.0
Other	6.6

Source: Wynne and O'Connor 1992.

Table 4.4   Importance of income sources in rank order

Income source	Importance to organization (1 = very important)							
	1	2	3	4	5	6	7	8
Sales	42	15	18	16	10	—	—	—
Commissions	11	21	5	16	11	16	16	5
Box office	47	19	15	8	7	4	1	—
Catering/bar	4	21	25	14	18	14	—	4
Local arts grant	17	25	25	14	14	3	—	2
Other public funding	44	27	14	7	4	1	1	1
Sponsorship	5	17	34	20	15	7	1	1
Other income	9	46	9	27	7	2	—	—

Note: Figures indicate the percentage of organizations indicating for each income source.
Source: Wynne and O'Connor 1992; with amendments.

Table 4.5   Networking characteristics of arts organizations

Type of contact/relationship	%
Personal, informal, for general purposes	53.1
Personal, informal, for specific projects	25.5
Formal, contractual, for general purposes	7.3
Formal, contractual, for specific projects	14.2

Source: Wynne and O'Connor 1992.

they perform and the services they provide' (1992: 112). This group is thus drawing upon a commercialized culture in the creation of cultural capital, and is dependent upon the market, rather than the state or education, to realize that capital in an economic form. The group is also challenging the operation of the art-culture system, and its assumption of the greater value of high culture as opposed to popular culture and the media.

However, these small businesses are obviously not the only players in the cultural economy. In most sectors of the cultural economy, activity is dominated by four or five major companies who produce most of the products in their field, and are able to pick up the successes of the small companies who thus supply a kind of inexpensive research and development function in the cultural economy as a whole (Garnham 1990). Susan Willis (1993), for example, argues that the market system is dominated by corporations which trade in, accumulate and hoard logos, brands and trademarks. These logos are a condensation of cultural capital as image-properties.

Corporations are highly protective of the images that form the basis of this corporate cultural capital, but they face a double-bind. On the one hand, the value of the logos depends upon their recognizability and they thus require constant use; on the other hand, value can be dissipated by the logo's misuse. In order to protect their value, many corporations turn to the law courts. So, for example, the Disney Corporation is continuously involved in lawsuits to protect the exclusivity of its property rights, challenging the legitimacy of others to use its corporate cultural capital. It also adopts a whole set of procedures, including a prohibition against photography in the backstage areas of Disneyworld, to ensure that only copyright-perfect images are circulated for public consumption. In this way, the integrity of its logos is protected from uses which might undermine their potential to be realized as economic capital.

There is a long history to the use of publicity images and logos in branding or creating a distinctive identity for products. An example of this tendency is documented in a newspaper report of the use of the scalp as a medium of display for advertisements: these are called 'cutverts'! And the question of how people use, or are made use of by, these logos in their own everyday activities has been much debated. This is an important question, since if the market is challenging the state as the arbiter of taste it matters whether or not consumers are able to appropriate its goods for their own ends to the same extent that they can as citizens of the state.

Wandering past the potted palms and plastic Christmas trees at the Lakeside shopping centre, near Thurrock in Essex, you might ponder man's evolution. Ten thousand years ago he would have brought back a slain deer or a skinful of fruit from a foraging expedition. Now he clutches a plastic bag.

At Lakeside, the truth dawns – we have become a species of advertising hoarding. Clan and totem

have given way to corporate logo. Are you Burtons, Benetton, Principles? Or Sweathog, Envy or Altered Image? Your bag, a brief visual essay on social aspiration and economic reality, has the answer. (Nicholson-Lord 1992: 3)

Hair space ... Michael Derrick sports the first in a new crop of adverts, this one for the modelling agency that dreamt up the idea   PHOTOGRAPH: MARTIN ARGLES

Close shave cuts dash in condom campaign

Angella Johnson

" I SUPPOSE some people will call me a dickhead," grumbled Leon Gregory as the barber shaved a condom advert on to the back of his head. "I'd rather look at it as imaginative advertising. Like wearing a sandwich board, only more hip."

Leon Gregory, a 17-year-old performing arts student, is a model. He has just spent 30 minutes having the word Durex trimmed on to the back of his head and is looking a little uncertain. "Oh well, at least I'm getting paid. And it does grow out after about a week," he reassures himself after a quick rearview glance. In the next chair, Michael Derrick, aged 21, settled for the word "Cutverts" on the back of his head — the name of the modelling and advertising agency both men work for.

Soon, Leon will be pounding the pavement, handing out free contraceptives, leaflets and advice on safe sex, as part of an advertising campaign for the London International Group, the manufacturer of Durex formerly known as the London Rubber Company.

On the one hand, there is a view which suggests that in sporting corporate logo – by wearing a T-shirt with Bugs Bunny emblazoned across the front, for example – we ritualize and humanize them, and in doing so, may be seen as contemporary poachers in logoland, appropriating a few rabbits for our own stews (see de Certeau 1988 for an elaboration of the metaphor of poaching). On the other hand, there is the view that by, for example, wearing clothing emblazoned with logos, we are merely providing free publicity to the benefit of commercial firms. Susan Willis adopts this more sceptical position, and asserts that a society 'where culture is indistinguishable from logo and where the practice of culture risks infringement of private property is a [society] that values the corporate over the human' (1993: 132–3).

Whichever view is adopted, it is clear that the commercialization of popular culture, including the creation of logos as image-properties, is a phenomenon which needs to be taken into account in any understanding of the cultural economy as a whole, since it suggests that the market, in conjunction with the law, is coming to be a rival to the state in its power to legitimate taste. In conclusion, it seems that the consolidation of the cultural capital of the new middle classes will require not only the backing of the state but also that of the market. Its principles of transformation, exchange and accumulation will not only be *like* those of a market, they will actually *be* a market.

Conclusion

This chapter has outlined a number of accounts of the interrelationship of class, the market and consumer culture. It began with the work of Bourdieu and Featherstone, who argue that taste – or consumer desire – is a social phenomenon and is the result of struggles between different class groups. As part of this struggle, they suggest that the new middle classes, whose size and significance in society is said to have increased as a result of a shift from a fordist to a post-fordist economy, have developed highly visible forms of lifestyle. The new and distinctive use of consumer goods this involves has, in turn, accelerated the shift from fordism to post-fordism as a consequence of the increasing importance attached by the new middle classes as cultural intermediaries to specialized and increasingly stylized forms of consumption. The determining or causal links between changes in production and changes in consumption can thus be seen to operate in both directions.

It was then pointed out that, as well as downplaying the role of other social groups, this kind of explanation tends to focus on the impact of a small number of circuits of exchange, especially those routed through education, high culture and the state, and has tended to ignore circuits of exchange that are mediated by the media, popular culture and the market. One example of the interaction between different circuits was given, drawn from the work of Wynne and O'Connor on cultural policy and urban regeneration, to illustrate the complexity of the relationship between cultural and economic capital. This can be linked to the speculation that the lifestyle of the new middle classes is bringing about a change not only in what can be accumulated as cultural capital, but in the nature of the organization of the art-culture system as a whole. While this change may, in (large) part, benefit the new middle classes, it may also have unintended effects which destabilize the system as a whole. Indeed, it may be the complexity of the processes by which cultural capital is being converted into economic capital that explains the ambivalence of the phenomenon of postmodernism.

5

Making Up and Making Do

Introduction

The last chapter introduced the work of Bourdieu and Featherstone as an example of the approach to the study of consumer culture which looked at the *two-way* links between changes in production for the market and changes in consumption, focusing in particular on their implications for the distribution of aesthetic knowledge.

The chapter looked at the expansion of the new middle classes and their active role as consumers, investigating the expressive aspects of their distinctive lifestyle in terms of the operation of taste, but situating this activity in a broader social context, specifically struggles between classes and changes in the organization of production for the market.

This chapter will introduce another example of the interactive or two-way approach to the study of consumption, focusing on the significance of gender in the development of consumer culture, and emphasizing the importance of looking at cycles of production and consumption. It is important to stress that the role of gendered groups – men and women – also has a double aspect, with changes in gender relations shaping changes in cycles of production and consumption and vice versa, and that the groups are simultaneously cross-cut by relations of sexuality, class, race and age.

In order to explore these two-way relationships, it is important to recognize that one of the problems with many arguments about the emergence of the so-called consumer culture is that they make use of a rather restricted notion of consumption, often only looking at consumption directly mediated by the market and the state (thus ignoring the significance of the family as a site of exchange), and assuming an asocial individual as the consumer. They also tend to adopt an understanding of the art-culture system which presumes that its operation has the same implication for all individuals, irrespective of gender, that is, that aesthetic knowledge or cultural resources are equally available to men and women. Yet many writers have pointed out the ways in which modernism was dominated by male artists (Huyssen 1986; Gilbert and Gubar 1988), while mass culture was historically denigrated as feminine. Andreas Huyssen, for example, notes that the novelist Gustave Flaubert is often attributed his status as the father of literary modernism on the basis of 'an aesthetic based on the uncompromising repudiation of what Emma Bovary [the heroine of his most famous novel] loved to read' (1986: 189). All this suggests that a more comprehensive consideration of gender will lead to a revision of the understanding of consumer culture presented so far.

However, this understanding has not yet been fully developed; this is partly because of the disparate nature of existing studies of gender and consumer culture. On the one hand, there are a number of studies which look at the gendered character of the activity of consumption as work, that is, at the acquisition and transformation of goods in housework. These approaches are not especially concerned with the question of culture. On the other hand, there is also a literature which directly addresses the question of gender, identity and consumer culture, but this does not often address the issues of work which preoccupy the first set of approaches. In what follows, therefore, a number of links are suggested between these approaches, but it should be recognized that they are tentative and require further exploration.

Gender and the Family Economy

Relatively little academic attention has been focused on gender and consumer culture; and what attention there has been is rather paradoxical. On the one hand, it is recognized in marketing and advertising that the role of consumer is constructed as a feminine one and that it is typically women who do the shopping (women implement 80 per cent or more of consumption decisions), that is, that it is women who actually tend to purchase most goods and do the 'work' of consumption. On the other hand, the vast majority of the entries on the topic of 'gender and consumption' in the Social Sciences Citation Index are concerned with what is described as 'deviant' behaviour, particularly the consumption of drugs, cigarettes, food and alcohol. It is as if the extent of women's participation in consumption practices is both taken for granted and a source of anxiety!

The few writers on gender and consumption who do not adopt either of these positions are at pains to point out that an individual's consumption is shaped by the social conditions in which they are embedded and that these social conditions include the interlocking sets of social relations that produce patterns of gender inequality between men and women. These writers point out that many 'consumer' goods are the object of further labour before they are finally consumed – so, for example, food that is bought in a supermarket is typically prepared, cooked and presented before it is eaten. This work or labour is generally performed by women, and is a large part of housework.

While the preparation of meals is readily recognized as an example of housework, a number of writers have argued that it is important to acknowledge that housework typically includes not only practical, but also emotional, sexual, reproductive and symbolic work done by women for men within family relationships (Delphy and Leonard 1992). It is not only work done on the house that is important here – the cleaning of the house, the stylization and ordering of its furnishings, and the preparation and presentation of food – but also caring work in relationships such as mothering, and work done by women on themselves, what might be called the work of femininity (Winship 1987), the work that women do on their appearance, manner and personal identity.

Housework defined in this way does not fit the common preconception of work as paid employment, but it can be seen as such once it is situated in relation to the notion of a family economy (Oakley 1976; Delphy 1984). This economy exists alongside and is interlinked with the industrial or capitalist economy. The family economy is structured by conditions of inequality, in which women tend to be in a position of economic dependence upon men. This dependence is socially structured by relations of power within the household, the state and the labour market, and has meant that the amount of time a full-time housewife with children spends on housework has stayed relatively constant during the course of the twentieth century: it is still 60–70 hours a week (Anderson, Bechhofer and Gershuny 1994). The amount of time that most men spend on housework has gone up slightly over this period of time; but it is still 5–10 hours a week, even when the woman in the shared household is not only doing the housework, but also doing paid work of some kind. The man may offer to *help*, but housework is still typically assumed to be the woman's responsibility.

Delphy and Leonard (1992) argue that, within the family, there are three types of economic activity: production, consumption and the accumulation and circulation of property. They write that the inequalities generated by these activities will be missed if the family is taken as a natural unit, in which all members equally participate, and argue that

> the fact that the family can be treated as a unit of production or consumption or of property-holding for certain purposes does not mean that the family (in the sense of all its members) produce and consume and hold property together as a block, nor that all have the same economic status and identical interests. (Delphy and Leonard 1992: 107)

As they go on to note, however, while it is often recognized that much production and property-holding is carried out by members as separate individuals, this fact is far less commonly noted as regards consumption. It is usually far from clear when authors speak of the family household as a 'unit of consumption' whether they are referring to the total consumption of all the members wherever it takes place, or just to that part of consumption which takes place within the home. Delphy and Leonard argue that even if 'family production' and 'family consumption' are used to refer to what is done or used by family members actually within the home, these processes are not the same for all the members of the family.

This last point, the existence of differences in the extent and quality of consumption of family members, is explained by contrasting the industrial economy and the family economy. Delphy and Leonard write:

> In the labour market, workers are paid a wage by their employer, but in the family-based household, members are maintained by its head. This means dependents have less choice as to what they get than if they were given money. What is provided for them is what is favoured (or at least agreed to) by the head. In addition, since much of what family members produce is consumed within the family, this in itself prevents goods and services consumed in the family being the same for all members. For example, when the husband and children consume meals served by the wife, she provides the services, so she cannot consume them in the same way as they do: as work done by someone else. She cannot both wait and be waited on. Hence, there are real problems in treating the family as a 'unit of consumption' in any analysis. (1992: 108)

The point being made here is that the separate statuses of men and women are marked out by their different places in what only *appears* to be the same consumption space. While he is watching television, she is getting dinner. Even at the dinner-table, the woman is likely to be the one serving the food. She is required to be a facilitator of other people's consumption rather than (or as well as) an active participant.

In short, while it is often noted that it is women who make up the majority of consumers, in the sense that it is women who actually purchase goods on a routine basis, it is not so often recognized that they will generally go on to work on the goods bought. Women are typically the *producers* of goods and services of which men as husbands are the *consumers* or final users. Indeed, given the relations of inequality within which much shopping and other housework is done, some feminists argue that it is inappropriate and misleading to consider shopping as an example of consumption, and suggest that it is more accurate to see it as part of family production – the work of selecting, transporting and transforming the raw materials or resources of housework. But it is possible to suggest that both interpretations are correct. Shopping may be seen as an instance of consumption in relation to the cycle of commodity production (that is, production of goods for exchange on the market), but as a moment of production in relation to household or domestic production (for exchange in the family). What this dual location of shopping illustrates is the importance of looking at *cycles* or circuits of production and consumption within society as a whole. It also shows that it is necessary to think of consumption not simply in relation to the market and commodification but also in relation to other economic systems, notably the family.

The domestic revolution and consumption

As a consequence of their recognition of the importance of inter-locking cycles of production and consumption, many feminist writ-ers are more suspicious than other writers of the term consumer culture. They argue that it should be understood not simply in rela-tion to the capitalist economy and class relations, but also simulta-neously in relation to family or domestic production and gender relations. Once this is taken into account, there is a question-mark over the notion that we live in a distinctively modern consumer cul-ture at all. The suggestion is that while there may have been changes in the commodification of objects, unless the interrelation-ship of these changes with the systems of production and exchange that operate in domestic life are explored it is difficult to say what their impact is upon society as a whole. It may be that the changes discussed so far, while an important aspect of social and cultural change, are not sufficient on their own to justify the suggestion that we are living in a qualitatively new era. One view is thus that a term such as *consumerism* is more appropriate than 'consumer culture' to describe the kinds of change that have occurred in relation to the consumption of objects exchanged through the market.

On the other hand, the emergence of consumer culture is some-times closely identified with what has been called a domestic revolu-tion in the making of the modern home, or what Game and Pringle, somewhat confusingly, call a 'major shift from housework as pro-duction to housework as *consumption*' (1984: 120). This shift is seen to be the result of a series of changes in the organization of the fami-ly economy, and is deemed to have brought about a fundamental reorganization in society analogous to that wrought by the industrial revolution:

> The change, for example, from the laundry to the washing machine is no less profound than the change from the hand loom to the power loom . . . the change from pumping water to turning on a faucet is no less destruc-tive of traditional habits than the change from manual to electric calculat-ing. (Cowan 1983: 223)

These changes included the steadily increasing purchase and use of commodities in place of home-made goods during the eighteenth and nineteenth centuries, and the transformation of the home itself into a kind of temple to consumption. From this point of view, it may seem appropriate to identify consumer culture as a distinctively modern form of material culture.

However, while this so-called domestic revolution has been closely linked with the rise of consumer culture, this does not mean that women, historically the custodians of the domestic sphere, have been the chief bearers or *intermediaries* of consumer culture. This is because, although women typically have responsibility in the family economy, they are not typically in control; moreover, they stand in a different relation to the art-culture system than do men. So, while women may have been the instruments of consumer culture, they have not necessarily been agents in its historical development.

This argument is developed by a number of writers, including Game and Pringle (1984) who suggest that, at the beginning of the twentieth century, there was a large increase in mass commodity consumption, and this created an urgent need for labour to acquire and transform these commodities before their final use. To this end, women were mobilized as what the economist Galbraith has described as a 'crypto-servant class', with the consequence that, as Game and Pringle note,

> There has been a growing uniformity of women's experience, at least in so far as women of *all* classes are occupied with consumption activities around their own homes, and the associated relational skills have become a defining characteristic of femininity. From about the 1890s . . . the new term 'housewife' came into use as a cross-class term that reflected this new reality. (1984: 122)

They thus argue that it is not women as such, but women as housewives, that is women subordinated within the family economy, who are the bearers of the emerging consumer culture.

It has sometimes been argued that the ever-increasing availability of finished goods for sale as commodities will lead to a decline in the amount of housework that is done by women; that is, as industrial production comes to provide more and more of the goods that used to be made in the home, women will be released from housework and increasingly enter the paid workforce, resulting in the end of the sexual division of labour both in the household and in paid work (see, for example, Braverman 1974). However, this kind of argument tends to ignore the continuing hold of power relations within the family. While more and more women have entered the labour market during the twentieth century, the broad patterns of the domestic division of labour have not changed very much. While there has been some change in the kinds of tasks that are done as part of housework – more and more tasks are associated with the transformation of commodities (shopping itself has become an increasingly important aspect of housework and now takes up one full day a week compared with two hours in the 1920s, as both more goods and a wider range of goods become available through the market) – it is still typically done by women for men on an individualized basis.

This is, in part, a consequence of the ways in which the process of suburbanization, while facilitating the entry of the market into the household, helped preserve hierarchical power relations between men and women. The unequal division of labour was fixed through the very architecture of the home and the geographical separation of home and work:

> Suburbia's socio-spatial patterns typically anchored in *place* the *market* arrangements of the postwar period . . . Buying a house, at least one car, and domestic equipment integrated households into a national landscape of mass production and consumption. (Zukin 1991: 140).

Similarly, in relation to the introduction of so-called labour-saving devices, Game and Pringle write:

> New technology in the home has contradictory effects. While it has removed a lot of the heavy work it has done little to reduce work frequencies and in some cases has created new forms of drudgery. For instance, no aspect of housework has been lightened so much as laundry, yet time spent on it has actually increased. Women can now be expected to wash clothes daily instead of weekly. (1984: 125)

Gershuny (1978; 1983) has also argued that the introduction of new technologies has meant a shift towards what he calls the domestic provision of services, a shift which rearranges but does not fundamentally disturb gender relations within the home. In other words, while the increase in consumer goods has contributed to a change in the content of housework, it has not removed gender inequality within the family.

Nevertheless, simultaneous with the increasing dependence of housewives on goods provided by the market, there have been changes in the organization of housework. These also relate to what is sometimes described as its *emotionalization* and *aestheticization*. So, for example, while it might have been expected that as housework was 'modernized' through the introduction of new domestic technologies, it would have become less emotionally involving, the reverse appears to be true:

> Laundering became not just laundering but an expression of love; cooking and cleaning were regarded as 'homemaking', an outlet for artistic inclinations and a way of encouraging family loyalty; changing nappies was not just a shitty joy but a time to build the baby's sense of security and love for the mother; scrubbing the bathroom was not just cleaning but an exercise of maternal instincts, keeping the family safe from disease. (Game and Pringle 1984: 127)

By the mid-twentieth century, housework had become not just a job, but an expression of love and warmth performed by each woman for her own family.

Significantly for the development of consumer culture, there has also been a process by which housework has been *aestheticized* in the sense that the standards by which housework is judged have come to include not only 'scientific' or 'technical' standards of hygiene and efficiency, but also those of style, harmony and 'atmosphere' (Forty 1986; Partington 1991). This aestheticization has been closely tied in with prevailing notions of masculinity and femininity. According to Forty, until the mid-nineteenth century, the choice of domestic furnishings seems to have been primarily a male activity. However, by the 1860s, the choice of domestic decoration and furnishing became an accepted and even expected activity for (first middle-class and then working-class) women. The principles women were encouraged to adopt by the many handbooks that began to appear were, first, that the home should be as unlike the husband's place of work as possible, and second, that the interior should express the personality of its occupants, especially that of the lady of the house. So close had the identification between woman and the house become in the late nineteenth century that a woman who failed to express her personality in this way was in danger of being thought lacking in femininity. In an essay published in 1869, for example, Frances Power Cobbe asserted:

> A woman whose home does not bear this relation of nest to bird, calyx to flower, shell to mollusk, is in one or another imperfect condition. She is

either not really mistress of her home; or being so, she is herself deficient in the womanly power of thoroughly imposing her personality upon her belongings. (Quoted in Forty 1986: 106)

More specifically, the activity of buying has itself come to be increasingly defined as worthy and significant, creating a new role for women as administrators of the home, directing consumption by their selection of the goods and services. In this way, women have been drawn into the development of consumer culture. So, for example, department stores – 'palaces of consumption' – were constructed as welcoming and inviting places for women in particular. At the Bon Marché in Paris, for instance, diaries, calendars, bulletins and even transport to the store were provided to encourage women to shop and feel at ease once they got there (Bowlby 1985). However, while shopping was seen as peculiarly feminine, it was not positively valued, but, rather, was constructed as irrational, fanciful and frivolous. Women shoppers were encouraged to think of themselves as being prone to become out of control, having an insatiable desire to buy. Managers of department stores helped create this perception through the way shoppers were treated once in the store. So, for instance, floor walkers, men who escorted women around the store helping and controlling their purchases, were common until the 1920s (Benson 1986). There were also medical studies which purported to show sexual dysfunction as the cause of kleptomania or shoplifting in women. Perhaps not surprisingly, there were also attempts to rationalize housework in general and shopping in particular. So, for example, this period sees the introduction and growth of domestic science in schools, the proliferation of housework manuals, and a torrent of advice to housewives on how best to look after their home and family in, for example, women's magazines.

According to Janice Winship (1987), this aspect of the development of consumer culture can be seen as part of an attempt to co-opt the early demands of feminism and the desire of the growing number of women who were participating in paid work to gain some degree of economic independence. Indeed, sometimes shopping was explicitly presented as an alternative form of liberation, as, for example, when Mr Selfridge suggested that he was aiding the cause of women's emancipation in opening his department store! More recently, Betty Friedan, author of one of the first manifestos of contemporary feminism, *The Feminine Mystique* (1965), quotes, with outrage, an advertising executive who had a similar, although more obviously condescending, view of the implications of consumerism for women: ' "Properly manipulated . . . American housewives can be given the sense of identity, purpose, creativity, the self-realization, even the sexual joy they lack – by the buying of things" ' (1965: 181).

Robyn Dowling (1993) provides a detailed study of how the meanings of both retailing and femininity were created in specific retail outlets in a study of the Woodward's department store in downtown Vancouver in Canada in the mid-twentieth century. She argues that, as environments in which commodities are bought and sold, retail institutions should be seen as places where the meaning of commodities is produced and negotiated. The retail context is seen to be a created place, one that is deliberately moulded by retailers in their attempts to sell commodities. She writes: 'Retailing is not only metaphorically a context in which the meaning of commodities is fixed, it is also *literally* a place where the meaning of commodities is produced' (1993: 298).

The store itself is a resource which retailers can use to make themselves and their commodities distinctive, and, Dowling suggests, retailers were routinely involved in a process of place-making. The importance of this is outlined by Benson:

> Manufacturers appealed directly to the consumer on the relatively narrow basis of the product alone, usually relying on a trademark or slogan to convey their message. But the newly self-conscious department store-manager spoke lyrically of developing a store image – presenting the store as a coordinated whole, harmonizing all its aspects, and doing so with a special twist that would distinguish the store in the mind of the public. (Benson 1986: 81, quoted in Dowling 1993: 298)

In other words, the lay out of stores, the location of goods in relation to others, and their display were deliberately intended to become part of the meanings of commodities. (This is explicitly recognized in today's retail vocabulary in which window-dressing is redefined as visual merchandising.) Place-making thus did not just provide the setting for the social interaction of selling and buying: it also aimed to mould elements of the sale, and constructed subject positions for both the sales clerk and the shopper. Through such practices, it is suggested, gender identities have been given a central place in the history of consumer culture.

More specifically, Dowling suggests that by the mid-twentieth century, luxury was not the main characteristic of most department stores; it had been displaced by the discourses of modernity and familialism. In the period 1945–60, the creation of a family place, a place welcoming to the entire family, was a paramount concern of Woodwards, and a number of strategies were adopted to promote a climate of familialism. These included: the use of the in-store journal to give information about employees' private lives, including 'romances', engagements, weddings, births and reports of collective social events; the organization of a store social club and an invitation to staff to participate in store outings; and the instructions to sales clerks to deal with consumers in a familial manner. As an example of the last of these, Dowling provides the details of the Woodwards' staff manual of 1948, a ten-point plan for 'successful selling' which included the following guidance to staff:

- treat customers as you would invited guests
- have a wholesome attitude
- watch your health
- keep your personal appearance neat and attractive (quoted in Dowling 1993: 305).

In these and other ways, then, the personal life of Woodwards' employees was made an integral component of their jobs, and Woodwards made itself a part of employees' 'private' lives. Both tendencies had the effect of enforcing a model of family life on employees and the store itself.

At the same time that this ideology of familialism was being promoted, shopping was defined as a modern activity. Unlike earlier department stores, Woodwards did not represent itself as modern through an emphasis on the luxurious, but through its organization of self-consciously rational lines. Its rationality was indicated by the design and architecture of the store itself, which was plain and functional. In keeping with this layout, commodities were displayed in an orderly, tidy manner and aisles were wide and linear. Thus, Woodwards represented itself as a modern place through its adoption of a rational and scientific mode of self-organization.

A discourse of rationalization also helped shape the positions of shopper and sales clerk. The sales clerk was equipped with 'rational knowledge' which he or she was instructed to impart to the shopper. The author of a column in the in-store journal claimed:

'This is the day of the expert.

Bewildered housewives, struggling to run their homes, feed and clothe their families as economically and efficiently as possible, can no longer keep pace with scientific evolution. They are baffled by the volume and intricacy of new consumer goods.

The retail salesperson has become an adviser, one who knows intimately the goods he is selling, who can protect his customers from fraud, who can explain to them how by proper use and care they can get the most satisfaction from their purchases. Study and training are as important for him as for doctors and lawyers.' (Quoted in Dowling 1993: 303)

This expert positioning of the sales clerk in relation to the shopper had a clear gender dimension. In contrast to the scientific and masculine rationality of Woodwards' management and staff, the Woodwards' shopper was positioned not only as a wife – she was constantly referred to as 'Mrs Consumer' – but also as stereotypically irrational and feminine. 'Bewildered' in the face of scientific evolution, she did not know what she wanted:

'Customers frequently will not tell you what is in their minds. They make a brief request. Behind that request is a host of needs-wants-desires. A skillful professional salesperson will tactfully, delicately, but determinedly, ferret out those needs and satisfy them.' (A 1949 column, 'Aggressive Selling' in the in-house store journal, quoted in Dowling 1993: 30)

In short, feminine shoppers were typically understood to be irredeemably irrational and inferior (although apparently susceptible to an implicitly sexualized interrogation).

A 5-year-old boy, out shopping with his mother, got lost in a crowded department store. 'Well, young man', said the salesclerk, 'what does your mother look like?' The youngster answered through his tears, 'She's the lady with a lot of packages and no money.'

(*The Beacon*, Woodwards' in-store journal, 1960, quoted in Dowling 1993: 311)

Shopping at Woodwards was presented as a way of enabling the (irrational) women of Vancouver to cook for and nurture their families in a modern, up-to-date way. However, food-floor shoppers, unlike shoppers in masculine departments such as sporting goods and hardware, had to be taught how to be modern. They were seen to be in need of education about new commodities through special promotions and displays, such as 'Brazilian Coffee Week' and the 'Salad Symphony' display. In 1954, a display kitchen was built for a home economist service. Here, the shopper was taught how to cook the modern foods she had bought, scientifically and hygienically, so that her family would remain healthy. In this and other ways, the techniques and standards for women's caring skills – cooking, cleaning and looking after her family, for instance – were increasingly tied to their use of commodities. So, at the same time that consumer culture was imbued with conventional understandings of femininity and masculinity, it reinforced gendered relations in the family economy of the household.

Dowling thus shows how, in contradictory ways, women were mobilized in the cause of consumer culture without being allocated the resources with which to become active agents in its development: they were continuously positioned as lacking certain key knowledges and capacities, and in Bourdieu's terms, denied direct access to existing cultural capital and the power to set their own standards to create alternative forms of cultural capital, let alone convert cultural capital into economic capital. They were necessarily involved in drawing the distinctions of taste, but were not recognized as its originators, and were not in a position to benefit personally from any status its display might accrue.

Winship (1987) adopts a complementary approach to Dowling in her emphasis on the ways in which definitions of gender have been linked to the development of consumer culture, illustrating how women's magazines in the twentieth century promoted particular kinds of femininity through the representation of consumption practices. In a study of British women's magazines, she identifies some broad shifts in the ways in which the role of the women reader as housewife, mother, wife and consumer was constructed, most notably, a shift from the representation of women in terms of their roles as wife and mother in the early and middle years of the twentieth century – along similar lines to those identified by Dowling – to an increasing stress on feminine individuality through an emphasis on glamour, sexuality and appearance towards the end. This argument has important implications for the issue of how consumer culture may have helped shape contemporary ideals of personal identity as a possession, reflexively created in practices of self-fashioning.

This shift towards an invitation to women to understand themselves in terms of feminine individuality is analysed by Winship by reference to the magazine *Options*, launched in 1982. This magazine was described in the publicity surrounding its launch as 'a magazine about choice', a choice which was later presented in terms of 'Better food, Better homes, Better fashion, Better living'. It is addressed to a reader who is invited to see herself as 'an entirely new breed of consumer', defined exclusively in terms of what she buys:

> She sees herself as the kind of women who should have a calculator in her handbag, a stereo in her car, a note recorder in her office. She is the generation for whom video and telecom were made. Busy women with open minds who will take advantage to make work more efficient and play more fun. The first generation of women for whom freezers, dish-washers and microwave ovens are not luxuries but essentials. (*Options* launch material, quoted in Winship 1983: 47)

This is the new woman who can be independent *and* feminine, who can look attractive *and* create a fulfilling family and home life even when carrying out a demanding job.

The representation of consumption dominates this and many other women's magazines. Not only is about half of the magazine taken up by advertisements, but almost all the colour photography, both in advertisements and features, illustrates commodities of some kind. In feature articles and advertisements, the modern woman is represented as a superwoman, enjoying the skills and pleasures of consumption, not in a passive way, but by actively appropriating and reworking commodities to construct a lifestyle which expresses her *individuality*. Winship writes that in *Options* 'the activities involved around consumption constitute a *creative skill* – the creation of a "look", whether with clothes, furnishings, food or make-up – which are both *pleasurable to do* and *to look at*' (1983: 48). The sphere of consumption is held up as the arena in which women can selectively choose 'options' to express their own unique sense of self by transforming commodities from their mass-produced forms into expressions of individuality and originality. The magazine provides optimistic encouragement to keep on trying, offering examples of women who have 'found themselves' through the adoption of an individualized lifestyle.

Winship argues that an important part of this latest stage in the representation of women in relation to consumption is the way in which women are invited to view their own lives as their *own creations*, and buy an identikit of different images of themselves created by different products. This latest stage in the constitution of women through consuming is linked by Winship to the growing importance of the *work of femininity*. Other writers too have argued that consumption practices have become an increasingly important source of the creation of the feminine self.

One instance of this is provided by the relation between the notions of beauty and femininity. Winship argues that, while beauty is not a new component of femininity, advertising in women's magazines has played an important part in redefining its meaning. She suggests that advertising has contributed to the idea that beauty is not a natural given – either absent or present – but instead is something that is achievable by any woman, though only through the application of the correct products. The way in which advertising has done this, according to Winship, is through its representation of women as 'the field of action for various products'. She points to the way in which in advertisements, women's bodies are broken down into different areas as sites for the actions of commodities.

Winship suggests that advertising builds on the creation of an anxiety to the effect that, unless women measure up, they will not be loved. They are set to work on their bodies labouring to perfect and eroticize an ever-increasing number of erotogenic zones. Every minute region of the body is now exposed to scrutiny. Mouth, hair, eyes, eyelashes, nails, fingers, hands, skin, teeth, lips, cheeks, shoul-

ders, elbows, arms, legs, feet – all these and many more
become areas requiring work. Winship sees this in terms of
imposition of a cultural ideal of feminine beauty and the multipl
tion of areas of the body accessible to marketing. It is the introd
tion of this idea that beauty is something that can be achieved, that
it is something to be worked on, that Winship identifies as the work
of femininity, and she suggests that consumer culture has been able
to feed on and extend this work through its promotion of a multiplicity of products.

Winship further suggests that through the representation of beauty as an achievable goal of self-transformation through the use of
commodities, women are constructed as consumers of themselves *as
possessions or commodities*. John Berger makes the same point when
he writes that, 'the publicity image steals [a woman's] love of herself
as she is and offers it back to her for the price of the product' (1972:
134). Kathy Myers (1986) catches this contradictory nature of consumption for women by describing it as a kind of cannibalism. The
point that is being made here is that women are both the *objects* or
signs of representation in advertising and the *market* for the majority
of products advertised. They are thus simultaneously located at two
moments of the cycle of commodity exchange – that of a privileged
sign in advertising and commodity aesthetics and the principal target market. They are also, in one sense, the principal actors in the
moment of use of commodities. From this point of view, the emotionalization and aestheticization of housework – including, most
importantly, the intensification of the work of femininity – may be
seen to have contributed to the emergence of the distinctively stylized nature of consumer culture in contemporary society and the
ideal of a possessive individual. However, the extent to which
women are active agents, in the sense of being in control of how to
use commodities, whether they are self-possessed or possessed by
others, is a much debated question.

As noted above, for many writers, women's role in the development of consumer culture must be located in relation to the family
economy. Here, it is argued, women are subordinated to men,
through the requirement to carry out housework, including the
work of femininity. To the extent that their use of commodities is
not conducted for themselves, but for others, women may be seen,
not as cultural intermediaries, but as bearers of a culture which they
do not own. From this point of view the idea of a feminine individual promoted in magazines such as *Options* is a contradiction in
terms.

Beauty

Making the most
of what
you've got

Part of looking good is knowing how to maximise your great points and minimise your bad ones. Charlotte-Anne Fidler shows you how with blusher, shader and a dash of lip liner

'When I was sixteen I worked in a cosmetics store. One day the manageress showed me how to make my small eyes bigger, my thin lips fuller and how to disguise my big nose. By the time I left I thought I must be really ugly. It's taken me all this time to realise that I'm not. Okay, I've got deep-set eyes and a big nose but I just make the most of what I've got.'
Bobbi Brown, make-up artist

Making the most of what you've got, 1990s-style, is about accepting who you are and realising that, while you're never going to look like Linda or Christy or Kate, you're going to look as good as you possibly can. If you're happy with the shape of your eyes, mouth and face, that's great. If you're not, then the latest contourers, eyeshadows and lipsticks can work wonders. We show you how.

FACES

'I'm definitely into contouring at the moment,' enthuses make-up artist Charlie Green. 'It really can give your face more shape.' Successful contouring takes practice, so invest in a proper brush – they're flatter and less round than blusher brushes – and experiment. Try Christian Dior Effets Blush Powder Blush Trio, £20, or Givenchy Blush Prism, £16. 'The way you shade and blend is very important,' says make-up artist Stéphane Marais. 'It has to be very light and transparent. No extreme contrasts or theatrical effects.' Charlie Green agrees: 'Always do your shading in daylight, not in the bathroom.'

WHERE'S THE BEST PLACE TO PUT BLUSHER?

For the most natural look, simply apply your blusher where you actually blush – on the apples of your cheeks. Roll it on using a large, fat blusher brush – the tiny ones that come in blusher compacts are useless for this – and bring the colour up from the centre of your cheeks to the hairline. For a really healthy look, flick touches of colour on the point of the chin, the forehead and over the temples, but don't overdo it – it's far easier to build up colour gradually than to wipe it off if you've been a bit slap-happy.

> **Expert's advice:**
> 'There are other ways to wear blusher, such as the Eskimo look I created for Gaultier by shading an upside-down triangle of rusted colour going from the cheeks to the jawline.'
> *Stéphane Marais*

HOW TO GIVE WIDTH TO A LONG FACE

According to Stéphane Marais, there are two ways of doing this. He either uses a bronzing powder to shorten the chin by brushing a touch of colour on the tip, and then blending it down to the throat. Or, he shortens the forehead by lightly shading the skin on the hairline with a bronzer or a blusher.

> **Expert's advice:**
> 'If you want to make your face appear shorter, try not to sculpt the cheekbones too much with blusher. Healthy colour in the middle of the cheeks will make your face look rounder.'
> *Stéphane Marais*

HOW TO GIVE YOURSELF CHEEKBONES

Diehard cheekbone-lovers can get the desired effect without having to have their molars removed. Using a powder blusher, create a triangle of dark

HOW TO MAKE A ROUND FACE LOOK THINNER

Narrow the forehead by lightly brushing a bronzer or shader on the temples. Then make the cheeks look more sculpted by creating a triangle of shadow under the cheekbones and highlight with a lighter powder on the top of the cheekbone.

> **Expert's advice:**
> 'You can diminish a double chin to a certain extent with bronzing powder. Lightly brush the powder along the weighty part of the jaw and blend it towards the throat.'
> *Bobbi Brown*

shadow from the ears down to the middle of the cheeks. If you want to make the cheekbones really stand out, highlight above and below the triangle with a lighter-coloured powder.

> **Expert's advice:**
> 'If you don't have cheekbones, don't worry about it, you're just one of the many who don't. And it doesn't matter. Just look how beautiful Isabella Rossellini is without them.'
> *Bobbi Brown*

HOW TO MAKE A BIG NOSE APPEAR SMALLER

This can be done by using two different coloured foundations – your normal one and another about three shades darker – but it's less labour intensive to use a ▷

EYES
Small eyes can be opened up with pale, frosted colours on the lids and darker shadow in the sockets, finished off with heaps of mascara

NOSE
Subtle shading down the side of the nose, using a slightly darker foundation or shader, evens up the shape and reduces width

CHEEKS
Peachy- coloured blusher brushed on to the apple of the cheek, the temples and the chin gives the skin a natural-looking glow

LIPS
Careful use of a natural-coloured lipliner blended with a paler lipstick gives the illusion of fuller lips

Beauty

For fuller-looking lips, outline with a skin-coloured liner

◁ shader or unshimmery bronzing powder. If you feel your nose is too long, lightly dust a shader or the darker foundation on the tip. If want to make your nose look thinner, you can put a line of highlighter down the centre of it, before brushing shader or darker foundation down each side. Make sure that the shading is as subtle as possible and that the two colours are blended very, very carefully.

LIPS

HOW TO MAKE LARGE LIPS APPEAR SMALLER

Big lips are great, but if you're determined to minimise the size of your mouth, throw out the lipliner – drawing a line inside the lip contour looks strange. It's better to play down the size with colour. Avoid pale, frosted lipsticks or glosses which will make the mouth look enormous. Opt for matt neutrals. Try MAC Deep Plum and Mocha, £8, and Helena Rubinstein Rouge Forever in Mat Rose, £13.50.

Play down full lips with neutral colours

HOW TO MAKE THIN LIPS APPEAR FULLER

Avoid very dark-coloured lipsticks which will only make your lips look smaller, while very pale colours can make the lips disappear altogether. Opt for something in between, such as Prescriptives French Fawn, £11, or neutrals from Ultima II The Nakeds, £10.50 each. Line the lips with a skin-coloured pencil – MAC Spice, £6.50, is a favourite with make-up artists. Then follow Linda Evangelista's lead and, starting at the corner of the top lip, draw a line upwards taking the pencil slightly over the edge of the lip in an arc, until you reach the cupid's bow. 'Don't make the cupid's bow bigger, it looks naf,' advises Charlie Green. 'But making the mouth wider from the corners creates a luscious look,' On the bottom lip, start at each corner, bringing the line into the middle. Only take the liner over the edge at the centre of the lip where it will look like a natural shadow – it looks fake if you go over the edge at the sides.

Finally, blot the parts that you've enlarged, otherwise they'll catch the light and look unreal.

EYES

HOW TO GIVE SMALL EYES A BIGGER LOOK

'Avoid putting make-up all around the eyes as you'll make them look closed and even smaller,' says Stéphane Marais. To open up the eye area, apply pale, even slightly frosted, colours on the lid itself and put dark shadow (greys or mid-browns) in the socket. Put a little shadow, or carefully blended pencil, under the eye and take it up to meet where you've shaded the socket. Use only neutral-coloured eyeshadows: 'Coloured shadow says, "here comes my make-up",' warns Charlie Green.

HOW TO ELONGATE ROUND EYES

To transform round, 'button' eyes into odalisque 'almonds', concentrate the colour on the outer corners. Take the eyeshadow up from under the eyes into the socket in a soft, V-shape and blend carefully so they don't look like wings. Avoid colour on the inner corners of the eye.

HOW TO LIFT DROOPY EYES

'First, don't think of yourself as having droopy eyes, they're "bedroom eyes" like Charlotte Rampling's or Tatjana Patitz's,' says Bobbi Brown. Avoid very dark or frosted eyeshadow altogether. Apply dark-brown shadow close to the lashes and use a skin-tone or neutral shadow over the rest of the eye. To finish, dab a little bone or white-coloured shadow under the browbone.

HOW TO BRING DEEP-SET EYES FORWARD

Avoid dark eyeshadows as they'll make your eyes recede even further. To make the eyes 'come forward', lightly line the top of the eye with a shadow liner then use pale, slightly shiny colours, such as pearl, on the eyelids.

Photograph by Hennessa

EYES
To lift slightly droopy eyes, a dark-brown shadow is applied close to the lashes and a neutral colour on the browbone

CHEEKS
Blusher or shader brushed just below the cheekbones will give a more sculptured look to a round face

LIPS
Neutral colours and no visible liner will make big lips look smaller

This line of argument suggests that women do not stand in the same relation to consumer culture as men. Myers writes:

> We, the audience, 'consume' meanings, and in so doing are able to inter-
> pret, complete the message of advertising. In the act of ingestion, we dis-
> cover ourselves, find meaning in our lives and – crucially – pace our lives
> through the purchase of products. Arguably this is a process which men
> experience as well. But the crucial point . . . is that women are more vul-
> nerable to the process because their upbringing and social expectations
> define them *as consumers and as images to be 'consumed' by the gaze of men.*
> Consumption, in this context, verges on cannibalism. (1986: 137;
> emphasis added)

Other writers have seen this work of femininity in relation to what is sometimes called the institution of heterosexuality (Rich 1984) and the ways in which women are sexually objectified by men. The argument here is that sexual relations between men and women are mediated through the construction of women by men as objects – in particular, as sex objects.

Relations of looking have been identified as a key aspect of this process of objectification by a number of writers including John Berger (1972) and Catherine MacKinnon (1983), thus pointing to the importance of images and the art-culture system in this aspect of the development of consumer culture; see also Mulvey (1975) for a psychoanalytic interpretation of objectification. Berger develops an analysis of the nude in oil painting which suggests that there is a gendered contradiction at the heart of this genre, which arose as a consequence of the fact that the painters and spectator–owners were usually men and the persons painted usually women. The contra-diction relates to the contrast between the individualism of the artist, the patron, the owner of the painting on the one hand, and, on the other hand, the person who is the object of their activities, the women who is treated as an object, a possession or abstraction. Berger suggests that this unequal relationship – between man as subject and women as object or possession of his gaze – is so deeply embedded in our culture – from high art to pornography to popular culture, advertising and everyday life – that it is possible to talk of a *male gaze.*

The operation of the male gaze means that women are conven-tionally depicted in quite different ways from men – not because the feminine body is different from the masculine body, but because the ideal spectator is always assumed to be male and the image of the

female is designed to flatter him. Furthermore, so widespread is the process of objectification that men have come to be defined in terms of their actions, while women are judged in terms of their appearance. This has had particular implications for individual subjectivity, which comes to have a gendered dimension. Men look at women. Women watch themselves being looked at. This, so Berger suggests, determines not only relations between men and women, but also the relation of women to themselves. From earliest childhood they have been taught to survey themselves continually, and so they come to consider themselves as objects or things. The use of commodities by women in, for example, the work of femininity, is thus shaped by their positioning as objects in relation to a male gaze.

An interesting example of this is provided by Beng Huat Chua's observation-based study of women shopping for clothes in Singapore (1992; this analysis makes interesting reading alongside the representation of 'trying it on' shown in the film *Pretty Woman*, starring Julia Roberts and Richard Gere). Chua suggests that designer shops offer an experimental stage in which clothing is tried on and assessed in terms of its 'fit' with the client's self-image and for its appropriateness for anticipated situations of display. Women, he suggests, appraise clothes in relation to an imaginary stage, on which they anticipate their own performance and the likely response of an audience.

Chua suggests that the first audience for the woman is herself, and claims that this self-referencing is captured in the psychoanalytic understanding of fashion consciousness as a symptom of narcissism – 'the tendency to admire one's own body and display it to others, so that these others can share in the admiration' (Chua 1992: 125). A second audience is the salesperson, whose judgement of the suitability of an item of clothing draws upon a range of criteria, including their understanding of a client's style and their knowledge of the appropriateness of the item in relation to the dress codes operating in particular social situations. However, a third audience is the male friend or husband of the client, whose (anticipated) opinion is most influential, even when he is not actually present. Chua notes:

> He tends to provide minimalist comments of either agreement or disagreement with 'the look' of the configuration on the client. These comments almost always amount to the decision to make or decline to purchase. One may say that he has a veto power over the client's decisions. (1992: 129)

According to Chua, this power is not only a consequence of the fact that it is often the husband who pays the bill, but also because he is the one whose social status stands to rise or fall with his wife's appearance when she wears the purchase on the occasion of the anticipated performance. It is almost as if the woman herself is an accessory to the man's self-presentation. This research thus provides some evidence to suggest that women survey themselves as objects in relation to a male gaze, and, paradoxically, actively work to create themselves as objects in a consumer culture.

From this point of view, then, while women have been central to the development of consumer culture, this centrality is as much a consequence of their objectification as it is of their role as intermediaries. This line of argument would thus also seem to imply that, in so far as consumer culture has contributed to the development of postmodernism, women, while necessarily implicated, are not likely to be recognized as active participants in its development. If women are denied the possibility of self-possession, and are unable to exercise ownership of their own selves, they cannot easily acquire other kinds of cultural capital either. They are the object of consumer culture at least as much as its subjects.

The pleasures of femininity

It has recently been argued that much of the work discussed so far presents an overly pessimistic view of the role of women in the history of consumer culture, minimizes their role as active intermediaries in bringing about changes in consumption practices, and overlooks the ways in which access to consumer culture may have provided resources to help women challenge gender inequality and their own objectification (Nava 1992). From this point of view, the opening of department stores may indeed have contributed to the emancipation of women!

This line of argument points out that, with the advent of the department store, shopping lost its previous automatic association with purchase and further use. It was no longer simply the purchasing of predetermined requirements, but became an activity in its own right, and as such provided an opportunity for women to explore their own desires outside the confines of the family economy. Rachel Bowlby catches this moment in the title of one of her books: *Just Looking* (1985). This development took place in the period that saw a dramatic increase in the use of transparent display windows, improved lighting inside stores, and a sense of theatrical excess in the display of items. As a result of these developments, stores can be seen to have provided a focus for women's fantasies, a site of entertainment, and a possible escape from the confines of domestic femininity. They provided a space within which (first middle-class and then working-class) women could participate in public life, in which they could experience some of the shocks, speed and spectacle of modernity, in which they could have brief encounters, and make 'unwise' purchases for themselves.

One way in which this argument has been developed is to look at the ways in which women have adopted resistant or subversive modes of consuming. So, for example, Mica Nava claims:

> Consumption . . . has offered women new areas of authority and expertise, new sources of income, a new sense of consumer rights; and one of the consequences of these developments has been a heightened awareness of entitlement outside the sphere of consumption. (1992: 166)

It has also been suggested that the construction of the female consumer as irrational has provided the basis from which women could wilfully challenge their subordination in relation to men. From this point of view, women do not simply passively adopt the versions of femininity which they are encouraged to emulate, but actively seek to redefine the meaning of these femininities. For example, it is argued that women have subverted the idea that beauty is something that can be achieved, put on and taken off, and have developed ways of seeing femininity as a *masquerade*, a performance, in ways which enable them to play with their personal identity, and take pleasure in the adoption of roles and masks.

From this point of view, masquerade, or the simulation which is femininity, enables temporary resistances to impositions of power, including the operation of the male gaze, and is a strategic response, adopted by women in situations that are not necessarily beneficial to them. It thus suggests that self-possession is not the only possible basis from which to participate in consumer culture, and that the masquerade offers other possibilities. This more active understanding of women's participation in consumption practices can be used to explain the emergence of the dynamic, ironic and self-conscious manipulation of style which is said to be characteristic of contemporary consumer culture. In this view, women are not only central to the stylization of consumer culture, but may stand to benefit from it, and can thus be seen as key cultural intermediaries.

One example of this approach is provided by Angela Partington's study (1991) of the pleasures British working-class women found in watching film melodrama in the 1950s. She writes:

> I will argue that a mass-market culture does not simply 'express' extra-textual differences, such as class and gender, but provides the conditions for the 'simulation' (reproductive transformation) of differences, which is carried out by consumers when they invest goods with meaning. (1991: 49)

Partington notes that one aspect of the distinctiveness of melodrama as a genre of film is the importance attached to the 'visualization' of its drama through an emphasis on styling, design and the aestheticized representation of emotion. Melodrama thus draws upon knowledges and competences which, historically, have been constructed as both specifically feminine and specifically consumerist and thus, argues Partington, have provided women with the cultural resources to explore and exploit femininity in new ways.

In a contextualized reading of a number of melodramas, Partington argues that melodrama's visualization was not interpreted by working-class women as primarily expressive of the characters' fixations, but provided an opportunity for them to exercise exclusive consumer competences. She argues that the characters in Hollywood melodramas are created through clothes, cars and houses, and that the use of these goods elaborates on 'always already signifying' star images. In the film *Written on the Wind* (1956), for example, there are four main characters played by stars of varying degrees of fame. Each character has a different style, indicated by the kinds of clothes they wear. Their clothes may be read as part of their characterizations, which will help to support a narrative reading of the film, but equally they may be read as elaborations of the stars' images, in ways which are not reducible to the sense of the narrative. Partington claims that 'reading the clothes constructs more "sense" than the narrative does, making the plot structure somewhat redundant':

> As Marylee, [Dorothy] Malone wears tight, brightly coloured dresses and trousers, stiletto heels and shirt-style blouses with the collar turned up, ostentatious jewellery and glamorizing accessories such as chiffon scarves worn as neckerchiefs. There are several scenes . . . where she 'poses' in front of the camera so that the image resembles a pin-up. The obvious

contrast with Lucy [played by Lauren Bacall], who is restrained and tasteful, signals to an audience who is attending to the characters and the narrative that there is no way Marylee is going to achieve happiness (i.e. win Mitch's [played by Rock Hudson] affections). But for a viewer who is interested in the clothes for their own sake, they do more than simply characterize. Dorothy Malone, while not as big a star as Bacall, was building an image of assertive sexuality, beautiful but tough and indomitable, striking rather than conventionally pretty. So, although her function in the narrative is to represent a weak, neurotic woman who does not deserve to be loved, this is contradicted by the suggestion, which the clothes make to viewers with specific consumer skills, that she does not need a man at all but is independent and self-sufficient. (Partington 1991: 62–3)

According to Partington, the working-class audience of this film was able to negotiate and resist the demure, tasteful 'housewife' identity as defined by experts and professionals, by subordinating it as simply one of the repertoire of femininities they might choose to adopt in a process of masquerade.

This understanding of femininity as a role to be put on and taken off is thus seen by Partington to be acquired by women in the application of consumer skills developed through their role as viewers of melodrama and other women's films. In this way, Partington provides an alternative interpretation – stressing women's active involvement – for the emergence of the view of feminine beauty as an attribute that can be acquired rather than simply being allocated at birth.

Women's pleasure in melodrama (and indeed in many other genres of film and other cultural forms) has sometimes been seen as evidence of a kind of narcissism (along the lines that Chua outlines above). In contrast to this negative view of women as passive accomplices in the process of their own objectification, and to their description as cannibals, Partington argues that objects are used by women as the accoutrements of femininity not just because they invite a voyeuristic male gaze, but because *looking at them* is the basis of women's shared knowledges and pleasures: 'Female subjectivity is acquired through learning-to-look as well as learning-to-be-looked-at. Indeed, the latter is made possible by the former' (Partington 1991: 54). Historically, in order for women to become skilled in inviting the male gaze, they have had to acquire skills enabling them to discriminate amongst objects, and to use them to adorn themselves and their surroundings. In order to exercise such skills in the expression of references and tastes, women have thus, she argues, become *subjects* of a (female) voyeuristic gaze, while simultaneously identifying narcissistically with objects (goods) since they are constituted themselves as *objects* of the male gaze. 'Just looking' has become an important part of feminine identity.

In the same vein, Evans and Thornton (1989) argue that, while it is generally assumed that women look at or read fashion magazines to find out what is currently in fashion and how they can get hold of the relevant clothes or otherwise adopt the look in question, looking at the fashion image is also an act of consumption in itself, not just a step towards consumption. They write:

> Magazines do not explicitly advertise or sell the clothes they feature in their fashion pages. The fashion magazine purports to represent a commodity – fashion – but in fact seeks to sell only itself – a look, an image, a world. This slippage is paralleled by a deviant, or perverse, consumption of the fashion image on the part of the reader. The women who cut their desire to the measure of the magazine image, practise a form of consumption that is both compliant and deviant. Women appear to be doing something with the images that they were not intended for, or not wholly intended for. Women do with these images both less and more than was intended. They may not (be able to) buy the clothes but they nevertheless consume the images. (1989: 82)

Other writers too have made use of the notion of narcissism, re-evaluating it positively as the source of a specifically feminine pleasure. Taking women's participation in consumption (rather than men's position in production) as the starting-point of her analysis leads Mary Ann Doane, for example, to argue that 'what we tend to define, since Marx, as commodity fetishism is in fact more accurately situated as a form of narcissism' (quoted in Radner 1995: 62).

Hilary Radner develops this argument further. She draws on Freud's understanding of feminine narcissism, in which feminine pleasure is held to be created in relation to the masculine gaze. According to Freud,

> Women, especially if they grow up with good looks, develop a certain self-contentment which compensates them for the social restrictions that are imposed upon them in their choice of object . . . The importance of this type of woman for the erotic life of mankind is to be rated very high. Such women have the greatest fascination for men, not only for aesthetic reasons, since as a rule they are the most beautiful, but also because of a combination of interesting psychological factors. For it seems very evident that another person's narcissism has a great attraction for those who

have renounced part of their own narcissism and are in search of object-love. (Freud quoted in Radner 1995: 63)

Radner points out that Freud appears to suggest that narcissism is a kind of failing. In contrast, she argues that while what she calls the 'New Femininity' created through product usage appears to construct a femininity that exists solely to confirm the projection of the masculine gaze, it also 'offers women a libidinal return on their investment that is in excess of the pleasure they may or may not receive as the object of the male gaze' (1995: 63). She writes:

> Within this new paradigm, represented by such women's magazines as *Self* or *Working Woman*, shopping is retained as a prototypical feminine activity, but is represented differently. Shopping is no longer the recreational activity of the bored housewife who must incarnate her husband's wealth and success. It becomes the means through which a woman externalizes her 'self-worth' as properly her own. Similarly, the magazine reader is encouraged to interpret the fit body as a a sign of feminine self-esteem, a mark of self-control and autonomy rather than submission to the gaze of a masculine subject. This new position of privilege is one of contradiction; it depends not on the generation of new models of femininity but on a rereading of old models. (1995: 63–4).

These kinds of analyses – of masquerade and narcissism – thus provide the basis for identifying a distinctively feminine relation to contemporary consumer culture, suggesting that feminine identity practices may have played a crucial role in its development. While it identifies women as subjects of a gaze, active in the creation and display of a simulated femininity, this is not the same relation between the individual and self-presentation as that described by Featherstone in relation to the new middle classes. While the (male) members of the new middle classes also have a playful attitude to their self-presentation in Featherstone's account, the individual is also created as a *hero* in a project or narrative of (usually) his own making, with all the connotations of mastery and self-possession that such a term, notwithstanding (or perhaps, as suggested below, because of) the irony with which it is adopted, implies. This process of heroization, now revealed to be not just part of the exclusionary project of the new middle classes, but also perhaps masculine, contrasts strongly with the feminine relation of simulation described by Partington and others in terms of masquerade. This is a relation of imitation, adopted as a strategy of resistance in situations in which women do not have the power directly to refuse the terms of their address by the male gaze, but may sidestep its force by turning it to their own ends. In this sense, it is not exclusionary but compensatory. It is also not a relation of self-possession but of displacement, in which the subjects and objects of consumer culture are confused.

However, the comparison between masculine and feminine modes of playing with self-identity is further complicated by the ways in which, so it is argued, masculinity is increasingly being represented as a sign in contemporary art and popular culture in the same way that femininity has been historically. So, for example, Evans and Thornton write:

> In Blitz culture, boys moved in on 'femininity', not only on the territory of narcissism but also on female masquerade. In postmodern culture, gender was not so much manipulated for special effect as played with as just one term among many. In the new magazines, read by both sexes, sexual difference was used in fashion spreads as just another historic, folkloric, cinematic or fashion signifier. (1989: 62)

They suggest that femininity has been replaced by, or made interchangeable with, masculinity in recent representations of subcultural style and *haute couture*, and also note that this principle of interchangeability was simultaneously applied to the use of blackness and whiteness as signs of identity. What are the implications of this?

In Paris, psychiatrist Martine Flament is conducting a study into the incidence of bulimia among men on military service. 'There are far fewer male than female sufferers in France but it looks as if the number is growing', she said.

Although a crisis in male gender identity has been blamed for the trend, the fashion and advertising industries must shoulder some of the blame. Fifteen years ago, it was rare to see a naked male torso on the screen. Now they are everywhere, advertising products from jeans to shower gel. And these are men who can flex their pecs with pride, flaunt stomachs taut as snare drums and boast biceps to boot.

Sales figures suggest that the male ego is no more resistant than the female to such images. Last year Europeans spent 4.7 billion on male toiletries. And according to Fabergé, ten years ago women bought two-thirds of male cosmetics; now men buy the same proportion. A recent study for the British Psychological Society confirmed men's impressionability in the matter of aesthetics. Students were asked to rate the attractiveness of models of their own sex. Men showed as big a loss of self-esteem and dissatisfaction with their body image as women. (Thomas 1993)

Evans and Thornton illustrate their argument by reference to *haute couture* and the magazines of street style such as *i-D*, including an advertisement in *i-D* for clothes by Katherine Hamnett which shows a black man and a white woman, both of whom wear only minimally differentiated crumpled and baggy garments. They point to some of the advantages of this for women, including the greater possibility of anonymity as a woman, since if gender is just one term among many the issue of difference recedes from the foreground. However, Evans and Thornton also suggest that the use of both masculinity and femininity as signs in the same way could be seen to have the effect of detaching the manipulation of masculine/feminine and black/white from any (possibly oppositional) political, cultural or sexual identity. It ignores the different material and social contexts within which men and women may simulate gender and sexual identity.

The New Man

Gay business men had long realised the spending power of men without kids. Straight business people did too, but tapping the market without scaring off the straights was a dicey business till the 'New Man' demanded to be treated as a sex object. (Kohn 1988b)

To summarize this, more optimistic, view of women's role as subjects in the development of consumer culture then, gendered relations of looking are central to the development of consumer culture, but they are not only relations of subordination, with men having the power to judge how women look, but are also associated with particular kinds of pleasure and can act as the source of specifically

feminine cultural competences. They are the subjects of a gaze in which objects are assessed for their usefulness in relation to the 'simulation' of femininity. Partington writes:

> Women's consumption of goods is a form of appropriation which can bring them into conflict with the intentions of producers and distributors, by conferring on goods 'the sacred aura denied [them] by the conditions and mode under which [they were] produced'. This is not a 'waning of affect' but an intensification of it. Women's relationships with goods transform them into objects which can serve many ritual and symbolic functions, meet many diverse and contradictory needs and elicit 'an excess of feeling, an undecidable mix of . . . emotions'. (1991: 67–8; references omitted)

It has also been argued that, as a consequence of the link between women and commodification, women's production of themselves as

an image in the process of masquerade becomes an increasingly important part of feminine subjectivity. This line of argument makes a case for a view of women as active intermediaries in the development of consumer culture, indicating how a specifically feminine subjectivity provides the basis for the emergence of an aestheticized mode of using objects and creating one's own identity. From this point of view, the gendered process of objectification and the associated relations of looking are not only a consequence of consumer culture, but also a causal factor in its development.

The implications of masquerade for women in consumer culture

However, it is important to point out that not all women have been able to take part in the pleasures associated with consumption in the same way. Black women, for example, have often been excluded from the relations of looking outlined above. So, for example, Jane Gaines (1988) points out that while some groups have historically had the licence to 'look' openly, other groups, such as black people, have only been able to look illicitly. Carolyn Steedman (1986) has also pointed out that only some women are able to buy new fashions and styles for themselves, while others – working-class women especially – know that their desires have to remain subordinated to the needs of others, usually men and children. These points indicate that different groups of women have participated unevenly in the development of consumer culture, both implicated and excluded from cycles of production and consumption in contradictory ways. They also suggest that the adoption of simulation, while it may offer a feminine mode of fashioning the self, is cross-cut by class and race (see Skeggs (forthcoming) and Tyler 1991 for further discussion of this issue; the latter also introduces questions of sexual difference).

Beverley Skeggs explores some of the complexities of the practices of imitation and masquerade in her study of young white working-class women. She suggests that while the women in her study had a clear knowledge about their 'place' they were always trying to leave it. To this end, they adopted the tactics of passing as middle-class through the display of certain kinds of femininity, in part developed in consumption practices. These tactics, she says, are those of denial, disidentification and dissimulation in relation to being working-class and simulation in relation to being middle-class. However, she argues that passing as middle-class did not and could not involve irony: the young women wanted to be taken seriously. She writes: 'In this sense their attempt to pass is not a form of insubordination; rather it is a dissimulation, a performance of a desire not to be, a desire not to be shamed but a desire to be legitimated.' What this suggests is that irony may be a strategy which is most useful in relation to the middle classes (both men and women), who can afford, and indeed may be able to profit from, the ability to make visible the playfulness of their passing.

Skeggs also points out that this non-ironic passing engenders anxiety and insecurity; so, for example, when the young women showed her round their homes, they apologized for the things she was shown:

> 'I know you're meant to have real paintings on your wall. but I love these prints [Athena's ballet dancers]. I just think the price for real paintings is ridiculous and frankly we've got other uses for our money.'

> 'When we moved in the kitchen was all white melamine, straight from the MFI so we ripped it out straight away. I put my foot down, I said we're not having that cheap stuff in here. The kitchen cost a fortune but I love it and I love spending time in here. But I'm afraid that to get it right in here means we've not been able to afford to do anything else, so I'm sorry the rest of the house dulls by comparison. I think I'd spend all my time in here if I could. It's my room. We would have done the rest but what with all the redundancies at ICI now you've just got to be careful.'

Skeggs suggests that these comments indicate the ways in which the young women's judgement of themselves – in terms of their ability to pass as having middle-class tastes – is filled with self-doubt and anxiety about the possibility of being caught out. Skeggs thus describes her analysis of the narratives of improvement through which the young women spoke of their class positioning as 'a study of unease'.

Skeggs further points to the difficulties these young women faced in attempting to secure legitimation for their tactics of passing. While they made investments in their bodies, clothes, leisure pursuits and homes to mark their difference from the working class, they were not able to use these strategies to secure material advantages because they were not able to gain access to any means to legitimate their practices. A number of other studies also support the view that tactics of passing or masquerade are somewhat limited in the rewards they offer. So, for example, Lisa Adkins's research on women employed in tourist industries (1995) shows how, in some workplaces, producing and mantaining a sexualized identity is a requirement of the job. So, for example, in a number of service organizations, Adkins found that if women were to get a job at all they had to fulfil criteria of visual attractiveness or beauty. Not only were women required to have an attractive, pleasing appearance to be employed, but part of the women's jobs once inside the workplace involved the maintenance of their looks. Yet in these organizations the skills involved in the work of femininity could not, as it were, be detached from their person, contracted out, and exchanged for economic rewards. The women were denied the possibility of mobilizing their femininity as masquerade in Partington's terms; instead, their identity practices were rendered intrinsic or natural to them through the relations of production within which they were employed. In contrast, men as workers could claim their selves or their workplace identities as their own cultural property which they contracted out and exchanged as a labour market resource. Adkins's research thus suggests that while men may act as culturally individualized workers, with performable identities, women workers are denied the ability to lay claim to their workplace identities as occupational resources. Women were denied the opportunity to exchange their cultural capital as economic capital on the same terms as men. In this way, the expression of taste or lifestyle by women is less likely to have significance for the market economy than the lifestyle of men, and women are less likely to benefit from consumer culture than men.

Conclusion

This chapter has explored the two-way relationship between changes in gender relations and changes in consumption. On the one hand, it has identified a number of ways in which relations between men and women have been transformed by consumer culture, specifically through the use of commodities in housework. On the other, it has considered the ways in which relations between men and women, including the family economy and the objectification of women, have contributed to the development of consumer culture, through, for example, providing a specific context for the emotionalization and aestheticization of consumption.

There is clearly some disagreement about the implications of this two-way relationship for women. Put crudely, this is a question of whether women can be seen as the subjects or the objects of consumer culture, the intermediaries or the instruments of its development. However, even in the most pessimistic accounts of the involvement of women in consumer culture, it is not intended to imply that women are passive in their consumption activities, for it is clear that they are not, but merely to point out that these activities tend to be carried out in sets of power relations which constrain women to act in certain ways. These power relations have been shown to operate not only at the economic but also at the cultural level. Cultural resources for the creation of the identity of a self-possessed individual are not equally available to all, and so, in many situations, a feminine identity may not be realizable as cultural capital at all, let alone legitimated as symbolic capital or exchanged as economic capital. In conclusion, it may be suggested that it is in terms of the occupation of a paradoxical position, simultaneously subject *and* object of consumption practices, that women's role in the development of consumer culture is best recognized.

This chapter has shown that if gender is foregrounded in the analysis of consumption it can provide a rival, or at least an additional, explanation for the growth of the consumer culture which Bourdieu and Featherstone relate to the rise of the new middle classes. This indicates that the development of consumer culture must be seen to have a number of interlocking histor*ies*, and cannot be understood in relation to a single overarching explanation. From this point of view, at least some of the processes discussed in chapter 4 might be better understood in relation to both class and gender, and not just class alone. The following chapters suggest that other issues too may be of significance.

6

Changing Races, Changing Places

Introduction

This chapter will explore the relationship between race and the development of consumer culture as a two-way process, looking at the dynamics of their interrelationship in the same way that earlier chapters discussed the relationships between class and gender and consumer culture. It will argue that the history of consumer culture is intimately bound up with the processes of imperialism, colonialism, and the creation of hierarchical categories of race, though these categories – variously expressed in understandings of self and other, whiteness and blackness, the civilized and the primitive – have themselves been transformed in the practices of consumer culture. In particular, it will be argued that racialized identity has increasingly come to be seen to be created in practices of imitation and that this is, in part, a consequence of the stylization that is characteristic of contemporary consumer culture. The mixed political implications of this will also be considered.

Commodity racism

In 1899 an advertisement for Pears' soap claimed:

The first step towards LIGHTENING THE WHITE MAN'S BURDEN is through teaching the virtues of cleanliness. PEARS' SOAP is a potent factor in brightening the dark corners of the earth as civilization advances, while amongst the cultured of all nations it holds the highest place – it is the ideal toilet soap. (Quoted in McClintock 1994: 132)

The advertisement depicts an admiral, decked in pure imperial white, washing his hands in his cabin as his steamship crosses the ocean, *en route* to some outpost of the empire. Soap is represented here as the cleansing agent of the imperial quest to bring 'light' to the 'darkest' corners of the earth. In 1910, another Pears' soap advertisement is divided into two panels. The top panel shows a little black boy in a cast-iron bath tub about to be soaped and scrubbed by a young white nursemaid. In the panel below, her look of happy amazement registers the effects of what has evidently been a miracle. Where the soap has been applied, the boy's skin has changed colour from black to white.

The selling-point of both advertisements relies on a casual and taken-for-granted identification of whiteness with cleanliness and purity and of blackness with dirt and pollution. In the first advertisement, whiteness is associated with civilization, and soap is identified as its carrier. In the second, through the identification of whiteness with cleanliness and blackness with dirt, the rule of white civilization, administered by the white nursemaid, is likened to an act of charity and goodwill. That the success of this hygienic civilizing process is represented in the second advertisement as a miracle is premised on the assumption that races are characterized by fixed natural or biological features, such as skin colour. The advertisement relies upon this for its 'comic' effect and its imagery reinforces social hierarchies between white and black through its association of these features with positive and negative values.

There are numerous other vivid examples of racism in early twentieth-century advertising, especially in advertising for so-called empire goods, including tea, coffee, cocoa and cotton. This racism is evident in, for example, the representation of black people as happy in servitude to white people, both in the fields and in the home, and in representations of black people as child-like or doll-like, and in the images of a feminine, mysterious or exotic otherness typically used to heighten a product's luxury or novelty appeal. However, the analysis of textual representations of race in advertising imagery is only a part of the broader project of documenting the historical relationship between race and consumption (McClintock 1994; Ramamurthy 1991; Willis 1990; Gilroy 1987, 1992, 1993; Hall 1992).

Much of this work looks at the representation of racialized differences in the advertising texts of consumer imagery, but this concern is integrated with an analysis of how understandings of race have historically been related to the social organization of circuits of production and consumption. An exclusive focus on the objects and images of consumer culture as texts tears them from their location in circuits of production and consumption. So, while textual analysis is an important form of analysis in so far as it offers a way of identifying either specific formal features which recur across a range of texts or especially influential formulations of a culturally resonant way of thinking, it does not provide a way of linking the text to either its context of production or its context of consumption. Textual interpretations may be given greater authority if they can be linked to these contexts; in relation to this body of work, this is most commonly the context of the histories of American slavery and European imperialism.

Anne McClintock's study (1994) provides a useful introduction to this approach. She argues that towards the end of the nineteenth century economic competition between nations had created a climate within which the aggressive promotion of products was becoming ever more intense. This competition contributed to the first real innovations in advertising and thus to the development of consumer culture. In 1884, for example, wrapped soap was sold for the first time under a brand name. This small event, McClintock argues, signalled a major transformation in advertising: items formerly indistinguishable from one another – soap sold simply as soap – came to be marketed by distinctive corporate signatures. Notable examples of these included Pears' and Monkey Brand – in Victorian culture, the monkey was an icon of metamorphosis, and therefore an apt choice to represent soap, with its alleged powers to transform nature (dirt, waste and disorder) into culture (cleanliness, rationality, industry).

Soap was also one of the first commodities to register a shift from myriad small businesses to the great imperial monopolies: in the 1870s hundreds of small soap companies had made and distributed soap, but, by the end of the century, the trade was monopolized by ten large companies. McClintock suggests that while this shift was undergone by many commodities, soap had a special place in this economic transformation. This is because, she argues, branded soap was credited not only with bringing moral and economic salvation to the lives of Britain's great unwashed, but also with magically embodying the spiritual ingredient of the imperial mission itself. She writes:

Soap did not flourish when imperial embullience was at its peak. It emerged commercially during an era of impending crisis and social calamity, serving to preserve, through fetish ritual, the uncertain boundaries of class, gender and race identity in a world felt to be threatened by the fetid effluvia of slums, the belching smoke of industry, social agitation, economic upheaval, imperial competition and anti-colonial resistance. Soap offered the promise of spiritual salvation and regeneration through commodity consumption, a regime of domestic hygiene that could restore the threatened potency of the imperial body politic and the race.

More generally, she claims,

Late Victorian advertising presented a vista of the colonies as conquered by domestic commodities. In the flickering magic lantern of imperial desire, teas, biscuits, tobaccos, Bovril, tins of cocoa and, above all, soaps beach themselves on far-flung shores, tramp through jungles, quell uprisings, restore order and write the inevitable legend of commercial progress across the colonial landscape. In a Huntley and Palmers' Biscuits ad, a group of male colonials sit in the middle of a jungle on biscuit crates, sipping tea. Towards them, a stately and seemingly endless procession of elephants, laden with more biscuits and colonials, brings tea-time to the heart of the jungle. (1994: 137, 142)

More than merely a symbol of imperial progress, it was as if soap became the *agent* of history itself.

This was also true for a number of other branded domestic products, as is made clear in an advertisement for Bovril, in which Lord Roberts' trek of colonial domination across South Africa is seen to spell out the letters B-o-v-r-i-l across the landscape. The text reads:

Careful examination of this map will show that the route followed by Lord Roberts in his historical march to Kimberley and Bloemfontein has made an indelible imprint of the word Bovril on the face of the Orange Free State.

This extraordinary coincidence is one more proof of the universality of Bovril, which has already figured so conspicuously throughout the South Africa Campaign.

Whether for the Soldier on the Battlefield, the Patient in the Sickroom, the Cook in the Kitchen, or for those as yet in full health and strength at home, Bovril is Liquid Life. (Quoted in McClintock 1994: 147)

In contrast to this animation of products in the colonial context, representatives of the colonized peoples were represented, not as historic agents, but as *frames* or *figures* for the exhibition of the commodity. In this way, the inclusion of a black person in an advertisement or other kinds of commodity imagery was not necessarily a reflection of, or an address to, a black person; his or her function in the image was to act as a cipher, enabling a white perspective on imperialism to be conveyed.

In some ways this is similar to the position of (white) women in relation to consumption, except that not only is the inclusion of a black person not necessarily a reflection of black people's lives, but black people are not even part of the assumed audience in this address to the consumer. White women, while not necessarily represented from a feminine point of view, were and are at least recognized as part of the audience or market in consumer imagery. The complexity of the relationship between race and gender is addressed by McClintock, who discusses their interlocking in the form of commodity racism.

Specifically, McClintock argues that there are two interlinked processes at work. On the one hand, the commodity is represented as the active agent in carrying out the civilizing work of the empire; on the other hand, the use to which the commodity is to be put – cleaning clothes, for example – is figured as magic. She writes: 'The working-women, both black and white, who spend vast amounts of energy bleaching the white sheets, shirts, frills, aprons, cuffs and collars of imperial clothes are nowhere to be seen' (1994: 144). McClintock argues that this omission attests to a fundamental dilemma in Victorian society: how to represent domesticity without showing women at work. This dilemma was a consequence of a widespread cultural anxiety about women's work. As women were driven from paid work in factories, shops and trades to private unpaid work in the home, domestic work became economically undervalued and the middle-class ideal of white femininity figured the proper woman as one who did not work for profit. Indeed, as noted in the last chapter, domestic work increasingly came to be represented as a labour of love towards the end of the nineteenth and the beginning of the twentieth centuries. In the mean time, the work of housewives and (largely female) domestic servants was either simply absent or represented as a magical process of transformation. The argument of McClintock and others here is that the representations of black people, while directed towards the creation of *white* subject identities, simultaneously marked these racialized identities (both black and white) in relation to a gendered hierarchy, in which masculinity was deemed superior to femininity.

This argument is not just mounted on the basis of textual analysis. McClintock locates these texts in relation to a wider set of cultural shifts, and argues that such advertisements were part of what she calls the shift from 'scientific racism' – embodied in anthropological, scientific and medical journals, and travel writing – to *commodity racism*. She writes:

> Commodity racism – in the specifically Victorian forms of advertising and commodity spectacle, the imperial Expositions and the museum movement – converted the imperial progress narrative into mass-produced consumer spectacles. Commodity racism . . . came to produce, market and distribute evolutionary racism and imperial power on a hitherto unimagined scale. In the process, the Victorian middle-class home became a space for the display of imperial spectacle and the reinvention of race, while the colonies – in particular Africa – became a theatre for exhibiting the Victorian cult of domesticity and the reinvention of gender. (1994: 133)

The so-called Imperial and Colonial exhibitions she mentions here were extremely popular marketing exercises sponsored by both commercial companies, such as Liptons and other manufactures of tea, coffee, cocoa and other colonial goods, and the British state. At their height in the 1920s, these exhibitions attracted up to 27 million people, offering them both the pleasures of funfairs and education in the ways of the empire through information displays and exhibits. They are just one illustration of the broader social and political climate in which the advertisements for soap McClintock discusses acquired their cultural appeal.

McClintock's general argument is that the economic interest in selling the new colonial products of cotton and soap-oils was intimately tied to the middle-class Victorian fascination with clean white bodies and clean white clothing. She stresses that both economic *and* cultural interests were at work in the branding of soap; it hygienically cleansed not just the white body but also the white race. Imperialism and consumer culture came together to produce what McClintock calls commodity racism, and, in the process, shaped each other. The next section demonstrates the ways in which this two-way relationship is still in operation in contemporary society.

The same difference?

First, consider the ways in which consumer culture has shaped understandings of the category of race. In her discussion of representations of race in consumer culture (1990), Susan Willis argues that during the course of the twentieth century there has been a shift away from the use of the representations of natural or biological racial difference that predominated in commodity design, styling and advertising at the turn of the century. This is not to suggest that earlier representations of race have completely disappeared. A number of brands still draw upon imperial and colonial iconography; contemporary examples include the continuing use of the image of an Indian woman uncomplainingly picking tea for PG Tips and the use of the 'golly' or 'gollywog', a representation of a black face which draws upon the stereotype of the happy dancing minstrel with deliberately blackened skin and enlarged mouth, in Robertson's jams and Trebor Black Jacks (Ramamurphy 1991; Chambers 1992). However, Willis argues that this kind of colonial imagery has largely disappeared, and, in its place, have emerged two contradictory tendencies: a move towards the representation of racial sameness and an emphasis on the celebration of racial difference. In both cases, race is represented as a matter of *style*.

Both tendencies arise, Willis argues, in relation to the *infinite seriality of commodification*, by which she means the combination of standardization and variation which she believes to be implicit in the commodity form. Following Marx, Willis argues that there is an inevitable flattening out, a levelling, of value in goods that are made to be exchanged on the market; they are all made to be exchanged for money and money, as the abstract medium through which they are exchanged, squashes differences between political, moral and cultural values. At the same time, however, the market requires novelty to stimulate demand, and as a consequence the imposition of the commodity form, that is, the production of goods for exchange on the market, is necessarily characterized by standardized variation, or repetition within certain limits. Race, Willis suggests, has been a primary figure, or trope, through which this standardized variation or seriality has operated. In this way, understandings of race have been central to the development of consumer culture, not simply through the ways in which the category has been implicated in the economic processes of transnational capital, but also through its centrality to the understandings of difference which structure everyday understandings and use of goods.

For Willis, the seriality of commodification emerges in two apparently contradictory ways in the representation of race: on the one hand, the move towards sameness and, on the other, the pursuit of difference. Willis sees evidence of the first strategy in the production of black versions of white cultural goods, what she calls black replicants (see Keegan 1992 for a discussion of the same tendency in advertising). One example of this phenomenon is the production of Jamaican, Hispanic and Chinese equivalents of Barbie, the white doll first produced by Mattel, the toy manufactures, in the 1960s. Black Cabbage Patch dolls have also been produced as copies of their white sister vegetables.

Children today are granted instant global gratification in their play – immediate hands-on access to both Self and Other. Or so we are told by many of the leading fantasy manufactures – Disney, Hassbro, and Mattel, in particular – whose contributions to multicultural education include such play things as Aladdin (movie, video, and dolls), G. I. Joe (male 'action figures' in black and white), and Barbie (now available in a variety of colors and ethnicities). Disneyland's river ride through different nations, like Mattel's Dolls of the World Collection, instructs us that 'It's a Small World After All.' Those once distant lands of Africa, Asia, Australia, and even the Arctic regions of the North Pole (yes, Virginia, there is an Eskimo Barbie) are now as close to home as the local Toys R Us . . . And lo and behold, the inhabitants of these foreign lands – from Disney's Princess Jasmine to Mattel's Jamaican Barbie – are just like us, dye-dipped versions of archetypal white American beauty. (Ducille 1994: 48–9)

In exploring this phenomenon of replication or the production of sameness further, Willis draws a parallel between what is happening in the production of toy dolls and certain developments in relation to their human counterparts – fashion models. She suggests that recent fashion displays are creating a 'new ethnicity' in which individuals who, in some way or other, represent all races in one are held up as ideals. She points to the use of 'beige' models in fashion shows and magazine features, and argues that their use indicates an attempt to erase the political significance of race. This racial homogenization is, she believes, paralleled by an attempted homogenization of gender through the use of androgynous-looking models (see chapter 5 for further discussion of this).

For Willis, this tendency raises the question of whether it is possible to give egalitarian expression to racial difference in a society in which whiteness is the norm against which all else is judged. She answers in the negative, arguing that, when all the models are white, the black copy is reduced to a mirror. The implication that Willis draws from this is that the commercial representation of black people simply enables communication between white people. She writes:

> The black replicant ensures rather than subverts domination. The notion of 'otherness', or unassimilable marginality, is in the replicant attenuated by its mirroring of the white model. The proliferation of black replicants in toys, fashion and advertising smothers the possibility for creating black cultural alternatives. (1990: 87)

A similar question arises in relation to the second tendency – the pursuit and celebration of difference for its own sake. This tendency is evident in the production of goods, images and identities that emphasize and multiply difference, including racial difference. One example that Willis gives here is the figure of the pop star Michael Jackson. She suggests that Michael Jackson's persona is constituted by his very instability and changeability, by the rapid turnover of differences in his styles of self-presentation. She argues that this notion of transformation draws upon the historical figure of 'the blackface' or minstrel:

> On the one hand, it is the overt embodiment of the southern [American] racist stereotyping of blacks, but as a theatrical form; blackface is a metaphor of the commodity. It is the sign of what people paid to see. It is the image consumed and it is the site of the actor's estrangement from self into role. Blackface is a trademark and as such it can be either full or empty of meaning. (1990: 90)

Jackson brings this ambivalent image up to date. He is a toy transformer in human form, continually creating new identities for himself through the use of make-up, clothing, surgery and music. Indeed, Willis suggests that Michael Jackson's physical transformations *are* his trademark. Her argument is supported by an analysis of the video *Moonwalker*, in which a dozen or so incarnations of Jackson, from his childhood onwards, merge into one another, like so many roles or masks. Once again, Willis raises the issue of whether this strategy makes difference meaningless and thus recuperates black alternatives. Her view is that the proliferation of representations of the difference of race and the celebration of the possibility of transformation devalues the meaning of what it is to be black, by relativizing it as just one more difference amongst others; everyone, it seems, is imagined to be equally 'raced'.

Putting on the style

Identifying a common element in these two tendencies, Willis suggests that race is increasingly represented in consumer culture, at the level of fantasy at least, as a matter of style, something that can be put on or taken off at will. She is thus implying that one consequence of the stylization of consumption in contemporary consumer culture is a shift from understanding race as a biological or natural category to seeing race as as a cultural or aesthetic category. It is a shift which has long historical roots. The examples discussed at the beginning of this chapter indicate that, even at the end of the nineteenth century, there was a fascination with the power of commodities to 'change' races in Western societies. Soap was attributed the magical power of 'washing away' the colour of blackness. But this fascination was underpinned by a belief in the biological fixity of race; it was this which made many of the advertisements of the time humorous in intent. However, Willis argues that this fascination with the power of commodities to change racial identity has continued throughout the twentieth century, and has contributed to a shift in how racial identity is itself understood. She believes it has not removed the possibility of racism, just transformed the terms of its operation.

Consider a recent example of the representation of racial difference in advertising. Judith Williamson (1986) analyses a number of contemporary advertising images which bring together representation of 'woman' and 'the colonial', 'the exotic' or 'the non-white other'. One advertisement she discusses is for a sun-tan lotion, 'Hawaiian Tropic'. It shows a woman, half-naked, standing in the sea, a garland around her neck; in the background is a tropical island, palm-trees fringing the frame of the image. Written across the sky is the claim, 'The natural tan of the islands'. The by line, either side of the brand name, 'Hawaiian Tropic', is 'Keep it dark' 'Keep it safe'. Williamson writes, 'This woman-in-sea-with-garland image is the typical representation of the exotic; conversely, femininity is represented by the "woman of the islands": half-naked,

UNITED COLORS
OF BENETTON.

SPRING / SUMMER COLLECTION 1993

dark-haired, tanned' (1986: 113). However as Williamson notes, the features of the woman in the image make her 'equally likely to be a white American or European woman who has *acquired* the "natural tan of the islands"' (1986: 113). The advertisement suggests that, through the use of the sun-tan lotion, white women may acquire, not simply a tanned skin, but also the implied mystique and exotic quality ascribed to dark-skinned people in white mythology. The caption offers the promise of its product 'to all skin types for a safe, dark, natural tan'. The fantasy it holds out is of 'acquiring' a 'natural' tan. This is a contradiction in terms: a 'tan' is not natural: by its very nature, the natural cannot be acquired, it is something you are born with. But in the fantasy world 'of the islands', the 'natural' colouring of 'the other' can be achieved through the application of a commodity. The risks in this process of calculated hedonism are made 'safe' by the product, which takes the danger out of racial metamorphosis and makes blackness not a lived reality but a realizable dream. As Williamson writes, 'If one were naturally dark, of course, one would be black – a contingency not anticipated by the ad, which clearly does *not* address "all skin types" but, like almost all public imagery, assumes its audience to be white' (1986: 113).

This fantasy of the potential of commodities to change race is also evident in the publicity for Benetton, an Italian clothing company. In much of their promotional imagery, the young people used as models are colour-coded: that is, they are juxtaposed to bring out colour contrasts (Back and Quaade 1993; Fernando 1992). As in Benetton outlets, in which stacks of jumpers are folded and piled up so as to seem as if they are paint colour charts, the overall effect of colour as the medium of difference in fashion is enhanced through the graduations in tone, the suggested compatibility of hues and contrasts in tints created by the endless repositioning of one shade against another. The question such imagery seems to invite is, what colour is your skin going to be today?

In an illustration for tights, for example, the viewer is confronted by a series of legs in profile, each slightly different in shape, completely encased in different-coloured tights. The invitation to the viewer is to select a different colour at her whim. Skin colour, a key marker of race, is not simply displaced, but replaced and reworked as an act of choice. As Sonali Fernando writes:

The legend United Colours [*sic*] of Benetton suggests a connection of skin colours and product colours, so that racial difference is commodified

merely as a trope of product difference, within a self-styled commercial
United Nations. (1992: 143)

In this imagery, it is argued, all races are presented, not as a biological category, but as a question of style, as a choice. But here again,
as in the last chapter where the contemporary invitation in fashion
magazines to see both masculinity and femininity as masquerade
was discussed, the question arises: is this a choice which is equally
available to all?

As many writers have noted, in this contemporary representation
of race in consumer culture the difference between being white and
being black is depicted as a question of aesthetics, and the political
reality of racism is eradicated. The contradictory implications of this
are revealed in a story told by the American lawyer Patricia
J. Williams about her experience when shopping in New York one
day soon after 'buzzers' were introduced into stores in order to control the entry of shoppers. She writes:

> The installation of these buzzers happened swiftly in New York; stores
> that had always had their doors wide open suddenly became exclusive or
> received people by appointment only. I discovered them and their mean-
> ing one Saturday in 1986. I was shopping in Soho and saw in a store win-
> dow a sweater that I wanted to buy for my mother. I pressed my round
> brown face to the window and my finger to the buzzer, seeking admit-
> tance. A narrow-eyed, white teenager wearing running shoes and feasting
> on bubble-gum glared out, evaluating me for signs that would pit me
> against the limits of his social understanding. After about five seconds, he
> mouthed 'We're closed' and blew pink rubber at me. It was two
> Saturdays before Christmas, at one o'clock in the afternoon; there were
> several white people in the store who appeared to be shopping for things
> for *their* mothers. (1993: 45)

The store was a Benetton franchise. This story suggests that the
choice of colour as a question of style is *not* equally available to all,
but other writers (see Gilroy 1987; Hall 1992 and below) have suggested there is more to this redefinition of race in consumer culture
than the use of representations of a stylized, colour-coded racial difference to increase the sale of products to white people and exclude
all others.

The arguments presented so far show the ways in which images
of black people and racial difference have historically been extremely influential in the development of the expanded circuits of production and consumption of imperialism, especially in the development

of new markets both in the colonies and within the imperializing nations themselves. This suggests that race is an important figure through which circuits of production and consumption and consumer culture itself have been organized. However, it has also been argued that, although images of black people have a special part in this, their use does not necessarily indicate a concern with speaking about or speaking to black people; rather, images of black people are typically used to facilitate commercial communication between white people. As Fernando puts it,

> As Black people in Britain in the 1990s we live a paradox; we are both part of society . . . and excluded from it (largely voiceless, under-represented and under-addressed) – so that our relation to representation is in no way straightforward or fixed. (1992: 141–2)

Furthermore, it has also been argued that what Willis describes as the two strands of seriality of the commodity or what Appadurai calls 'the mutual effort of sameness and difference to cannibalize one another' (1993: 287), may have the effect of intensifying the political problem of racism. However, while the arguments discussed so far show that consumer culture has been implicated in the creation of hierarchical categories of race, they also suggest that it has contributed to shifts in how racism operates, specifically to the shift *from* a racism tied to a biological understanding of race in which identity is fixed or naturalized *to* a racism in which race is a cultural category in which racial identity is represented as a matter of style, and is the subject of choice. In the next section the political implications of this will be considered.

Making races

The arguments discussed so far are important in so far as they show how imperialism, commodity production, images of race and consumer culture are interlinked. However, they tend to be production-led and tell us very little about how not only the images but also the objects of consumer culture are actually used in the everyday activities of people to create racial identities (although they provide evidence for the argument that white people have been invited to use commodities to reinforce a sense of whiteness as superiority). In exploring this it is important to recognize that culture is itself a contested resource in the fashioning of identity, and that black and white people are likely to have different relations to the art-culture system. In particular, it is necessary to bear in mind the ways in which the distinction between high and popular culture in the art-culture system has worked to the disadvantage of black people (Weedon and Jordan 1995). However, it is also clear that the use of cultural goods by black people has been an important way in which they have challenged their marginalization in Euro-American societies.

A number of writers have been concerned to show that consumption is not a passive process for black people, and that consumption activities are not fixed by producers and advertisers. Paul Gilroy, for example, documents 'the richness of cultural struggle in and around "race" ' and identifies 'dimensions of black oppositional practice which are not reducible to the narrow idea of anti-racism' (1987: 154). He emphasizes the ways in which what Willis calls the seriality of the commodity is *opposed* in the consumption practices of black people. He suggests that these practices indicate that black people not only refuse the racism of many advertising images, but that they also create alternative understandings of race, through their participation in consumer culture. In doing so, he identifies the use of cultural goods as especially important in the creation of these oppositional understandings. He thus points to the importance of the art-culture system in the mediation of black people's relation to consumer culture, and identifies a different way of thinking about racial identity.

One example of this is what Gilroy describes as the refusal and reversal of a white cultural economy of time and space; this is an economy in which the night-time is set aside as the period allocated for recovery and rest from work. He points out that for some black people, in contrast, the night-time is the right time. The night-time, he argues, is assertively and provocatively occupied by black people for the pursuit of pleasure. Gilroy also suggests that, in many black consumption practices, there is a refusal and reversal of the dominant white tendency to privatize consumption, to make it a matter of individual preference, carried out in the domestic sphere. In black culture, consumption is celebrated, not as a private or individual practice, but as a collective, affirmative practice in which an alternative public sphere is brought into being. He gives the example of music consumption: records are used as cultural resources in processes of creative improvisation in response to the requirements of specific public occasions – religious, political and cultural.

This process of giving meaning to records takes different forms across different sites. So, for example, Gilroy points out that the record shop often acts as a popular cultural archive and repository of folk knowledge:

> It stores some of the key cultural resources of the racial group and provides an autonomous space in which the music, language and style that enable people to bring meaning and order to their social lives can be worked out and worked on. (1992: 136)

In the black dance-hall there is an orientation towards improvisation, spontaneity and live performance – the musical commodity is never finished, but always open to being reworked. Gilroy writes:

> records become raw material for spontaneous performances of cultural creation in which the DJ and the MC or toaster who introduces each disc or sequence of discs, emerge as the principal agents in dialogic rituals of active and celebratory consumption. (1987: 164)

In Britain in the late 1960s and early 1970s, competition amongst the sound-system DJs led to a practice in which they removed labels from the records which they used. This act both allowed the DJ to keep the information contained on the label secret – information hard to come by through any other route because of this subculture's dependence upon imported records – and thus keep one step ahead of rival systems, and expressed the distance between the consumption practices in which these records were used and their context of production. Gilroy writes:

> The removal of labels subverted the emphasis on acquisition and individual ownership which the makers of black music cultures identified as an unacceptable feature of pop culture. This simple act suggested alternative collective modes of consumption in which the information essential to purchase was separated from the pleasure which the music created. The record could be enjoyed without knowing who it was by or where it was in a chart. Its origins were rendered secondary to the use made of it in the creative rituals of the dance-hall. (1987: 167)

The rivalry between sound-system DJs over records was paralleled on the dance-floors by intense rivalry amongst their followers, expressed in dance competitions. It is through such collective practices, Gilroy suggests, that the users of black music have managed to combine both a strong sense of fashion and a respectful approach to the historical status of their musical culture which values its longevity and its capacity to connect them with their historical roots (1987: 1992). In this way, alternative understandings of race are sustained in black people's participation in consumer culture.

Finally, Gilroy also argues that a further consequence of black people's participation in consumer culture is that they have played an important role in dissolving the distinction between art and life that has historically been a feature of European culture in general and concert music in particular. On many occasions in black culture, listening to music is not just a cerebral process of contemplation as is typically the case in classical concerts, but also a bodily process of immersion in sound. As was noted in chapter 4, the erasure of the distinction between art and life is associated by Bourdieu, Featherstone and others with the adoption amongst the new middle classes of the project of turning their life into a work of art, but black people, Gilroy suggests, have played an especially important, but often unrecognized, part in this process.

The relationship between race and the redrawing of the boundary between high and low culture is a complex one, in part because white middle-class lifestyles have sometimes drawn upon racialized notions of 'the primitive', 'folk culture' and 'authenticity' to enhance their own standing (see below). In one sense, this can be seen to have contributed to the dissolution of the boundaries between high and low cultures, but, in another way, it can be seen as an appropriation across the boundary which works to reinforce the hierarchy between them. However, Gilroy's claim is independent of the white appropriation of racialized objects across the high–low divide. He argues that it is the activities of black people themselves which are contributing to the dissolution of the boundary between high and popular culture. One example he gives to support this claim is that of the relationship between the crowd and the performer in black cultural practices. This has historically often been one of dialogue and interchange. More generally, as Kobena Mercer argues,

If . . . postmodernity . . . refers to the dominant cultural logic of late capitalism, which 'now assigns an increasingly essential structural function to aesthetic innovation and experimentation' as a condition of higher rates of turnover in consumer culture, then any attempt to account for the gradual dissolution of boundaries between 'high' and 'low' culture, between taste and style, must reckon with the dialogic interventions of diasporic, creolizing cultures. (1994: 124)

However, Gilroy is at pains to point out that, when looking at these activities, it is important to recognize that what is involved here is a set of interlinking processes in which meanings – of objects *and* of the people that use them – are in flux. The two approaches to the study of consumption introduced in the first chapter of this book may make this clearer. There it was argued both that 'social lives have things' and that 'things have social lives'. On the one hand, people, in networks of friends, relatives and work colleagues, are continually being defined and redefining their identities and political commitments through their use of objects; they acquire their social identity, including a racialized identity, through their use of things. On the other hand, racially coded objects – that is, objects that have public or conventional racial associations, such as a Malcolm X T-shirt or cap – move across different sites, bringing meanings with them, but also acquiring new meanings in the process of their use, and in this way acquire their own life, or cultural biography.

But once these two approaches are set alongside one another, a number of questions begin to emerge in the context of the stylization of consumption. A key issue in the first approach is how 'race' is to be understood as a category of identity: what does it mean to be white or black? There are a number of dimensions to this problem, including the questions of whether the racial identity of the user should be seen as fixed or as fluid, and of what the sources of that identity may be – are they biological, political or cultural? The second approach intersects with the first, since it raises the question of whether the use of racially coded objects can transfer aspects of racialized identity to users. This might seem an odd idea to consider, but, as noted in the earlier discussion of studies of the images of commodity racism, a fantasy of the power of commodities to change racial identity has persisted throughout this century. Indeed, as the following arguments suggest, while Gilroy is keen to show how black people's participation in consumer culture has contributed to a transformation in the organization of the art-culture system, it is also true that the meanings of 'black' or 'white' have also been subject to change.

Indeed, there is much debate about whether there is a core to black and white identities, and if so, what that core is. The belief that there is a biological basis to race has been widely discredited, but there is much dispute about whether it is possible to identify other foundations for a racialized identity. These debates often hinge on the question of 'authenticity'; however, what counts as authentic is notoriously difficult to define, not least since, as noted earlier, the art-culture system is a machine for *making* authenticity. However, the notion of authenticity is often tied to a quest to identify the cultural origins of a particular form or practice. Cultural origins are seen to provide an alternative foundation to race to that of biology.

Imitation and authenticity

Black authenticity, however, is the source of both fear and fascination amongst many white people. Norman Mailer provided a classic expression of this ambivalence in the essay. 'The White Negro', but something of the same longing is expressed by the beat writer, Jack Kerouac:

> At lilac evening I walked along with every muscle aching among the lights
> of 27th and Welton in the Denver colored section, wishing I were a

Negro, feeling that the best the white world had offered was not enough ecstasy for me, not enough life, joy, kicks, darkness, music, not enough night . . . I passed the dark porches of Mexican and Negro homes; soft voices were there, occasionally the dusky knee of some mysterious sensuous gal; and dark faces of the men behind rose arbors. Little children sat like sages in ancient rocking chairs. (Quoted in Ross 1989: 68–9)

Andrew Ross is one of a number of writers who describes some of the ways in which 'blackness' has been taken up as a symbol of authenticity in white American popular culture. He writes that the romanticization of black authenticity is 'part and parcel of the long transactional history of white responses to black culture, of black counter-responses, and of further countless and often traceless negotiations, tradings, raids and other compromises' (1989: 67).

Ross gives a potted history of the complicated set of responses and counter-responses between black and white cultures, which can be seen as a chain of borrowings, in which each group takes it in turn to *imitate* or out-manoeuvre the other:

The racial questions of rock'n'roll – How much of a white component (country, rockabilly) was *truly* present in 'white' R&R's versions of 'black' R&B? Did Elvis *imitate* or did he *sing* 'black' music? – were only the latest chapter of a history in which hybrid cultural forms have themselves begged the question of imitation to the point of absurdity. To cite only a few convoluted examples: ragtime – a 'clean' black response to white imitations of the 'dirty' black versions of boogie-woogie piano blues; the cakewalk – a minstrel blackface imitation of blacks imitating highfalutin white manners . . . Dizzy Gillespie's satirical imitations of his white bohemian disciples who imitated the beboppers' own version of hipster 'cool' Howlin' Wolf – an 'authentic' bluesman . . . whose name is taken from his failure to emulate the yodeling of Jimmie Rogers, the white hill-billy musician of the thirties whose own vaudeville-inspired yodelling was spliced with a variety of powerful blues influences; and Elvis's rockabilly hair, greased up with Royal Crown Pomade to emulate the black 'process' of straightening and curling, itself a black attempt to look 'white'. (Ross 1989: 67–8)

These examples are used by Ross to support the claim that the plagiaristic commerce between white and black musical cultures is an everyday phenomenon, not an exceptional practice. He also argues that this interchange is not an equal exchange between the two different cultures; rather this history is one which is weighted towards dominant white interests. In this context, he suggests that 'imitation' may be better understood as 'theft' and 'appropriation', and that black authenticity has very different meanings in the two cultures.

Caryn [Franklin]   Yes. Caucasian culture is bankrupt in many ways.

Hassan [Hajjaj]   Hip hop has given heroes to young black people. And now it's crossed over to mainstream fashion – Gucci have done desert boots.

Judy [Blame]   Cultural vampires!

Fiona   [Cartledge]   Cultural groups who haven't got power in society will use fashion to give them power, and that's what black culture does.

Judy   America hates hip hop because it's influencing young white youth.

Hassan   Hip hop is important because it's known as a black music, but all kinds of people are buying into it. Like jungle is the first thing that's come out of Britain that's exclusively black.

Russell [Waterman]   I don't think you can say that black culture leads white. All that needs to be said is that black culture is as valid as any other, and for the first time people are recognising the influence it's had.

Judy   Our generation is the first generation to understand that. (Enninful 1994: 38)

As Ross goes on to argue, in relation to the history of popular music, black authenticity is often identified with uncommercialized music, while white music is associated with commerce and consumer culture. This contributes to the somewhat paradoxical situation in which, as Gilroy notes, authenticity has become 'a notable presence in the mass marketing of successive black folk-cultural forms to white audiences' (1993: 99). Indeed, Gilroy suggests that authenticity has become an important element in the racialization necessary to making not only black music but also non-European and non-American musics acceptable items in an expanded pop market, citing the example of so-called World music as a case in point. He argues that authenticity is actually a product of a white nostalgia for an imagined past, fixed in a fantasy of a time that never was, in which mind and body were in harmony.

This romanticization of black authenticity ignores the ways in which nearly *all* popular musical taste – with its shifting definitions of white and black music – is actually negotiated in response to commercially produced music. As both Gilroy and Ross point out, commercial forms, whether on record or in performance, were the means through which black meanings were made widely available, and were received and used by a popular audience, including a black audience. Moreover, the nostalgic interpretation of authenticity provides a context in which black performers stand condemned as selling out if they are actually seen to benefit commercially from their performances (Mercer 1994). This condemnation is evident, for example, in the arguments of some critics of Michael Jackson, who pathologize his self-transformation, and dismiss his metamorphoses as merely an attempt to adopt a more white, European, look. Ironically, then, this nostalgic, sentimental understanding of black authenticity is one way in which black people are blocked from laying claim to the economic capital (to return to Bourdieu's terminology) which their cultural practices create. Gilroy emphasizes the disenfranchisement this involves, arguing that there is a racism at work here which denies the capacity of black people 'to bear and reproduce any culture worthy of their name' (1993: 97).

An example of the mobilization of authenticity via representations of other cultures is provided in a recent Habitat catalogue (1994: 2–3). This catalogue, shot 'on location in India, Poland and the UK', begins, by way of introduction, with the claim that 'Experiencing different cultures and ways of life is now an everyday occurrence. In this catalogue we celebrate the skills and visual inspiration of many countries, with simple designs that can reflect how you live' (Habitat 1994: inside front cover). Many of the items are named in relation to a place, such as, for example, 'Brighton teaspoon', 'Sienna armchair', 'Mandalay sectional seating', 'Baltimore bedlinen', 'Skye mug' and 'California guntuft wool rug', examples all taken from the first few pages of the catalogue. In these cases, the meanings conventionally associated with a particular place are transferred to the domestic object in question through the act of naming. Giving an object the name of a place implies that the object is *like* the place. This is a *metaphorical* placing of the object. In principle, it applies to all the place-named objects illustrated in the catalogue, whether the place is Brighton or Mandalay, although its effectiveness will clearly depend on the consumer's geographical knowledge.

However, other objects are given a place-identity in another way: they are *actually*, not simply metaphorically, placed. So, for example, many of the textiles used in Habitat products are located in the place of their production, placed in relation to their 'origins'. The

place of production – 'somewhere' in India – is represented in such a way as to signal its authenticity, its relation to a way of life which seems untouched by the processes of commodification, that is, to a folk culture. So, for example, the first such image shows a woman's hand trimming a durry with a pair of scissors, her face and body invisible, her 'Indianness' indicated by the colour of her skin, the accessories of silver bangles and rings, her bare feet just visible underneath a sari. On the facing page is a photograph of 'Frame dyed cotton hanging out to dry in the desert breezes of Rajasthan' (Habitat 1994: 3). The authenticity of the product is achieved through its placing in a culture in which production for use (rather than the market) still apparently prevails, in which man (or rather, *pace* McClintock, woman!) works in harmony with nature ('the desert breezes').

In another double-page spread (Habitat 1994: 124–5), the left-hand page is once again filled by falling sheets of vividly coloured cotton cloth, hung from what look like wooden slats. On the right-hand side is the image of the entrance to a tent, made out of similarly vivid material, in the dark interior of which it is possible to see the backs of two figures, both wearing turbans. The text on the left-hand page encourages the viewer to see the cloth as a reflection of the culture it comes from, symbolized by the wedding we are told is occurring in the tent on the right-hand side. It reads, '*The bright intensity* of drying cotton lengths is mirrored by the tenting of a Rajasthani wedding celebration' (Habitat 1994: 124). In buying the product, the consumer is encouraged to buy another culture, another, 'authentic', way of life. The placing of the products in a setting which foregrounds a threshold – the opening to a tent – puts the products in between two cultures; Habitat is represented as the mediator of their differences, the bringer of 'authenticity'. Such images produce the promise that, through consumption, the Habitat individual can acquire the 'simplicity and informality that we seek' (Habitat 1994: 87).

Some other products that are located in this way are glass-ware and furniture; these too are presented in their place of production – 'somewhere' in Poland. The images that place these products are tinted monochrome photographs of men and women, their faces visibly worn, lines etched by a life of physical hard work. Once again, many of the images show the products to have been made in what is presented as an artisanal mode of production, with men shown blowing glass (Habitat 1994: 113), and making furniture by hand. It is as if, following the collapse of communism, former east

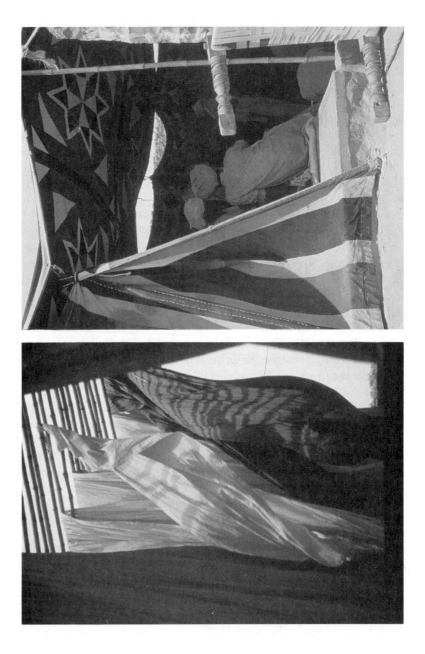

European countries can be assimilated to the fantasy of the pre-modern, the time before commodification and the market to produce 'authentic' products for the West. In these ways, the selection of certain products for authentication is achieved through an apparent dissolution of the high–low cultural divide (these crafts are authenticated through their selection and stylization in the Habitat catalogue and can be seen to produce artworks of aesthetic value), but done in a way which sustains racialized representations of others for a white audience. As the newspaper article 'Worldly Goods' confirms, Habitat is not alone in employing this strategy to promote its goods. This article is followed by details of further reading, including books with the following titles: *Ethnic by Design*, *Ethnic Style: From Mexico to the Mediterranean*, *Mittel Europa: The Interiors of Central and Eastern Europe* and *India Modern*, and with information about 'where to buy – specific looks'.

However, the racialized authenticity of products is not simply an effect created by producers for white people. (And indeed, it should not be forgotten that the black middle classes may well appropriate the images of 'the exotic' or 'folk culture' exemplified here by examples from the Habitat catalogues in the expression of their own lifestyle.) More generally, authenticity has been important for black people who seek to lay claim to an autonomous identity, uncontaminated by white racism. Gilroy argues that music and its rituals can provide a basis for another such authenticity. As noted above, he argues that the study of the circuits of the production, circulation and consumption of music shows that an authentic black identity is not something that can simply be adopted as a style, but something that, instead, is 'lived as a coherent (if not always stable) experiential sense of self' (1993: 102).

However, at the same time he argues that the very terms of analysis – production, circulation and consumption – by artificially separating out different moments of meaning-making, obscure the complexity of race as a category of identity. He argues that the term 'consumption' is especially problematic in this respect, since it emphasizes the passivity of its agents and plays down the value of their creativity as well as the political significance of their actions in the resistances of everyday life. He suggests that it is important to recognize that as black styles, music, dress, dance, fashion and languages become a determining force shaping the style, music, dress, fashion and language of Britain as a whole, black people are taking a defining role in the shaping of popular culture and consumer culture.

Worldly goods

Starting our four-page special, Elspeth Thompson explores the ethics of ethnic

UNTIL RECENTLY, a room filled with tribal masks, rattan furniture and hand-painted ethnic ornaments meant one of two things. Either you were a global explorer in the 19th-century tradition, surrounding yourself with trophies from your travels, or you were an unashamed old hippy (in which case the objects would be seen through a joss-stick haze). Nowadays, ethnic style is the latest fad in interior design – and you don't have to go abroad or knit it yourself to get it.

Every high street is full of the stuff, from designer galleries selling hand-thrown African pots and antique textiles to Habitat's folksy painted crockery and Indian bed linen. The glossy design magazines exhort us to go neo-peasant and kit out our kitchens in Mexicana.It doesn't matter where it's from, so long as it's handmade, breezily decorated in bright colours and doesn't look like it's been anywhere near a Midlands conveyor belt.

It would be nice to say that this trend was a reflection of Britain's rich multicultural society, but it still tends to be white western businessmen who are behind the latest upmarket profiteering. Coinciding with the first bites of the recession, this change in style – from the designer-label, status-conscious 1980s towards a different set of values embracing hand-crafted objects – had to be cheap, so it ruled out most of the indigenous craftspeople working in this country. When the current Habitat catalogue includes photographs of women embroidering pillowcases in India or Polish glass-blowers making wobbly glass goblets, the message is meant to be: 'This is handmade; this brings with it the innocence of a less industrialised society.'

The labour involved is, nevertheless, very intensive and intricate. Hand in hand with the demise of the machine-made aesthetic came a return to decoration. Whether it's carved wood from India or punched tin from Mexico, the new ethnic style is marked by a strong element of surface pattern. Nearly a century after Adolf Loos decreed that 'Ornament is crime' and 'tantamount to remaining on the level of a Red Indian', we have come full circle. Now we seek the Red Indian within us between the stripes of a Navajo blanket.

The appeal of this decorating is more than simple pattern, or of colours that remind us of other climes. In it we see an integrity that is missing in our own soulless culture. These objects are made and embellished with love, sometimes with prayer – or, at least, they were before the days of mass production for tourists. The pattern on Indian carvings and Turkish kelims if never quite finished – because only God can create perfection.

Such furnishings were an integral part of the societies that produced them. Indians painted their houses – and still paint everything from lorries to the horns of their cows – because they belong to a certain caste, or for good luck and protection. In almost every culture, rugs, chests and other pieces of furniture played a vital part in courtship and dowry giving. When we furnish our homes with these objects, we often misunderstand them. Global Village, for instance, has sold travelling sitars from Indonesia which are converted by their customers into drinks cabinets, and The Conran Shop did a brisk trade in 'primitive rice pounders' from the Philippines that could double as jolly unusual (and, at £125 a throw, expensive) fruit bowls.

Do these bizarre changes of use and context matter? Richard Evans, external affairs director of Traidcraft, a company that ploughs its profits from sales of carved wood, textiles and other products back into the developing countries where they are made, thinks they do. 'Buying something from another culture for aesthetic reasons is like visiting a zoo,' he says. 'Until you see a giraffe in its natural context – having to crop leaves from tall trees – you can't understand why it looks the way it does.' In Traidcraft catalogues, there are short explanations of every item's history.

The Observer

ELLE DECO

ORIENT EXCESS

CHINA IS BACK IN FASHION. SPICE UP YOUR HOME WITH DECORATIVE DETAILS

£3.50
Mirror from Loon Fung supermarket

£950
Antique lacquer cabinet from Liberty

£175
Chair from The Conran Shop

£2.50 Box of tea from Loon Fung supermarket

£2
Satin slippers from Ying Hwa

£4.50
Parchment parasol from ATOZ

COMPILED BY SUE PARKER, SHOPPING EDITOR OF ELLE
DECORATION. NOVEMBER ISSUE ON SALE OCTOBER 20

218

Wool coat (£453.75) by
Bella Freud. Cotton shirt
(£129) and wool tank top
(£115), both by Joseph.
Sari from a selection
from Variety Silk House.
Mittens (£3.82) by
Laurence Corner. Socks
(£2.95) by John Lewis.
Leather brogues (£79.99)
by Russell & Bromley

However, there have been relatively few studies of the ways in which cultural practices inform other dimensions of social life. Angela McRobbie (1994), while recognizing the importance of 'the space of fantasy . . . the state of distraction . . . the daydream' in the formation of identity, argues for the necessity of investigating (rather than simply assuming) their significance in, for example, the practices of education, training and employment. The few studies that there have been indicate the force of the limits within which understandings of racial identity are negotiated. So, for example, Fuller (1982) and Mac an Ghaill (1989) document the tightrope along which young black girls walk in their bid to succeed in school without surrendering their ethnicity. McRobbie further points out that Hewitt's study of interracial friendship patterns among boys in south London (1986) shows such friendships to be strained to the point of breaking when the short-lived shared space of the school gives way to the more segregated space of adult life and employment. What these studies point to is the need for further investiga-

tion of the significance of consumer culture and the stylization of identity outside the sites of leisure, recreation and relaxation.

Race and diaspora

Nevertheless, Gilroy argues for the advantages of a black identity created through activities of consumption; it is neither essentially fixed, nor a stylized authenticity that can be chosen or discarded at will. He argues that such activities can be used to create an identity which 'can be understood neither as a fixed essence nor as a vague and utterly contingent construction to be reinvented by the will and whim of aesthetes' (1993: 102). Stuart Hall, too, argues, for the radical possibilities inherent in understanding identities as created in processes of cultural self-construction (1992). He suggests that processes of understanding products in terms of an authenticity are not necessarily nostalgic but may be future-oriented, not necessarily fixing but transformative. It is important to recognize here that 'identity' is being understood as a kind of cultural capital in itself. Racial identity, which for many white people is so taken for granted that their whiteness is invisible to themselves, is here constituted as an achievement and as a source of value. As Cornel West writes, 'people, especially degraded and oppressed people, are . . . hungry for identity, meaning and self-worth' (1992: 38).

An alternative way of thinking about authenticity and racial identity is provided by Homi Bhabha and his use of the term *mimicry* to describe the borrowings between different races (1994). For Bhaba, this is not a straightforward borrowing or dependence of colonized upon colonizer, of black upon white; instead, the colonial mimic enjoys, or plays with, a necessary ambivalence within the process of imitation. This is because mimicry, for Bhabha, indicates something 'not quite right', and expresses the displacement of which it is an effect. Amit Rai (1994) identifies this displacement, this something not quite right, in the appropriation of the cultural form of the film in India. He writes: 'In India the codes of film – both within the symbology of western aesthetics, and western technology – were appropriated, broken and remoulded to resist, dominate and survive' (1994: 52). He quotes Ani Saari:

> Existing in no-man's land, the popular Indian film or, as may be a more appropriate definition in aesthetic terms, the Indian Pop-film, is an eclectic, assimilative, and plagiaristic creature that is constantly rebelling against its influences: Hollywood and European cinema and traditional Indian aesthetics and life-styles . . . Everything that it borrows from the Euro-American film scene it distorts and caricatures. (Rai 1994: 56)

Using the notion of mimicry, Rai shows how, in many Indian films of the 1950s and 1960s, the symbol of Elvis, often combined with that of the god Krishna, was imitated by the Indian male star as a device to represent distinctively Indian concerns of nationalism. He describes this as the creation of a post-colonial hybrid. Today, he suggests, images of Elvis have been replaced by images of Rambo, the Terminator, Robo-cop and Madonna, continuing a tradition of hybridity, or *masala*, that he believes is part and parcel of the post-colonial experience. The production of these hybrid-mimics is seen by Rai not as a strategy for overcoming domination, but as a form of resistance that survives or negotiates its domination. As a form of resistance, mimcry can be seen, like the feminine strategy of masquerade, as an alternative way of understanding the ironic playfulness that characterizes contemporary consumer culture. It provides the basis for a hybrid, yet authentic, identity.

For Gilroy, the sense of connectedness which underpins this

identity is related to the notion of a diaspora. It is the black person's connection to a disapora which provides a context within which consumption can contribute to a politically enabling or expressive authenticity. Writing in relation to the black population in Britain, he argues:

> Here, non-European traditional elements, mediated by the histories of Afro-America and the Caribbean, have contributed to the formation of new and distinct black cultures amidst the decadent peculiarities of the Welsh, Irish, Scots and English. These non-European elements must be noted and their distinctive resonance must be accounted for. Some derive from the immediate history of Empire and colonization in Africa, the Caribbean and the Indian sub-continent from where the post-war settlers brought both the methods and the memories of their battles for citizenship, justice and independence. Others create material for the processes of cultural syncretism from extended and still-evolving relationships between the black populations of the over-developed world and their siblings in racial subordination elsewhere. (1987: 156)

Stuart Hall, too, stresses the importance of an understanding of diaspora for understanding the conditions in which racialized authenticities are made and remade:

> Selective appropriation, incorporation, and rearticulation of European ideologies, cultures, and institutions, alongside an African heritage . . . led to linguistic innovations in rhetorical stylization of the body, forms of occupying an alien social space, heightened expressions, hairstyles, ways of walking, standing, and talking, and a means of constituting and sustaining camaraderie and community. (1992: 28)

In relation to the notion of diaspora, the understanding of a 'usable past' (Hazel Carby, cited in Gates 1992) is important. A dialogue with the past, a process of cultural retrieval, provides the basis of a counter-history for a diaspora. The very name of the black British film collective 'Sankofa' illustrates this ambition well. The word means 'go back and retrieve it' and refers to a bird with its head turned backwards. However, this is not a return to a fixed past, but is understood as a dialogue between present and past, a reconstruction of the past, what Kobena Mercer calls 'the artistic commitment of archaeological inquiry' (cited in Gates 1992).

However, this is recognized to be an uncertain process, open to many different determinations, and liable to lead to conflict as well as constructive creation. So, for example, Appadurai warns that, because of the disjunctive and unstable interplay of commerce, media, national politics and consumer fantasies, ethnicity or race, 'once a genie contained in the bottle of some sort of locality (however large)' has now become a global force, 'forever slipping in and through the cracks between states and borders' (1993: 285). Appadurai argues that this global culture cannot be seen in terms of a simple, stable (even if large-scale) system, but as a series of disjunctive flows which are better understood in terms of a human version of chaos theory.

Nevertheless, Hall (1992) and Cornel West (1990) have argued that the practices of black diasporas (and it is important to stress the plural here) have the potential to contribute to a radical reconfiguration of what is meant by culture in general, and by consumer culture in particular. This has involved what they see as the displacement of European models of high culture, including the understanding of the cultural work as a unique, auratic object, to be held apart from everyday life. This is related by Hall to the emergence of the United States as a world power, and, consequently, as the centre of global production and circulation. He writes:

> This emergence is both a displacement and a hegemonic shift in the *definition* of culture – a movement from high culture to American mainstream popular culture and its mass-cultural, image-mediated technological forms. (1992: 21–2)

This American popular culture, as noted above, has always contained within it black American popular vernacular traditions. At the same time, there has been an uneven process of decolonization, which has been marked by the emergence of decolonized cultures, and the impact of these cultures – including the popular Indian film – is not confined in space, but is circulated through an increasingly globalized market economy.

Hall, with reservations, chooses to describe this shift in terms of a 'global postmodern' culture; this is what he calls, in a phrase which has similarities to Featherstone's definition of postmodern culture (see chapter 4), 'modernism in the streets' (Hall 1992: 22), a shifting of the terrain of culture towards popular, everyday, practices, away from the specialized sites of art galleries and museums to the high street and the dance-hall. He believes that this displacement indicates a 'momentous shift' in the balance of relations between high and popular culture. In contrast to Featherstone's emphasis on class, however, Hall argues that this is a shift in which black cultures have a special place, as indicated by the emphasis on style, the displacement of writing by music as the definitive form of contemporary culture, and the emphasis on the body, which can be seen as one of the forms of cultural capital black people have historically won back from colonialism.

Hall argues that European high culture has, on the whole, shown a blindness and hostility towards racial difference, which is evident in its silent, indirect and usually unacknowledged incorporation of other styles, other artistic movements and other ways of life. He writes of 'its inability even to speak ethnicity when it was so manifestly registering its effects' (1992: 23). As discussed above, contemporary consumer culture which is closely tied to the global postmodern culture of which Hall writes displays, in contrast, a fascination with difference. While recognizing that the proliferation of difference illustrated by 'Benetton and . . . mixed male models . . . doesn't make make a difference of any kind' (1992: 23), Hall argues that the fascination with difference in the global postmodern culture is not simply cynical, but is also an indication that culture has been transformed 'by the voicing of the margins' (1992: 23). This voicing is the work of imagination:

> No longer mere fantasy (opium of the masses whose real work is elsewhere), no longer simple escape (from a world defined principally by more concrete purposes and structures), no longer elite pastime (thus not relevant for new forms of desire and subjectivity), the imagination has become an organized field of social practices, a form of work (both in the form of labour and of culturally organized practice) and a form of negotiation between sites of agency ('individuals') and globally defined fields of possibility. (Appadurai 1993: 273–4)

Conclusion

This chapter has presented a number of different arguments about the relationship of race and consumption. It was first argued that images of black people were historically very important in shaping the development of both imperialism and consumer culture. It was pointed out that these images were not typically either a reflection of or an address to black people; rather, they were figures chosen to enable commercial communication between white people. It was then argued that images of black people continue to have a similar function in contemporary society, although the content of the images has changed. Nevertheless, it was suggested that, despite not being actively recruited to consumer culture, black people have been active in its development. This was documented through studies of their use of cultural products in distinctively stylized ways. Examples were given to show how the development of popular music has been a complex interchange of borrowings and practices of imitation between black and white cultures. In this sense, black people can be seen to have acted as key cultural intermediaries in the development of consumer culture.

Within this dynamic, the notion of authenticity was identified both as a medium through which white people gain access to the ways of life developed by black people through the stylized use of particular products, *and* through which black people develop a complex expressive identity. The importance of the cultural activities of black people was recognized in what was described as a shift from European high culture to a postmodern global culture. This change in the organization of the cultural field provides a different context from which to view consumer culture, and shows, once again, that class and the process of commodification is only one dimension of contemporary consumer culture. It also suggests that not only is consumption to be understood in relation to multiple circuits and histories, with divergent trajectories and different scales of operation, but that the art-culture is an important site for the development of consumer culture.

7

Back to the Future and Forward to the Past

Introduction

In late 1994 the Victoria and Albert Museum hosted a show, sponsored by Perrier and *The Independent*, called 'Streetstyle: From Sidewalk to Catwalk, 1940 to Tomorrow'. Not surprisingly this exhibition, sponsored by commerce and held at one of the sacred temples of the British art establishment, was reviewed throughout the press, including *The Independent on Sunday*, who selected Peter York, a well-known commentator on youth culture and author of *Style Wars* (1980) to give his opinion. The headline of the review, 'The dead beat of the street', suggests he found the show – which with its title indicated its aspiration to be ahead of the times – to be rather dated. He begins the review by describing the organizer, Ted Polhemus, and his wife in the following, somewhat unflattering, terms:

> Ted Polhemus, co-organiser of the V&A's new *Streetstyle* exhibition and author of the accompanying book, is Triple A – an American Albino Anthropologist. A paler man you couldn't hope to meet. *Mrs* Polhemus, so he said when he turned up at the Cultural Studies sort of event that attracted people from his discipline in the late Seventies and early Eighties, was a stripper. I always took this to mean that Mrs Polhemus stripped in a Post-Modern, participative-observer, Spirit-of-Inquiry fashion rather than for the usual more proletarian motives. But who is to know. And perhaps she has now given it up for a Chair in Youth Studies somewhere. (York 1994: 24)

The rivalry between commentators, discussed in relation to struggles over taste in chapter 4, is, it seems, at its most vicious in relation to the field of youth and consumption. This rivalry is a testament to the centrality of the activities of young people to understandings not only of consumer culture but also of contemporary cultural change more generally. It may also be a consequence of the bitterness arising from the fact that commentators, like everyone else, get older, while youth cultures stay young. There is, apparently, nothing, so damning in an indictment of an exhibition on youth cultures than to say it is 'a bit dated', to imply that it it belongs, with its begetters, in some previous decade.

There is now a long and well-known history of youth subcultural styles, from the teddy boys and the mods, to the skins and punks, to hip hop and rave, which has occupied the attentions of sociologists, journalists, and music and fashion commentators alike. The distinct styles of post-war youth subcultures have been interpreted as symbolic or magical solutions to age and class domination, and as a means of marking out and winning cultural space for young people. Such styles have been applauded for their creativity in borrowing and transforming everyday objects or fashion items – the teds' appropriation of the Edwardian suit or the punks' borrowing of safety pins, bin liners and zips – recoding them according to the internal aesthetics of spectacular subcultures. And while only a small minority of young people may have adopted the complete ensemble of subcultural style, large numbers are seen to have drawn on selective elements, creating their own meanings and uses from them.

Since punk, the range of stylistic options open to an increasingly reflexive youth has greatly expanded, with revivals of many of the major subcultures occuring in the late 1970s, the 1980s and continuing into the 1990s.

> Before Pulp and after Sparks, there came THE HUMAN LEAGUE, straight outta Sheffield Electro City, the original Great Northern Pop Group. They used cheapo synths. They had lopsided haircuts. They had pierced nipples. And they sold millions. Now, just in time for the Eighties Revival, they're back . . . (Pope 1995: 10)

> **DECADE BLENDING**: In clothing, the indiscriminate combination of two or more items from various decades to create a personal mood: *Sheila = Mary Quant earrings (1960s) + cork wedgie platform shoes (1970s) + black leather jacket (1950s and 1980s)*. (Coupland 1992: 15)

The wardrobes of past subcultural styles have been exhumed and recombined in endlessly different combinations. It is not only goths who look like ghosts. Indeed, the raiding of the past – in the spirit of retro and nostalgia – is paradoxically sometimes identified as one of the most important 'trends' in contemporary youth style. Clothes and accessories are worn as though in quotation-marks, their wearers self-consciously evoking a past epoch in which their parents' countercultural heroes declared that time was on their side. Has Mick Jagger been proved right?

Youth subcultures

It was not until the post-war period in Britain that 'Youth' became a focus of media attention and the basis of a common identification.

Young people have not always been treated in this way. There have not always been clearly defined characteristics of appearance or tastes in music, films or clothes special to the young; there has not always, in other words, been a distinctive youth culture or subcultural style. This suggests that youth cultures are not the inevitable manifestation of hormones or the expression of a particular stage in a biological life cycle but are, rather, social constructions.

So, what factors account for the emergence of youth cultures and the identification of youth as a separate social category and a distinctive phase of life? One of the most important factors is that the transitional period from dependent childhood to independent adulthood has been greatly lengthened in modern industrial societies. The gradual rise in the school-leaving age during the course of the twentieth century and the increasing insistence upon educational qualifications for many jobs has extended the period between childhood and entry to the workforce. Also many young people in the immediate post-war period were better off than those before the war, whether they were in full-time education or at work. For example, in one of the first studies of the so-called teenage consumer in Britain, Abrams (1961) calculated that, compared with 1938, the real earnings of teenagers in 1958 had increased by 50 per cent (twice as much as their parents' increase during the same period) and that their real discretionary spending power had almost doubled in the same period. The young, therefore, came to be recognized as 'youth' in part because they became a significant consumer market.

However, these economic changes did not directly translate into the emergence of spectacular youth subcultures. There was also a series of interrelated social and political changes in post-war Britain which redrew the contours of everyday life. These included the breakup of traditional housing patterns, including the building of new housing estates and a process of suburbanization; changes in economic organization, with the widening of a gap between old manufacturing and new service industries and the increasing employment of women; and the racialization of the issue of migration in political and public debate. At the same time, there were transformations in the culture and leisure industries, which were being restructured, partly in response to the emergence of youth as a market, contributing to an increasing breakdown in the national boundaries of British culture as American popular culture further extended its increasingly global reach.

These changes are seen to have contributed to a period of uncertainty and instability, resulting in a time in which the contradictions between the traditional values of puritanism, responsibility, thrift and pride in a job well done and the new values of hedonism and the spectacular consumption of the so-called affluent society became increasingly acute. The changes destabilized the everyday conventions of social life for many people, but were felt especially strongly by young people, who experienced both the difficulties – dislocation, forced mobility – and the benefits – increased disposable income, liberation from tradition and freedom of movement – more acutely than their parents. At the same time, the hopes of post-war Britain were clearly fixed on the upcoming generation: 'youth' emerged as the society's favourite age, a visible group on whom the anxieties of society as a whole were focused. As a consequence, young people experienced themselves and were experienced as somehow different, not least in their responses to what was seen to be an intensification in processes of commodification. Youth was thus both a reaction and a response to consumer culture: young people were both intermediaries and symbols of the changes in the organization of cycles of production and consumption.

The youth subcultures that emerged in response to these conditions shared three general characteristics (Abercrombie and Warde 1988). First, they were cultures of *leisure* rather than work. Second, the social relationships of youth subcultures were organized around the *peer group*, and were as much collective as individual. This contrasted with the adult orientation to families or individual friends. Third, youth subcultures were characterized by a concern with *style*. More specifically, the emergence of different styles specific to young people, inflected by the cross-cutting claims of class, gender and race, has been seen by a number of writers in terms of the creation of imaginary or magical solutions to the anxieties raised by the contradictory changes facing society as a whole (Jefferson and Hall 1976; Hebdige 1979).

This analysis of style as a process of transformation is rooted in the belief that creativity is an integral aspect of everyday life. However, given this belief, what was seen to distinguish the activities of young people was the *internal coherence* of the style to which their creativity gave rise, the active articulation of objects with activities, expressions of belief and ways of life in a distinct ensemble. New meanings were seen to emerge as the elements of the style were combined into a unique whole or assemblage. This ensemble was seen to have its own internally generated unity in which dress, appearance, language, rituals, modes of interaction and genres of music gained their meaning in relation to one another. Each element of the style was seen to exist in a state of *homology* with every other. It is this homology, or structural symbolic fit, between the elements which is seen to have given youth subcultures their internal coherence.

The homologous coherence of youth subcultures is said to be created through the process of *bricolage*. Bricolage is a term taken from the work of the anthropologist Lévi-Strauss and is used to describe the process in which objects acquire new meaning through recontextualization. So, for example, the mods were said to be bricoleurs (thieves of style) as a consequence of the ways in which they transformed the meaning of a whole range of commodities – including the scooter discussed in chapter 2, as well as the conventional insignia of the business world – by creating a style that erased their original straight meaning. As a device, bricolage has parallels with some of the innovative artistic techniques adopted in the avant-garde art movements of the early twentieth century such as Dada and Surrealism, a parallel that became self-conscious in punk, with, for example, the elevation of the most unremarkable, mundane and inappropriate items – safety pins, razor blades, tampons, plastic clothes-pegs – to the status of 'the ready-made' of Surrealism, the found object as artwork. In this respect, youth subcultures have been seen to be central to the challenge to the boundary between high and popular culture which is said to be a characteristic of contemporary postmodern culture.

In this analysis, the stylization of consumption is in large part the outcome of creative practices by young people; it is a mode of consumption which itself comments upon the anxieties more widespread in society about the political and cultural implications of living in a period in which more and more people came to believe that they had 'never had it so good'. Youth cultures are thus seen here as the sites of struggles over the control of meaning in a rapidly developing consumer culture, struggles played out in dress, demeanour, music and language. The notion of resistance was central to these early interpretations of youth sub cultures – style was seen as a form of defiance, political protest or semiotic guerrilla warfare; Hebdige writes:

> The 'subcultural response' is neither simply affirmation nor refusal, neither 'commercial exploitation' nor 'genuine revolt' . . . It is both a declaration of independence, of otherness, of alien intent, a refusal of anonymity, of subordinate status. It is an *in*subordination. And at the same time it is also a confirmation of the fact of powerlessness, a celebra-

tion of impotence. Subcultures are both a play for attention and a refusal, once attention has been granted to be read according to the Book. (1988: 35)

This identification was also a crucial part of the claim that youth subcultures represented an authentic response to the intensification of the market and its apparent disregard for earlier ways of life.

However, the resistance identified as part of youth sub cultures was held to be being continually recuperated through both a process of *commercialization* and a process of *redefinition* in the media, either through *condemnation* and the creation of so-called moral panics (Cohen 1972) or *incorporation* by normalizing certain behaviours as typical of young people. Indeed, some have argued that youth subcultures can no longer exist in today's commercially predatory environment: that they no sooner emerge than they are swallowed whole by contemporary consumer culture.

| **CLIQUE MAINTENANCE**: The need of one generation to see the generation following it as deficient so as to bolster its own collective ego: '*Kids today do nothing.* | *They're so apathetic. We used to go out and protest. All they do is shop and complain.*' (Coupland, 1992: 21) |

Punk, which emerged in the late 1970s and early 1980s, is sometimes seen as the last authentic youth culture. Certainly, in many ways, punk seems a likely end-point to the history of youth sub cultures as presented so far. It was a contradiction in terms: self-styled as a celebration of meaninglessness – there were 'no more heroes' – it required the living-out of nihilism. At the same time that it turned its back on authenticity, the history of youth sub cultures was ransacked for meaning. From this point of view, punk can be seen as a kind of implosion, a black hole of cynicism from which there could be no back to the future. This is the view of youth subcultures that would support Baudrillard's claim that the 1990s don't exist, that we are moving directly from 1989 to the year 2000 (Baudrillard 1988, cited in Redhead 1990): in this analysis, we have already started the 'end of the century' party (Redhead 1990).

The argument here is that the increasing commercialization of popular culture has led to the demise of youth subcultures, or rather their subsumption within what is called alternately called pop or youth culture. Commercialization is seen to make it impossible to sustain authenticity and means that resistance is no sooner expressed than sold back to young people. At the same time, it is argued that the previously existing generational or age-linked identity of youth subcultures has been undermined. The audience for rock and pop music, for instance, now cross-cuts generations – on one side, young people's parents listen to it in the car on the way to work, academics write books about it, and newspapers are filled with gossip about its stars, while on the other children's magazines and television programmes are increasingly taken up with the details of the life histories of the personalities of the pop music scene – so how can music – or any other consumer good – mark a difference, indicate authenticity or express any kind of generational resistance?

It is further argued that being young in the 1990s, that is between 18 and 24, is a profoundly different experience to what it was even in the 1970s. There are, it is noted, 25 per cent fewer teenagers in Britain now than in 1983. Moreover, since the 1970s, deindustrialization, unemployment, economic restructuring, AIDS and a resurgence of racism have created fundamentally new realities for young people. Writing in the American contexts, Lipsitz says that 'While youth music and youth fashions fare very well in the marketplace of postindustrial America, young people are faring very badly' (1994: 18). (See 'Young Grufties' for an account of the situation facing young people in Hungary). One explanation of this paradox – the numerical, political and cultural decline of young people and the rapid expansion of youth culture – suggests that it is not simply that young people are especially vulnerable to economic misfortune, but that the cultural significance of youth itself is undergoing a profound transformation.

This argument suggests that the erosion of the significance of youth in the West may be linked to the commercial success that the 'babyboomer' generation of the 1960s – including its contemporary heroes Steven Spielberg, Oliver Stone, and Richard Branson – have achieved through failing to grow up. More generally, as Redhead (1990) notes, the fascination with subcultures as a thing of the past can be linked to the presence of a large group of people between 40 and 50 for whom the moment of the 1960s counterculture is a significant point in their own personal as well as generational autobiography. In films such as *Close Encounters*, *ET*, and *Peggy Sue* for instance, youth is lived out again in an attempt to sidestep or forestall adulthood. In his films, Spielberg travels back in time to the era of his childhood in ways which bring him 'back to the future' richer in cultural and economic capital: time is apparently on Spielberg's side, at least.

Young Grufties find solace in shadow of suicide

Nick Thorpe visits Budapest's Black Hole club to find some of the several hundred teenagers who see their lives only in shades of black.

'IT MAKES me mad, that I'm so deathly calm,' reads the slogan scrawled on the wall in the lavatory of the Black Hole club in Budapest.

This is Grufty graffiti: the teenagers who take their identity from a German word for 'tomb' wear black leather jackets, dye their hair black and are all, patiently or impatiently waiting for death.

There are several hundred Grufties in Hungary. In Budapest they meet at the Black Hole club; in the small mining town of Tata, they meet at the Hoof. Some keep rats as pets. Many cut their veins. All of them frequent cemeteries, staying there to drink or sleep when the weather is warm enough to do so.

'I used not to be able to cry, and then I scratched my veins; since then I can, and it's much better,' says one girl in Gabor Dettre's documentary film about the Grufties, *Tomorrow Has Been Cancelled* ...

'If I cut my veins I can concentrate my thoughts on death, and it helps,' said her friend.

'Many people are loved only after death, not during their lives,' another girl explains. 'Cemeteries are so beautiful — they're always clean and well-tended. I have a friend who sleeps in a coffin and his whole room is like a crypt.'

A third girl adds: 'In the cemetery we can ponder life — we're not hurt or kicked around, and we don't take anything, though we're sometimes mistaken for those who do.'

At Budapest central police station, the officer in charge of the section dealing with youth crime, Gyorgy Gabriel, clearly distinguishes the Grufties from other youth groups.

'We never have any trouble with them. They strike me as simply being depressed.' Suicide, he says, is not a police problem.

The Grufties emerged in Hungary six years ago. Their philosophical approach to death makes them more serious than their friends who are Gothics, Darks (post-Gothics) or punks. Unlike Satanists, they do not worship devils or rob graveyards.

They have no political ideology. In the shadow of death they have found a sense of community, which saves many of them from the suicide they feel drawn to. Most come from broken families and live at home, with their mothers.

Zoli spends his days with fellow Grufties around the statue to the nineteenth-century romantic poet, Mihály Vörösmarty, in the square named after the poet situated at one end of Budapest's smartest pedestrian street. 'Many of us have died,' he says. 'Others have got married, or changed ...'

During the shooting of Dettre's film, two of the characters committed suicide. Hungary, with more than 4,000 suicides a year in a population of 10 million, has one of the highest rates in the world. One third of suicides are teenagers between the ages of 15 and 17.

A group of German skinheads provides the entertainment one afternoon in the square; some small gypsy children who have just stolen salami from a supermarket do so the next day.

As the sun moves off the square, somebody finds a telephone card, and with the proceeds from its sale, a two-litre carton of red wine is bought, and everybody retires to the warmth of the oldest underground railway line on continental Europe, to celebrate.

Friends come and go, always with three kisses on the cheeks, between the boys as well, unlike the usual two. The stranger sit-

No future now: Europe's disenfranchised and hopeless urban youth is increasingly intoxicated with the nihilism that made the Sex Pistols millionaires.

ting with them, asking stupid questions, is kissed as well, for good measure. 'I was often in mental wards, and saw the patients treated like animals,' said a girl whose suicide attempt was foiled by a stomach pump. 'I'd like to work with sick people and children. I know I could look after them better than that.'

But their chances of ever getting work are slim, because of their appearance and lack of education. The girls are mostly still at school or evening school and the boys unemployed. One tells how he lost his job at a building site in the summer because he couldn't bear to keep his hat on in the heat, — and it hid his hairstyle (black, yellow and red, falling in collapsed spikes).

On a Sunday night, the Black Hole in Golgotha Street in a Budapest suburb — as remarkable for its abandoned industry as for its entirely cobbled streets — resembles something between the engine-room of a tramp steamer and the dungeon of a medieval castle. The walls are painted with images of hallucinations from a bad LSD trip.

The kids — mostly of school, that is, potentially suicidal age — are dressed in black, dripping with safety pins, earrings, nose-rings and lip-rings.

People stumble rather than dance to a roaring music relieved by moments of surprising melody.

There is no sense of danger or hostility. Tobacco and alcohol are the only visible drugs. Some seem completely sober, others far gone. Sandbags are stretched out, ominously, for people to lie, rather than sit on. Most are occupied. A terribly thin girl steers another by the arm across the dance floor as if it were a cliff-ledge. It is only a week since a 16-year-old punk girl died after visiting the club. The police called it a heroin overdose, but the Grufties maintain that it was 'some other shit ... they rarely sell you what they say it is'.

One girl in a white dress dances with another — the only person smiling in the room — like a fairy from another planet. Only the bouncers, fat and ridiculous in their padded jackets, start getting rough about closing time, smashing bottles and looking for a fight.

But the Grufties are already gently kissing one another goodbye, then, finding they cannot part, setting off together across the cobbles into the wintry night.

The Observer

N is for Nostalgia

Finally casting off the legacy of Lot's wife, we spent much of the decade looking over our shoulders as nostalgia turned into a marketable concept. Adverts were particularly culpable with Levis, Holsten Pils, Brylcreem and a host of others trying to convince us that behaving like a picture postcard version of your parents was infinitely more credible than living for the present. One suspects that the dominant rationale behind such persuasion was nothing more than the crusty desires of thirtysomething advertising execs to slap their we-lost-our-virginity-to-this favourite records onto soundtracks for commercials. . . . And what did we get from all that looking back? Sore necks. (Mathur 1989: 63)

This argument suggests that while the expansion of the mass media was a necessary condition for the emergence of youth subcultures, their continuing growth has eroded the understanding of youth upon which they were built. Youth, in this view, is not an age-linked category and youthfulness is not a biological attribute, but neither is it simply a social construction; it is, rather, an attitude, and is the result of the manipulation of time as a cultural resource. Youth may still be society's favourite age, but this is an age to which almost everyone can gain access if they have the know-how.

A related argument suggests that the conditions which gave rise to not only youth subcultures, but also the counterculture, were exceptional, and that young people today face a different set of circumstances. This is the implication of the view proposed by those who argue that the 1960s were characterized by the resurgence of a specific set of cultural values, whether those be the values of an expressive individualism identified by Berneice Martin (1981) or those associated with the revival of romanticism posited by Colin Campbell (1989). In these views, the 1960s provided a set of cultural resources which animated the youth subcultures of the period, and helped constitute a movement – the counterculture – that was generationally specific and has come to be enormously influential, but is not available on the same exclusive terms for young people in the 1990s that it was in the 1960s.

However, while all these arguments have some validity in so far as they point to changes in the constitution of the category of youth, they may not be accurate in the claim that youth subcultures have disappeared: if what it means to be young is changing, then it seems likely that so too are youth subcultures. Indeed, some sort of change seems inevitable given the escalating expansion of the media over the last twenty years or so; as Jody Berland argues:

> Broadcasting and the cultural industries are increasingly privatized . . . a process which has helped to create an expanded market for newer technologies in the form of consumer durables – not literally of course, as they are more and more – and in equal measure – widely available and rapidly obsolete. These consumer technologies function as distribution systems for entertainment and consumable information which enables their producers to 'occupy and produce a space' that is newly capitalized in both national and individual terms. Such technologies are becoming more and more refined in their ability to adapt to increasingly individuated uses, parts of the body, parts of the home, parts of the city, to separate and reunite their users in differentiated and expanded space. Their functional precision offers another expression of entertainment's mode of address, a kind of liberating fabulosity, a mode of possible excess superimposed upon the normal. (1992: 46)

In other words, while there may be something to the argument that youth no longer exists, its proponents may simply be searching for youth culture in the wrong place – by hanging out on the street corner or at the V&A – while it may be happening elsewhere – on the screen or in what McRobbie (1994) calls the 'enterprise subcultures', such as the ragmarket for example. Or then again, it may be that the authenticity, internal coherence and political challenge of the early youth cultures has come to be inflated by commentators, both academic and commercial, whose own reputations are enhanced in line with the exoticism of the subcultures with which they are identified.

Certainly the role of commentators in constructing what they appear only to document should not be ignored. While the accounts that follow give some indication of how contemporary writers conceptualize the activities of young people, it is possible to identify a shift in the centrality of youth to studies of culture and consumption. In the early studies, the activities of young people themselves occupied central stage, although it was the class-based dimensions of youth subcultures that principally concerned early commentators, while issues of gender and race were marginalized (McRobbie 1991; McRobbie and Nava 1984; Gilroy 1987; Mercer 1994). However, as McRobbie (1994) notes, during the 1980s the couplet of youth and class was often displaced, rather than supplemented, by concern with questions of race, gender and sexuality. In the 1980s work on young people the consumption activities of young people were the object of study, but youthfulness was not explicitly addressed; instead, gender, race or class was the focus. So, focusing on the literature of race, McRobbie writes:

> It is after all black *youth* who have been making much of the music Paul Gilroy examines . . . Despite this, the process of what Stuart Hall has described as 'becoming not being' have not been explored in relation to the experience of being black or Asian young people. This is a pity because the whole question of identity which is posed by the new ethnicities work has a special resonance for youth. There is a particular intensity to the processes of separation and detachment from parents and the simultaneous attachment to symbols of freedom and adventure such as those provided in music and found in the spaces of the street and night-club . . . thus the Was Not Was remix (two white American producers, with black musicians) of the soul classic 'Papa Was A Rolling Stone' has 'Papa's children' rapping back at him for failing in his parental obligations, for leaving 'Mama' to work to provide for her family and for letting his children down. This example of 'generational consciousness' is indicative of a desire to rewrite the classics from the viewpoint of youth who have grown up aware of questions of sexual inequality. (1994: 182, 183; references omitted)

Significantly, it is still rare to find studies which address the interrelationship of youth and other dimensions of social identity; many studies still focus on one aspect of social life at the expense of others, rather than exploring the relationship between them.

The culture of youth

In general terms, however, it has been suggested that the commercialized media environment has transformed the social and cultural space within which young people's cultural activities take place. Once again, it is the art-culture system which is seen to have taken on a special significance in the mediation and development of consumer culture. While this view can be overstated, the following figures give some indication of the significance of cultural activities in young people's lives.

5 per cent of the UK population attend the theatre, opera or ballet.

4 per cent of the UK population attend museums or art galleries.

2 per cent of the UK working class attend any of the above.

2 per cent of all young people (excluding students) attend the theatre (the most popular traditional arts venue).

0 per cent of the young unemployed attend the theatre.

98 per cent of the population watch TV on average for over 25 hours a week.

92 per cent of 20–24-year-olds listen to the radio.

87 per cent of 20–24-year-olds listen to records/tapes.

75 per cent of 16–24-year-olds go to pubs on average about four times a week.

40 per cent of 16–24-year-olds go to the cinema at least once in three months.

38 per cent of 11–25-year-olds go to discos.

26 per cent of 11–25-year-olds go to nightclubs.

Willis 1990: p.ix

In an environment in which, it is claimed, the average British person now sees 140,000 ads between the ages of 4 and 18, it is not how young people make a spectacle of themselves that is definitive of youth culture, but how they move within, how they live 'immersion' in spectacular space.

The rest of this chapter discusses some of the ways in which this lived immersion is described. Each one can be seen as an attempt to highlight the distinctive characteristics of contemporary youth culture by exploring its relationship with either the market and/or postmodernism. Consumer culture is typically the implicit or explicit medium of this relationship. These accounts propose different interpretations of the two-way relationship between young people and consumer culture, exploring both how young people have acted as key cultural intermediaries in the development of consumer culture, and suggesting ways in which youth and what it is to be young have been transformed by consumer culture.

I The market and common culture

Paul Willis, on the basis of a study of young people in Wolverhampton in the late 1980s, argues that notions of postmodernism are inappropriate to describe the symbolic work and creativity of young people's informal cultures. He argues that while it may make sense to speak of postmodernism in the domains of fine art or architecture, where there is a body of modernist artworks to react against – there is no such body (and no need for one) to mediate the effects of modernism in young people's everyday or common cultures. Instead, he asserts:

> Common culture is not (as 'post-modern' culture is held to be) chaotic or meaningless even if it is invisible or baffling to outside formal eyes. Its inherently democratic impulses, its variety and complexity, above all its social connectedness, show us . . . how 'ordinary' identities creatively and 'commonly' articulate with, and are developed through, the restless, dramatic and contradictory themes of modernization. (1990: 140)

N U M B E R S

Percent of U.S. budget spent on the elderly: 30
on education: 2

ROLLING STONE, APRIL 19, 1990, P. 43.

Number of dead lakes in Canada: 14,000

SOUTHAM NEWS SERVICES, OCTOBER 7, 1989.

Number of people in the workforce per Social Security beneficiary ...
in 1949: 13
in 1990: 3.4
in 2030: 1.9

FORBES, NOVEMBER 14, 1988, P. 225.

Percentage of men aged 25–29 never married ...
in 1970: 19
in 1987: 42
Percentage of women aged 25–29 never married ...
in 1970: 11
in 1987: 29

AMERICAN DEMOGRAPHICS, NOVEMBER 1988.

Percentage of women aged 20–24 married ...
in 1960: 72
in 1984: 43
Percentage of households under age 25 living in poverty ...
in 1979: 20
in 1984: 33

U.S. BUREAU OF THE CENSUS.

Number of human deaths possible from one pound of plutonium if finely ground up and inhaled: 42,000,000,000
1984 U.S. plutonium inventory, in pounds: 380,000
These numbers multiplied together: 16,000,000,000,000,000

SCIENCE DIGEST, JULY 1984.

Percentage of income required for a down payment on a first home ...
    in 1967:   22
    in 1987:   32
Percentage of 25–29 year olds owning homes ...
    in 1973:   43.6
    in 1987:   35.9

FORBES, NOVEMBER 14, 1988.

Real change in cost of a one-carat diamond ring set in 18-karat gold between 1957 and 1987:
    (in percent): +322
    of an eight-piece dining-room suite: +259
    of a movie admission: +180
    of an air flight to London, England: −80

REPORT ON BUSINESS, MAY, 1988.

Chances that an American has been on TV: 1 in 4
Percentage of Americans who say they do not watch TV: 8
Number of hours per week spent watching TV by those who say they do not watch TV: 10
Number of murders the average child has seen on television by the age of sixteen: 18,000
Number of commercials American children see by age eighteen: 350,000
The foregoing amount expressed in days (based on an average of 40 seconds per commercial): 160.4
Number of TV sets ...
    in 1947:170,000
    in 1991:   750 million

CONNOISSEUR, SEPTEMBER, 1989.

Percentage increase in income for over-65 households (senior citizens) between 1967 and 1987: 52.6
For all other households: 7

Percentage of males aged 30–34 married with spouse present ...
    in 1960:   85.7
    in 1987:   64.7
Percentage of females aged 30–34 married with spouse present ...
    in 1960:   88.7
    in 1987:   68.2

U.S. BUREAU OF THE CENSUS, CURRENT POPULATION REPORTS, NO. 423, P. 20.

Percentage of U.S. 18–29 year olds who agree that "there is no point in staying at a job unless you are completely satisfied.": 58
Who disagree: 40

Percentage of U.S. 18–29 year olds who agree that "given the way things are, it will be much harder for people in my generation to live as comfortably as previous generations.": 65
Who disagree: 33

Percentage of U.S. 18–29 year olds who answered "yes" to the question "Would you like to have a marriage like the one your parents had?": 44
Who said "no": 55

FROM A TELEPHONE POLL OF 602 18–29 YEAR OLD AMERICANS TAKEN FOR *TIME/CNN* ON JUNE 13–17, 1990, BY YANKELOVICH CLANCY SHULMAN, SAMPLING ERROR 64%. AS REPORTED IN *TIME*, JULY 16, 1990.

Source: Coupland 1992

It seems that while arguing that a hierarchy between high and popular culture still exists, Willis wishes to redefine popular culture, as lived by young people, as a *common culture*.

Willis appears to be asserting here an underlying continuity between early youth subcultures and contemporary youth culture. However, this is a continuity which is marked by the increasing interpenetration of creativity and the market, for Willis's common culture emerges from the interstices of the market. Indeed, it is not in spite of this interpenetration but as its consequence that common culture challenges what Willis sees to have been the one-way power of communication exercised by a cultural elite in the past. He argues that 'sent message' communication is being replaced by 'made message' communication. He gives as an example the following chain: a message is sent out by A to B, by whom it is re-made (not simply received) and then sent out again through a reworking of its meaning, either back to the original sender, A, or as a communication to another person, C, or people, D, E, etc. Each of these people will then do the same. The process is no longer a linear two-dimensional one, since the meaning and the direction of the message are persistently subject to change. Moreover, Willis also believes that made messages provide the basis for emergent communication communities, what he calls 'proto-communities', communities which are at present either unrecognized, misrecognized or only partly recognized.

These proto-communities, he claims, are 'flatter' than many previous kinds of community, in that they do not have the depth of daily face-to-face interaction, but instead arise out of new forms of communication. Such communities are serial – metaphorically, they can be seen as a spaced-out queue rather than a talking circle, but represent the new connectedness of contemporary youth culture. They are created by the fans of music, television, cinema, comics, computer games and 'the net'; in the last case, these connected webs of consumers have been described elsewhere as virtual communities (Rheingold 1994), communicating with each other through the dispersed flows of the electronic media.

Willis argues that the market brings with it enhanced possibilities in so far as it unsettles tradition and unpicks convention, providing materials which can be used to question the authority of 'made messages'. Indeed, he argues,

Questions can also be aimed at that very market system which produces the consumerism which produces the questions. . . . Even as 'the market' makes its profits, it supplies some of the materials for alternative or oppo-

sitional symbolic work. This is the remarkable, unstable and ever unfold-
ing contradiction of capitalism supplying materials for its own critique.
(1990: 138, 139)

He believes that the market's constant search for something new
raises the popular currency of symbolic aspiration, and that young
people continue to quicken the pulse of the cultural economy.
However, it sometimes seems that, for Willis, while young people
are especially adept in negotiating this economy, their identity is
defined outside consumer culture. In this sense, Willis appears to
suggest that while young people are significant cultural intermediaries, the meaning of youthfulness has stayed relatively untouched
by consumer culture.

II The image and postmodern culture

Dick Hebdige (1988) offers an alternative interpretation of contemporary youth culture. Like Willis, Hebdige was one of the earliest
commentators on youth subculture as style (1979). However, unlike
Willis, he argues that there has been a transformation in the nature
of youth cultures, a shift which he identifies from a distance, the
distance between the planet he inhabits – represented by the academic journal *Ten-8* for which he sometimes writes – and the next
planet in the galaxy, the world of the magazine, *The Face*. He writes
with appreciation and sensitivity of this second planet, but explicitly
associates himself with the first, in part through an act of identification which overcomes the generation gap that was said to have contributed to the emergence of youth subcultures in the first place: by
identifying with the sentiments of his own parents' generation.

This distance between these two planets is measured by a post,
the post of postmodernism. For Hebdige, postmodernism is a culture of the image:

Truth – insofar as it exists at all – is first and foremost pictured: embodied in images which have their own power and effects. Looking takes
precedence over seeing ('sensing' over 'knowing'). Words are pale ('speculative') facsimiles of an original reality which is directly apprehensible
through image. This reality is as thin as the paper it is printed on. There
is nothing underneath or behind the image and hence there is no hidden
truth to be revealed. (1988: 159)

Once again, this is a flat world, in which the vertical axis of hierarchical evaluation has collapsed and the organization of sense is horizontal and is extended through the multiplication of differences. Cultural intermediaries – amongst whom the young are visible but by no means dominant – are not the priests of a sacred culture; instead 'knowledge is assembled and dispensed to the public by a motley gang of bricoleurs, ironicists, designers, publicists, image consultants, *hommes et femmes fatales*, market researchers, pirates, adventurers, *flaneurs* and dandies' (1988: 159). Neither time nor space exist: both have been dissolved in an eternal present as 'elsewheres' and 'elsewhens' are brought into the 'here' and 'now'. Sense, in so far as it exists at all, resides at the level of the atom, the element, the fragment and the *combination* of fragments. The permutations are unlimited: 'high/low/folk/popular culture; pop music/opera; street fashion/advertising/*haute couture*; journalism/science fiction/critical theory; advertising/critical theory/*haute couture* . . .' (1988: 161).

At times, it seems as if Hebdige concurs with the gloomy prognostications of Baudrillard, who renounces the possibility of escape from this combinatory culture. Instead, Baudrillard formulates a series of what he calls 'decadent' or 'fatal' strategies, including hyperconformity. For Hebdige, *The Face* is hyperconformist: 'more commercial than the commercial, more banal than the banal . . .' (1988: 173). This is a view of the relationship between youth culture and consumer culture in which the cultural intermediaries of the art-culture system play a hugely significant role, but with unanticipated and uncontrollable effects. In this view, young people are caught up in profound cultural changes which are not of their own making.

Yet, so Sarah Thornton argues, this is to misrepresent the way in which, for example, style and music magazines are appropriated by young people. She points out that at the end of the 1980s, over thirty magazines addressed youth, featured music and style editorial, and drew advertising from the record, fashion, beverage and tobacco industries. However, rather than seeing these magazines as strategies of hyperconformity, as incorporation or selling out, she argues that they are integral to subcultural formations. She writes:

> Magazines like *i-D* produced acid house subculture as much as the participating dancers and drug-takers. The subcultural consumer press regularly pull together and reify the disparate materials that subculturalists might turn around and interpret as revealing socio-symbolic homologies.

> While not random, the distinct combination of rituals that came to be acid house was certainly not an unmediated reflection of the social structure. Media and commerce do not just *cover* but help *construct* music subcultures. (1994: 187–8)

Angela McRobbie, too, argues that the media can no longer be understood as antagonists; rather, they are accomplices:

> youth cultures make an explosive entrance into the world of the image and the text through a frenzy of communication, in style, in sound, in posters, fanzines, video, and in flyers and other publicity information. Without all of this and alongside the pretensions of preferring to remain pure and uncontaminated by the media, youth cultures require this kind of self-publicity to provoke the reaction they do. (1994: 214)

And, at times, Hebdige too argues that the fragmentary, or what he calls 'tesselated surfaces and plural textures of contemporary popular culture' (1988: 211) indicates that there remains a possibility of contradiction and resistance in youth culture. He suggests that it is no longer possible to confine subcultural resistance to the 'ghetto' of discrete, numerically small subcultures. In their place, he sees a heterogeneous field, organized around contradictory and conflicting aspirations, inclinations, dispositions and drives. In contrast to the Baudrillard-inspired view of hyperconformity as the only possible response, he tentatively identifies other strategies, insisting, for example, on 'the imaginative sweep, the sheer daring, the will to organise, to mobilise and intervene' exhibited in the execution of the Band Aid project (1988: 218).

In a move not unlike that made by Willis, Hebdige understands the radical potential of Band Aid in terms of the articulation of a version of *the common*. In Hebdige's case, this is a common-sense drawing on 'traditions of co-operation and mutual support, rooted in the human(e) values of good fellowship and good neighbourliness . . . to imagine a community beyond the boundaries of the known' (1988: 219). Like Willis, Hebdige argues that this will require a reconceptualization of culture itself, away from a view which sees it as made up of the relations between discrete texts or objects and readers towards a view which understands it in terms of processes, flows and networks of meaning, in which art and everyday life are inextricably mixed. In this version of 'the common', however, as the example of Band Aid illustrates, the media are not external to the category youth but are intricately involved in its construction.

III   The counterculture and the time of post-political pop

In *The End-of-the Century Party* (1990), Steve Redhead offers another view again of the relationship between youth and consumer culture through a study of popular music. Once again, it is the interpretation of the media which acquires a pivotal status in the account offered. Redhead argues that the 1990s are unlikely to see a slowing down of the accelerating speed of the turnaround of fashion and style in popular music (an argument which parallels the theme of Douglas Coupland's first novel, *Generation X*, which is subtitled 'tales for an accelerated culture'). Yet while he argues that the acceleration is so great that what he calls Pop Time will, eventually, go backwards, he also argues that 'it is not so much a case of back to the future, as forward to the past' (Redhead 1990: 6).

Redhead claims that contemporary popular music is no longer simply 'youth' music; indeed, he suggests that the music that became associated with the post-war construction of notions like the teenager, the generation gap, youth subcultures and even youth itself is now assisting in the imminent destruction of the selfsame categories. He quotes Frith with approval: ' "Youth" is now just a marketing device and advertiser's fiction; the myths that matter have different sources: American funk and hip, the archives of psychedelia and folk-rock' (1990: 26). At the same time, Redhead too appears to suggest that new communities are also being created in a continuing recombination of synthetic and authentic elements.

Like Willis and Hebdige, he points to the interpenetration of popular and consumer cultures; indeed, he writes, 'Counter-cultures, as it is used in this book, is a phrase pregnant with double meaning. Its use here has at least as much to do with shopping and consumption as with opposition and the 1960s counter-culture' (1990: 17). More significantly, he argues that popular music and its associated cultures have always been tied to the market. So, for example, he claims that the characteristics of youth culture which Hebdige identifies with life on the planet inhabited by readers of *The Face* – including the obsession with pastiche, parody, quotation and the theft or piracy of the debris of earlier times – have always been part of pop. He writes, 'since the 1940s, Pop Time has, in many ways, been circular rather than linear: the speed of what comes around again may change but the cyclical motion is embedded in pop's genealogy' (1990: 25). Indeed, he suggests that there is no time outside Pop Time, no place outside the reaches of the market, no identity – including that of youth – which is already given before consumption.

In this sense, Redhead can be distinguished from Willis, who, while arguing that the market provides the materials for young people's creativity, seems to assume that what it is to be young is in some way independent of the workings of consumer culture. At the same time, Redhead also differs from Hebdige, who, while arguing that what it is to be young is increasingly created in the market, adopts a largely pessimistic view of the implications of this for subcultures. Redhead is not pessimistic; as noted above, he seems to concur that subcultures as discrete entities have more or less disappeared, but he does not see this as a loss. This is, in part, because he thinks that the existence of subcultures as self-generating and internally coherent entities was overstated in the first place, but, perhaps more importantly, because he believes that the pop culture of the market now, as it has in the past, provides a fluid, constantly shifting terrain for the creation of identities. In order to describe this culture, he suggests, it is necessary to be responsive to acceleration or speed, or what, quoting Paul Virilio, he describes as 'the depletion of time':

> The twin factors of time's reduction to an instant, but being *everywhere*, are precisely the facets of pop and rock music culture which should attract our critical attention in the age of instantaneous electronic communication. (1990: 46)

It is as if time has been disengaged from age in consumer culture, and, as a consequence, in the time of post-subcultural pop, anyone can buy youth as a commodity in the global hypermarket. This is not seen as the liberation of youth, for that would be to presume a youth in need of liberation, but instead, Redhead argues, provides 'the scope for invention and adoption of . . . new subjectivities', and it is this, 'rather than the attempt to 'represent' divided or non-existent communities' which 'makes Post-Political Pop significant today' (1990: 89).

What Redhead suggests is that the concern of previous commentators with *age* has masked the significance of *time* in understanding the changing relationship between youth and popular and consumer cultures. From his point of view, it was young people's ability to symbolize the capacity for social change that made them society's favorite age-group in the immediate post-war period. In this sense, youth subcultures were not simply a sign of the times, but a sign of time itself, of how time might be (re)organized. The development of consumer culture – in which, in his view, young people are important cultural intermediaries – has extended this capacity to others in ways which have made age, if not redundant, certainly less important as a source of identity. In this sense, young people's role as cultural intermediaries has undermined the social category of youth. 'Youth' culture is now a culture in which time, not age, is revealed to be the newly stylized medium through which the anxieties of society approaching the end of the second millennium are given a magical solution to the problem of 'progress'. Lipsitz provides an apt example:

> In Public Enemy's music video 'Fight the Power' Flavor Flav, the group's free-spirited trickster, displays a stopped alarm clock, pinned to his shirt and explains that 'this means we know what time it is.' He does not elaborate on how the broken clock conveys this information, but from the context of the video his meaning is clear. The group believes that time has stopped, that progress is not being made, that the need for social change is so urgent that it obscures everything else about our time. (1994: 17)

While Redhead focuses on the activities on young people in his study of popular music, it seems that he believes almost anyone can be young, that is, if they can not only go forward to the past, but, once there, also get back to the future. Perhaps, though, this ignores the issue of who owns the time machines. In this respect, the organization of the art-culture system (and in particular, the media), and its ability to determine who has access to the time machines, acquires a special importance. How are young people themselves positioned in relation to time travel?

HISTORICAL UNDERDOSING: To live in a period of time when nothing seems to happen. Major symptoms include addiction to newspapers, magazines, and TV news broadcasts.

HISTORICAL OVERDOSING: To live in a period of time when too much seems to happen. Major symptoms include addiction to newspapers, magazines, and TV news broadcasts. (Coupland 1992: 7 and 8)

In order to address this question it is necessary to consider what might be described as the political economy of pop culture. The first point to make here is that this economy is immensely complex, and comprises a whole host of networks, some of which link together, but others of which operate in relatively discrete enclaves. Angela McRobbie (1994) characterizes one set of networks in the following terms:

> the magazines produced by fans, the music produced by DJs, the clothes bought, sold and worn by subcultural 'stylists', do more than just publicize the subculture. They also provide the opportunity for learning and sharing skills, for practising them, for making a small amount of money; more importantly, they provide pathways for future 'life-skills' in the form of work or self-employment. To ignore the intense activity of cultural production as well as its strong aesthetic dimension (in graphics, fashion design, retail and music production) is to miss a key part of subcultural life – the creation of a whole way of life, an alternative to higher education (though often a 'foundation' for art school), a job creation scheme for the culture industries. . . . In this undocumented, unrecorded and largely 'hidden economy' sector subcultures stand at one end of the culture industry spectrum and the glamorous world of the star system and the entertainment business at the other. (1994: 161–2)

However, while McRobbie presents a positive view of this economy – 'I would suggest that this involvement can be an empowering experience . . .' (1994: 161) – it is not clear that her account of the cultural economy recognizes the special features of an economy which is dominated by the media and multinational businesses. Redhead himself, while acknowledging the importance of young people in pop culture, does not attempt to map the relative contribution of young people as either producers or consumers to its economy. However, other analysts suggest that 'the culture industry spectrum' is not linked in a direct chain of enterprises as McRobbie implies (although see the discussion of Wynne and O'Connor in chapter 4), and that the potential for young people to act as cultural intermediaries is restricted by the interests of multinational companies (Amin and Goddard 1986; Amin and Thrift 1994).

IV The culture of choice and the spaces of the screen

Youth cultures of the past are often described as spectacular, meaning that they were deliberately created to be looked at, to be a spectacle. In these spectacular youth cultures, the distinction between being young and being old(er) was created by the deliberate use of visual and other markers, the adoption of a certain style, the project of turning oneself into a coded image, a spectacle for others. The young defined themselves as different by their self-creation as a spectacle. It is argued by writers such as Frith (1992), Nava (1992) and Lury (1995) that today's young people do not create subcultures by making themselves into a spectacle, but in the ways in which they operate within a society which is itself a spectacle or hyper-reality. In this view, young people are central to struggles over meaning because by highlighting the role of audiences, they *redefine* the role of cultural intermediaries in the light of ongoing changes in the art-culture system.

The society of the spectacle is one in which the media predominate; however, this domination is complicated by the fact that the distinction between the media consumer and producer is both indeterminate and of great commercial importance. The viewers (or users might be a more appropriate word) of what Umberto Eco calls 'neo-television' (1984) – which now potentially includes VCRs, various film, music, sport and other narrowcasting cable and satellite services, videotapes, educational and other software, games and so on – may be in pubs, shops, bus stations, corner stores and dance clubs as well as the living room and the bedroom. Moreover, since, as noted in chapter 4, post-war generations have grown up with a style of television programming and mode of address that typically adopts self-referential forms which exploit and play upon the evolved forms of television itself, they are familiar with strategies for discovering new significance in the already well known, and maintaining a playful distance from established styles (King 1989). At the same time, music is pervasive; it is played on tapes, radio, cds and videos in homes and cars, on walkmans and telephones, in television advertising and films, and is the principal component of the background soundscapes of most stores and many workplaces. As Redhead claims, 'Combined with fast-flickering subliminal images, it appears to be forever selling, soothing, celebrating, hustling, commiserating and titillating' (1990: 8). And pop music continually reflects back upon its own past to conjure up a future, each genre reviving, reworking, quoting, parodying and pirating the others.

In this environment, young people are principally defined as an audience (rather than or as well as a market), but this is an audience of a new kind. In this view, then, it is *the distinctive activities of young people as members of an audience* that both marks them out as young, or at least as youthful, and makes them key cultural intermediaries. As Sarah Thornton notes

various media are integral to youth's social and ideological formations. *Micro*media like flyers and listings are means by which club organizers bring the *crowd* together; *niche* media like the music press construct as much as they distort youth *movements*. Contrary to youth discourses, then, subcultures do not germinate from a seed and grow by force of their own energy into mysterious movements to be belatedly digested by *the* media. Rather, media are there are effective right from the start. They are integral to the process by which, in Bourdieu's terms, we 'create groups with words.' (1994: 176)

It is in relation to a revised conception of the importance of an active audience that this view explores the relationship between young people and consumer culture. However, this conception is a multi-faceted one.

On the one hand, this definition of young people as a distinctive audience is seen to be a consequence of their targeting as such by the media, in particular the music, television and advertising industries. So, for example, Frith argues:

For the mid-80s alliance of the new television, the music industry and global advertisers, 'youth' was constituted as a pop audience, a social group with an identity – a lifestyle – expressed through rock sounds and stars and styles. (1992: 12)

He suggests that the interest in youth as a special audience was especially intense in the mid-1980s because of the restructuring of the culture industries that was occurring in this period as a consequence of the introduction of cable and satellite and the increasing marketization of the media as a whole. This interest involved, in part, a 're-ageing' of youth:

Pop viewers, TV youth as traditionally defined by the music industry, by *Top of the Pops*, 12–24-year-olds, were certainly not the 'better-off' youth British advertisers were now after. Their ideal audience was made up of 18–34-year-olds, and in commercial TV terms the 'crisis' in youth broadcasting in 1988 actually described the attempt to redirect pop programming from the former to the latter. (Frith 1992: 15)

Significantly, this also involved a regendering of the audience, with a change of gender address, from one directed to young women to one directed to young men. This move, Frith suggests, is related to a shift in the producers' conceptualization of the audience, from participants in a domestic leisure pursuit to users of media technology.

According to Frith, in the media producers' desperation to hang

on to market share of the audience, youth became not only an especially valuable market for sale to advertisers, but also the section of
the audience whose ways of viewing were believed to anticipate how
the population as a whole would view television in years to come.
Winning the youth audience would thus ensure a successful commercial future. As Frith says, in the context of an intensification of
market processes within the media, this involved an understanding
of youth which no longer saw it as a symbol of change, but as *a symbol of choice*, of audience choice in a commercialized media environment. He writes:

> In this model 'youth' became a category constructed by TV itself, with
> no other referent: those people of whatever age or circumstances who
> watched 'youth' programmes became youth, became, that is, *the future of
> television*. (1993: 75)

Youth, in this account, no longer describes a particular type of person, who is attracted to a particular type of programme, but, rather,
describes an attitude, a particular type of viewing behaviour. Frith
quotes a revealing extract from an interview with Janet Street-Porter
who at the time was head of youth programmes at the BBC:

> I don't really think I make youth programmes. I think the word youth has
> become this ghastly term. I don't know why I call myself 'Head of Youth
> Programmes'. I wanted to be head of a department because I wanted to
> have the clout, but I couldn't think of what else to be head of . . . I'd like
> to be called head of 'different' programmes or 'youth*ful* programmes' . . .
> I suppose the programmes we make are for people who don't have a lot
> of responsibilities. The minute you have a *lot* of responsibilities, you stop
> being receptive to new ideas. (1989, quoted in Frith 1993: 75)

As Frith points out, Street-Porter's definition of youthfulness in
terms of irresponsibility indicates the extent to which this new conception of youth was tied to the advertisers' conception of the ideal
consumer. Ultimately, then, Frith suggests, the revived invocation
of youth in the mid-1980s was a way of bringing into play new discourses around the television audience which were to do with the
legitimation of political changes in the media in terms of consumer
choice.

The concern with young people as an audience can be seen as
part of a more long-term process on the part of producers and
advertisers which Ien Ang (1991) calls 'desperately seeking the
audience' in which the audience is constructed as a resource in the

First, some questions: what did you and your friends do last Saturday night? Have you got any interest in politics? What's your favourite advert on TV at the moment? Assuming that you still remember last Saturday night, these should not be very difficult questions to answer. Which means that you may be somewhat bemused to learn that, with the right contacts, you could actually sell this information to advertising agencies – and then charge them £150 an hour to come and talk it over with you. Really.

This is because many of the people who make advertisements, and specifically those who make advertisements aimed at you (that's you, as in 'the youth' are currently in a state of mild panic. (Benson and Armstrong 1994: 54)

organization of the culture industries through the measurement of audience 'ratings' and 'appreciation' of specific programmes. However, as Ang points out, these measurements of the audience have very little to do with the actual activities of viewers. Similarly, Frith suggests that in contradistinction of producers' representations of watching as an activity of choice, 'one of the pleasures of television viewing . . . is that one doesn't have to "choose" anything at all, doesn't have to take one's TV screen as any sort of sign of one's identity' (1992: 28).

However, it is also argued that while producers may systematically misrepresent the audience activities of young people in accordance with their own commercial and political needs, there is nevertheless something distinctive about the activities of young people *as an audience*. For writers such as Turkle (1986) and Lury (1995) these activities take place in the new spaces of media-saturated environments; so, for example, Karen Lury argues:

it may be possible to recognise the ways that young people orientate themselves today as different from previous generations . . . partly as a result of the methods through which they find out '*where* they are' rather than '*who* they are'. (1995: 39)

In this approach, it is argued that negotiating and using modern communications technology is not only appropriate, but a vital experience for young people in that the performance of their selves 'is bound up with the proliferation of media opportunities and "travel" possibilities'. The audience for these performances of identity are typically 'enabled, distanced and connected by media technologies'; indeed, Lury suggests that at certain points, 'the "others" who make up the audiences for these performances of identity may be "hardwired artefacts", that is, the technologies themselves (1995: 41). Similarly Turkle (1986) claims that in young people's use of video games 'conversation gives way to fusion'. Contrasting this experience with that of playing a pinball machine (think of Roger Daltrey in *Tommy*), she says:

> The video game is different: here all of the action is in a programmed world, an abstract space. In an important sense, it is a space where the physical machine and the physical player do not exist. It is not easy for pinball players to describe their feelings of what makes the game respond. Some describe it as a 'conversation': there is a sense of give and take. But although it has become a cliche to speak of the video game as 'interactive', players describe the experience of being with one as less like talking with a person and more like inhabiting someone's else's mind. . . . In pinball you act on the ball. In Pac-man you are the mouth. (1986: 69–70)

In this view, being young is living in an altered state. It is a state in which the individual's relation to objects is not one of calculated decontrol (as in Featherstone's account), but one of distraction, in which the 'original' or 'natural' is no longer the location of the true 'self'. However, as Lury also points out,

> this is not also to say that such distinctions are no longer important or relevant, but instead that the processes of cloaking, merging, the sniggers of embarrassment, and the confessional styles engaged in, and abandoned by, young people reveal clearly that identity functions *as process*. A process that is open more or less anxiously, more or less consciously, to contradiction. (1995: 41)

It is this set of relations of viewing – of being an interactive audience and performing an identity in interaction – which is held to characterize contemporary youth culture, and it is in making visible identity *as a process* that young people create themselves as youth.

Moreover, young people are seen to occupy inner spaces of the self and outer spaces of urban life simultaneously. Here too, technologies play a central role. In his discussion of youth culture in the United States, Lipsitz argues that young black people answered 'a culture of surveillance with a counterculture of conspicuous display' (1994: 20). He writes:

> Hemmed in by urban renewal, crime and police surveillance, young people write graffiti on subway trains and buses so that their names and

images can travel all over the city and be seen by strangers. . . . Dancing calls attention to the movements of the body as metaphors: a dance step like 'the running man' aestheticizes the danger of being chased by the police, while electric boogaloo 'robot' moves and 'vogue' gestures build dramatic tension through continuities and ruptures in movement. Cyborg-like effects in dancing and music enable people whose oppressions are inscribed on their bodies (because of racism, sexism and homophobia) to imagine their bodies as flexible technologies with prosthetic properties. Large car speakers adjusted to pump-up-the-bass 'jeep beats' of rap music travel freeways and city streets, claiming space while projecting out sound . . . (1994: 21)

In these ways, Lipsitz argues, rap music, graffiti-writing and car customizing 'turn consumers into producers, and they contest prevailing definitions of property and propriety' (1994: 22). While he argues that it is sometimes 'hard to tell the difference between critique and collaboration' (1994: 25), he concludes 'It is not so much that young people are under the "thrall" of commodities, but rather that the power of commodities inevitably shapes the contours of personal and collective identity' (1994: 26).

The value of youth cultures

But what is the significance of these interpretations of youth culture for understanding young people's role in relation to the development of consumer culture? Are young people able to act as cultural intermediaries? As they get older, will they be able to lay claims of ownership to the culture they mediate or simply hold on to the cultural goods of their past? In her discussion of the youth cultures of the 1960s Berneice Martin (1981) suggests that the expressive individualism that underpinned their emergence is also responsible for the later success of this generation of young people in certain sectors of the economy, including many of the so-called service occupations such as, advertising, finance and the media. Indeed, expressive individualism is often linked to the notion of lifestyle used by Featherstone (1991) to help explain the rise of the new middle classes. This would suggest that it was a combination of class and generation that contributed to the changes associated with the new middle classes identified by Featherstone.

There are very few studies of whether the values developed by young people in the context of consumer culture today are likely to be taken up in the same way in the sphere of paid employment. However, David Cannon (1994) believes that today's young people – who, following Douglas Coupland, Cannon calls Generation X – have developed a distinctive set of values in response to the changed circumstances of their lives, and that these values will come to shape work culture. He identifies a number of processes as especially influential in shaping the values of this generation, including 'invasive media', 'worldwide consumer products', 'accessible communications and computer tools', 'global issues' and 'travel'. He writes:

> Invasive media has been used to promote brand names such as Benetton, Haagen Dazs, Nike, Esprit and Windows which are now part of the everyday language of *Generation X* around the planet. Described by some as the first global generation, they are joined together not by a common ideology but rather a sophisticated knowledge of consumer products.
>
> This is true for individuals in all tiers of the educational and socio-economic ladder. Research shows that young people who drop out of school with little grasp of mathematics or history have in fact detailed stores of information on computer gear, fashion products, and recreational equipment. (1994: 2)

On the basis of a large number of focus group discussions with young people in the UK, North America and the Netherlands – most of whom have experienced some higher education – he identifies what he describes as a new 'attitude'. He suggests that this attitude is shaped by young people's perception that trust has disappeared from the world, and identifies a number of sometimes contradictory responses to this perception, including a 'mortal fear of boredom', a desire to learn 'how to', a craving for continuous feedback and external validation, a high degree of awareness of appearances, a belief in the importance of gender equality, emotional suppression and secretiveness, and a demand for honesty.

These responses are only loosely characterized by Cannon, but he believes they provide some indication of the values which may come to inform the work culture of the early twenty-first century. They are clearly shaped by the emergence of consumer culture, and suggest that the skills developed in the consumption activities of youth culture have the potential to be transferred to other areas of life. Cannon writes:

> Common to all the younger people in the study was a delight in collecting bits of information, facts, jargon and trivia. In their personal lives this might translate into a sophisticated knowledge of music or mountain

bikes. In their working lives it includes things like Windows or Internet. Special knowledges are constantly traded among young people and represent a kind of status symbol to those who possess them. Monitored conversations between young people from school leavers to Oxford firsts show less emphasis on the sharing of thoughts and feelings, and more on exchanging information about consumer products and services which they know a great deal about. (1994: 7–8)

Cannon also provides some evidence to support the view that the skills that young people acquire in 'the processes of cloaking, merging, the sniggers of embarrassment, and the [adoption and abandonment of]confessional styles' (Lury, 1995: 41) said to be characteristic of youth culture are put to work in their presentation of self. So, for example, Cannon writes,

Almost any parent will tell you adolescents are a bit secretive. This is not new and is part of the normal development of young adults. In the UK groups we found that young people still share their inner feelings and fears with close friends and siblings. This is not the case in our US and Canadian groups. North American *Generation X* for the most part believe they are on their own. Many have developed what they call '*the tape*' – a prerecorded message about their dreams and plans that they play to parents and even girlfriends and boyfriends '*to stop all the questioning*'. (1994: 9)

At the same time, young people are said to be hyper-sensitive to *managed truth*. This complex, some might say contradictory, set of values clearly has the potential to confuse current understandings of authenticity in self-identity.

ANTI-SABBATICAL: A job taken with the sole intention of staying only for a limited period of time (often one year). The intention is usually to raise enough funds to partake in another, more personally meaningful activity such as watercolor sketching in Crete or designing computer knit sweaters in Hong Kong. Employers are rarely informed of intentions. (Coupland 1992: 35)

Whether the values of Generation X will not only come to shape the self-presentation of young people, but also form the basis of a lifestyle which can accumulate cultural capital is as yet uncertain. As Cannon points out, some young people may alternatively choose to adopt the life of a 'slacker', a term from Richard Linklater's film of the same name. It refers to those young people who live off parental hand-outs, working briefly here or there in what Coupland calls McJobs. Its ethos of 'why bother?' is promoted by the recently launched magazine *The Idler*. Is this the counterculture of the 1990s?

McJOB: A low-pay, low-prestige, low-dignity, low-benefit, no-future job in the service sector. Frequently considered a satisfying career choice by people who have never held one. (Coupland 1992: 5)

Conclusion

It has been argued here that 'youth' emerged as a social category of identity in the post-war period in close association with the distinctive use of material objects by young people. However, the visibility of this distinctiveness in subcultures was also a result of the role that youth played as a symbol of change in the post-war period. As we approach the end of the twentieth century, these two dimensions of the visibility of youth cultures have affected each other so that youth is now both a symbol of choice and a category of identity created through a reflexive relation to objects as carriers of space and social change or time more generally. A number of different approaches to the study of contemporary youth have been introduced, ranging from those in which biological age is still articulated with youth, to those in which it has been disarticulated, until, in some accounts, it appears as if more or less anyone can display youthfulness by adopting a reflexive relation to time and space mediated through the use of consumer goods, especially those of the media technologies.

In discussing this reflexive relation to time and space, these accounts identify the role of the market and consumer culture as critical. In some accounts, such as that of Willis, the market, while transmitting the resources of a common culture is still, in some senses, external to the category of youth, that is, it does not inform the way in which people inhabit youthfulness. In many other accounts, however, it is as if the market, and its culture, has entered into the very terms of how an identity is done or performed. This is explained in terms of the way in which consumer culture provides an environment in which age – specifically what it is to be young – is constituted as a style rather than a biological or even generational category.

For Hebdige, who ties in this stylization with the emergence of postmodernism, this has unfortunate political implications, in so far as it cuts youth subcultures free from their moorings in specific struggles. However, for others the implications are less clearly identifiable: Redhead and Karen Lury, for example, believe that the recognition of the constructedness of identity that this stylization reveals brings at least the potential for scope and innovation at a fundamental level, that of the self. However, while for Redhead it seems as if this potential has the (radical) power to undermine the category youth, for Lury and others this potential is being exploited by young people to reconstitute youth subcultures in a distinctive way. Nevertheless, in both cases this potential is seen to be linked to the dynamics of the contemporary art-culture system in which the media are taking on a more and more significant role. While Redhead, implicitly at least, highlights the role of young people as producers, Lury and the others foreground the creative potential of a conception of young people as a new kind of audience. It is in this capacity that young people can be seen as key intermediaries in the development of consumer culture today.

8

Consumer Culture, Identity and Politics

Introduction

This book has investigated the phenomenon of consumer culture from a number of angles. The first chapter considered the view that consumer culture should be seen as a contemporary manifestation of Euro-American *material culture*. This approach highlights the importance of exploring the interrelationship of economic and symbolic aspects of material goods or objects in the organization of all societies. However, it was also argued in this chapter that the symbolic or cultural aspects of material objects have come to take on a special importance and distinctive organization in contemporary Euro-American societies, so that consumer culture is said to be drenched in meaning. This organization is what marks out *consumer culture* as a specific form of material culture.

In the second and third chapters, it was argued that this distinctive organization could be described in terms of *stylization,* and is brought about as a consequence of the interrelationship of a number of factors, including:

1   changes in the processes of commodification associated with production for the market;
2   changes in the relation between the different cycles of production and consumption existing in contemporary societies;
3   an increase in the relative power of consumers *vis-à-vis* producers in some cycles;
4   the increasing impact of the art-culture system and the significance of the use of cultural goods, not only in itself, but as a model of consumption for other goods.

The last factor was identified as especially important in the emergence of consumer culture. It was argued that the art-culture system has come to take on a crucial role in the mediation of the relation between an individual's social position and his or her practices of consumption, in large part because of its significance as 'a machine for making authenticity' (Clifford 1988). The following chapters then went on to investigate the ways in which consumer culture has come to provide new sources of identity, and has contributed to the emergence of a politics of identity.

Chapters 4, 5, 6 and 7 explored the relationship between changes

lture and key social groupings, highlighting in each
cance of the art-culture system in this interrelation-
of these chapters, the specialized roles of hierarchically
ial groups – defined by class, gender, race and age – in
ese changes was emphasized. The notion of the cultural
y was introduced as a way of exploring these roles,
was found that different groups function as intermediaries to greater or lesser extent and in different ways. One interesting feature of these chapters is that they suggest that it is not only
the dominant groups that have influenced the development of consumer culture; subordinate groups are sometimes active intermediaries, although others have been relatively uninfluential. This points
to the relative independence of consumer culture from economic
and social relations of power and inequality, although, as was noted
in the first chapter, this independence is limited, and, in any case,
consumer culture can be seen as the site of new relations of power
and inequality (see below).

The isolation of the activities of each social grouping in a chapter
of their own was an artificial device, intended to illuminate the different ways in which individuals are positioned in relation to consumer culture as a consequence of their membership of these
groups. The aim was twofold: to show that our participation in consumer culture is uneven – it brings benefits and disadvantages to
different people in different ways; and, conversely, that consumer
culture is the consequence of some people's or some groups' actions
more than others. However, given that concrete individuals are
members of *each* of these groupings, it needs to be remembered that
any individual's participation will be contradictory, comprised of a
set of interacting, sometimes conflictual, relations. These relations
are always negotiated in different ways by the multiply positioned
individual.

As an example of what Fine and Leopold (1993) call a *horizontal*
approach to the study of consumption, that is, one which attempts
to look at consumer culture in relation to consumption of all material goods, the approach presented here has tended to play down the
significance of *vertical* approaches based on systems of provision.
Fine and Leopold argue for the importance of such vertical
approaches on the grounds that the way in which consumption is
determined is fundamentally dependent upon the integral combination of the vertical chain of structures and processes that are
attached to particular groups of commodities, such as food, clothing, energy, transport systems, and so on. Each of these is seen by

Fine and Leopold to be characterized by its own distinctive history and organizing principles. Their work thus provides a refinement of the view discussed in chapter 2 which indicated the importance of looking at how the mode of provision of goods – in particular, the use of either market or state mechanisms – shapes their consumption and creates specific forms of inequality.

However, while Fine and Leopold's book shows important differences between organized systems of production, the vertical approach has not been foregrounded here because it has not yet been sufficiently developed to provide a basis from which to consider the emergence of consumer *culture*. Moreover, it is not entirely clear how Fine and Leopold establish the basis on which vertical systems of provision come to be isolated from each other. The approach adopted here has sought to show the ways in which consumer culture, as a distinctive organization of material culture, operates *across* different systems of provision. This broadly horizontal approach has to some extent pointed to the importance of looking at the art-culture system as a vertically organized system of provision because of its centrality to the emergence of consumer culture (just as Fine and Leopold's study of the clothing industry as a vertical system of provision provides an interesting analysis of its significance in relation to the taking up of 'fashion' as a mode of provision across other sectors). More generally, further studies in the vertical organization of consumption would both provide a basis for evaluating the thesis posed here and offer a complementary approach to the study of consumer culture.

In the rest of this final chapter, some of the implications of the development of consumer culture for society as a whole will be considered: first, by returning to the discussion of its role in the supposed decline in the distinction between high and popular culture; second, through an exploration of its implications for understandings of the individual and the exercise of will; and, third, in its relation to contemporary forms of politics through a consideration of the relationship between consumer culture and understandings of collective identity and social sources of community and solidarity.

Consumer culture and the art-culture system

One of the themes of this book has been the centrality of the dynamic relationship between cycles of production and consumption and the art-culture system for understanding contemporary consumer culture. It was pointed out that at the same time that the art-culture system has contributed to the development of consumer culture, consumer culture has brought about changes in the organization of the art-culture system, including contributing to an alleged erosion of the distinction between high and popular culture. But it was also pointed out that there are a variety of different views on whether this erosion has in fact occurred.

Featherstone's argument (1991) is that the much hypothesized demise is actually more complicated than it seems. On first impression, he seems to suggest that the boundary between high and popular culture is becoming less rigid, permeable even, in part as a consequence of an intensification of the commodification of culture. On a closer reading, however, it seems what he is actually saying is that what has changed is that some individuals – namely members of the new middle classes – are acquiring the ability to move between high and popular culture in ways that are beneficial to them. More specifically, he is suggesting that the ability to move between the two is currently being defined in such a way as to make this movement one of the sources of an exclusive and exclusionary lifestyle amongst the new middle classes. In the exercise of calculated hedonism, this movement is represented as *a capacity of the individual,* as a function of his or her (good) taste, but this capacity is, in fact, only realizable by some individuals and not others as a consequence of the restricted access to strategies of legitimation for some groups in society. In other words, while certain individuals – in the legitimating context of middle-class lifestyles – may cross the boundary between high and popular culture the distinction itself is upheld, and with it the institutionalization of an uneven distribution of aesthetic knowledge.

Certainly, as chapters 5, 6 and 7 have illustrated, the capacity to move between high and popular culture is not as easily recognized as the exercise of individual taste when carried out by members of other groups; rather, it is typically seen in terms of people being swept up in the indiscriminate world of the market in which the principle of exchange arbitrarily flattens all value and removes the possibility of individuals knowingly participating in distinctions of taste. This perception illustrates the continuing force of the boundary between high and popular culture, itself created through the opposition between authenticity and commodification sustained in the art-culture system, and through the exclusion of subordinated groups from the processes of authentification that the system deems legitimate.

However, it is important to point out that the opposition between authenticity and commodification is not one of mutual exclusiveness; rather, authenticity and commodification have historically always been sustained as *apparent* opposites through a complex set of processes in which they are actually intertwined. This book has proposed not only that it is this complex mix of opposition and dependence that has provided a dynamic which has fuelled the development of consumer culture, but also that consumer culture has provided a new context in which this opposition is played out – through, for example, the reflexive, ironic practices of the new middle classes. However, this does not mean that consumer culture has made the opposition itself redundant.

One consequence of its enduring hold is that the participation of members of subordinate groups in consumer culture is not typically understood in terms of the exercise of judgement or taste, but is, rather, described in terms of *masquerade, imitation* or *incorporation,* all terms indicating that the decontrol of emotion involved is not seen to be as calculated or as strategic as that required for the self-possession of the new middle classes' social identity and political authority. This is, in part, because of the ways in which such practices are not deemed to be sufficiently knowing or self-consciously reflexive, but are, rather, seen to be natural, unknowing or deceptive. As a consequence, they remain tactics rather than strategies (to use a distinction proposed by de Certeau 1988). At the same time, however, it may be that the boundary between high and popular culture is at least weakened as an unintended consequence of the activities of the new middle classes; if this is so, then consumer culture may be seen to offer subordinate groups new resources in the making of authenticity and the creation of social and political identities of their own. However, debate on this question is often further complicated by the use of the term postmodernism to describe contemporary culture.

As outlined in chapter 2, postmodernism is a term which, in its more limited definition, identifies a number of distinctive characteristics of the contemporary art-culture system. These include not only the alleged erosion of the distinction between high and popular culture, but also the displacement of a relation of contemplation with an artwork by a relation of immersion (Lash 1990). Consumer culture has been argued here to be one of the chief purveyors of these changes (at least for limited social groups) to spheres of social life outside the art-culture system through its promotion of the stylization of consumption. However, while postmodernism (in this limited sense) and consumer culture are sometimes assumed to describe similar phenomena (and, indeed, are sometimes used more or less interchangeably, as in Featherstone's work) they have also been distinguished on the basis that while the latter is principally concerned with changes in the use and appropriation of goods (cultural and otherwise), postmodernism includes a range of other processes, including challenges to the authority of science and technology and their construction of the relation between nature and society. It can thus be seen to be concerned with broader questions of the authority of all sorts of knowledge, technical and scientific as well as aesthetic. It is in this broader sense that postmodernism has been linked to the so-called implosion of the social, that is, its internal dissolution. This book has suggested that consumer culture should not be elided with postmodernism in this respect. However, this does not mean that consumer culture has not had widespread implications for contemporary understandings of the self or, indeed, for society as a whole.

Consumer culture, the individual and the exercise of will

A recent series of advertisements for the lager 'Schlitz' displayed the contents of the rubbish bins of a number of celebrities. In the ad which features Lisa Bonet's garbage, the text notes 'we can figure out . . . that she's into health food, owns a dog and gets sent stacks of scripts. She also drinks Schlitz.' What else can the viewer figure out? Is the display of the final detritus of consumption to be read as evidence of identity? Is garbage, the husks of a personal selection of consumer goods, to be understood as a self-portrait?

This section will explore the question of how significant consumer culture is in defining *our sense of ourselves* as individuals and as a society. This is a difficult question to answer, not least since, as pointed out earlier, participation in this culture is both uneven and contradictory. Moreover, as the earlier chapters show, an individual's relation to his or her self-identity may be different in different social groups, and the emergence of consumer culture may thus have different implications for different social groups.

A study carried out by Peter Lunt and Sonia Livingstone (1992) provides one way of answering the question. These two social psychologists set out to explore the hypothesis that consumer culture provides the conditions within which most people work out their identities. In order to do this, they carried out a study which directly asked people about how consumption informed their everyday life. This study consisted of an in-depth postal survey with 279 respondents, a series of nine focus group discussions, and a series of twenty interviews to provide material for the construction of individual life histories. The general finding of the study was that people's involvement with consumer culture is such that it infiltrates everyday life not only at the level of economic decision-making, social activities and domestic life, but also at the level of meaningful psychological experience. It affects the construction of identities, the formation of relationships and the framing of events.

However, this finding of the widespread significance of consumer culture for personal identity does not mean that everyone is a shopaholic. Rather, Lunt and Livingstone's study suggests that it is possible to divide people up into different groups, according to their shopping habits. They identify five such groupings:

Alternative shoppers   12%
These people use the alternative market, buying second-hand books and clothes and attending jumble sales. They seem to stand outside the pressures and pleasures of modern consumer culture. They find little pleasure in shopping.

Routine shoppers   31%
These people shop on the high street whenever they need something, but seem disengaged from consumer culture. They rarely buy on impulse and do not use the alternative market. They find little pleasure in shopping. Shopping is a routine activity.

Leisure shoppers   24%
These people come closest to the stereotype associated with consumer culture ('I shop therefore I am'), enjoying a range of shopping experiences, enjoying window shopping and using consumer goods in their social relationships as rewards, promises and bribes.

Careful shoppers   15%
These people find shopping fairly pleasurable, but seem to be careful shoppers, enjoying the use of the products bought rather than the process of selecting them. They avoid the alternative market and are moderately economical in their shopping habits.

"ON THE WEIRD REQUEST SCALE, YOU GUYS JUST SCORED A NINE."

LISA BONET

True, it's not exactly normal to rake through a girl's garbage. But at least we asked her first.

When actress Lisa Bonet finally agreed, it was our eyebrows that were raised.

Why, for instance, did she throw away a perfectly good pair of jeans? What was on the video tape? And why book a double room at the swanky Beverly Hills Hotel when she lives just a block away? We can't say. Lisa could. But she won't.

What we can figure out is that she's into health food, owns a dog and gets sent stacks of scripts.

She also drinks Schlitz. (This ad would have looked pretty dumb if she didn't.) Only ever brewed in the U.S. of A, the light, refreshing taste of Schlitz is now available in the U.K.

Ordering anything less authentic could get you a ten on the weird request scale.

IN AMERICA, YOU ARE WHAT YOU TRASH.

Thrifty shoppers   18%

These people find some pleasure in shopping, especially enjoying shopping for clothes, food, presents and shopping with the family compared to window shopping. They are thrifty, shopping around for the best buy, waiting for the sales for expensive purchases. They use all forms of the alternative market to buy goods.

(Adapted from Lunt and Livingstone 1992: 89–94)

Rather than assuming that everyone is preoccupied with shopping, then, what Lunt and Livingstone mean when they say that people's identities are constituted in relation to consumer culture is that their identities are bound up with the negotiation of a set of oppositions deriving from consumer culture. These oppositions include:

cash	credit
simplicity	complexity
budgeting	borrowing
institutional control	individual responsibility
necessities	luxuries
being careful	having pleasure
second-hand	new
control	loss of control

(Adapted from Lunt and Livingstone 1992: 149)

Lunt and Livingstone are keen to stress the variety and complexity of the views people hold in relation to consumption, and point out that most people formulate a set of strategies or rules to guide their consumer decisions. They suggest that these strategies are motivated by the desire for control over the social environment; they have a strong rhetorical component, expressing people's aspirations, hopes and fears as well as their actual practices. The rules are a way of negotiating the oppositions between opportunity and danger, freedom and responsibility, pleasure and the moral order. Lunt and Livingstone identify the following common strategies or rules of resistance:

1   make appropriate social comparisons – do not think a good is a necessity for yourself just because someone else has it;
2   follow guiding principles – follow abstract principles of consumption which provide a framework for taking numerous specific decisions;

3   adopt coping actions;
4   maintain self-control;
5   follow warnings.

These everyday rules or resistances are seen by Livingstone and Lunt to be a response to the push and pull of the oppositions at work in consumer culture.

But how are these oppositions identified? Lunt and Livingstone suggest that certain objects characteristic of consumer culture – such as, for example, the credit card, the cash dispenser or the shopping mall – act as key symbols in the setting up and negotiation of these oppositions.

The cash dispenser

The modern wayside shrine – never mind rewards in heaven: a moment's devotion produces cash upfront right now! Drawbacks: sin punished by having your card eaten, and pilgrimages to find a machine in working order. (Kohn 1988a: 180)

The credit card, for example, was frequently attacked by their interviewees as a symbol of decline, although most people interviewed had one, because it symbolized a perceived lack of self-control and a perceived loss of traditional community feeling. More generally, the credit system was seen as a major source of loss of individual control, satisfying the desire for ownership of possessions but leading to a lack of self-discipline. There was a belief that the so-called traditional values of thrift, prudence and patience were being replaced by personal debt, avarice and impatience (epitomized by the character Gordon Gekko in the film *Wall Street*, who claims 'Greed is good'). Yet, as Lunt and Livingstone point out, credit cards are, in fact, responsible for only a very small proportion of personal credit in

Britain today. They thus conclude that it is the *symbolic meanings* of the credit card that are really significant in defining these opposi-tions and point to the relation between these symbolic meanings and anxieties about personal or self-identity, especially the dimen-sion of identity to do with self-control or lack of self-control.

It is perhaps not surprising then that it is the playful manipulation of the dimension of identity to do with self-control that Featherstone (1991) identifies as fundamental to the lifestyle of the new middle classes. As noted earlier, Featherstone describes what he calls calculated decontrol, or the calculated capacity to move into and out of involvement with things or objects, as an especially important component of the distinctive lifestyle developed by the new middle classes. The term refers, not to 'losing control', but to the capacity of the individual strategically to de-control the emo-tions, to open him or herself up to an extended range of sensations and enjoy the swing between the pleasures of immersion in an object and those of detached distance. It is related by Featherstone to the aestheticization of everyday life. It can be seen as the capacity to enjoy moving from being in control to out of control back to being in control again, that is, *to move between* the oppositions which Lunt and Livingstone identify as especially significant in contempo-rary understandings of the self.

The manipulation of this movement is seen by Featherstone and others as the source of what they describe as the playfulness of con-temporary culture, explaining its parodic, nostalgic and kitsch impulses as the individual moves in and out of the multiple histories or cultural biographies of goods, making and unmaking authenticity as he or she chooses. It can also be seen, however, as a magical solu-tion to what is described by Helga Dittmar (1992) as a fundamental contradiction in contemporary understandings of self-identity: the idealism–materialism paradox.

In describing this paradox, Dittmar points out that the dominant Western ideal of personal identity is that it is unique and autonomous, uninfluenced by other people and socio-cultural sur-roundings. Idealistically, then, personal identity should be indepen-dent of material context in the sense that *we are who we are no matter what we possess.* Yet, as she notes, this view is in apparent conflict with the fundamental axiom of contemporary consumer culture: that identity is defined through the exchange, possession and use of goods (the subtitle of her book is *To have is to be*). What is being suggested here is that the manipulation of the dimension of identity to do with control or lack of control in the lifestyle of the new middle classes appears to provide a (magical) solution to this paradox in that it suggests that the link between identity and possession is simply a matter of play. In so far as the link can legitimately be defined as one of play the paradox can be made to disappear: possessions can be used to express, transform, even create identity, but this creation is not to be taken seriously – it is only play – and thus does not contradict the belief that we are who we are no matter what we possess. Indeed, as Featherstone notes, in the context of the lifestyle of the new middle classes to take the link too seriously would be to reveal oneself as a person without discrimination, style or taste.

However, as noted above, while the new middle classes have sought to legitimate this magical solution to the idealism–materialism paradox in the elevation of their taste as a lifestyle, the manipulation of the dimension of self-control by other groups has not so easily been accepted as playfulness. Moreover, the (mythical) figure of the 'abnormal consumer' or 'addictive personality' indicates the extent of public anxiety about the consequences of the unchecked spread of this calculated decontrol of emotions beyond the enclaves of the new middle classes. Furthermore, as Dittmar points out, the magical solution to the idealism–materialism paradox identified by Featherstone obscures a situation in which

> the argument that all are much freer to acquire the lifestyle – and thus identity – of their choice runs the risk of slipping into an imaginary world of equal opportunities, and thus of becoming a rhetoric that all are equal, even if some remain more equal than others. (1992:201)

It is thus a magical solution which is potentially the site of much political conflict.

This view that the individual can fashion him or herself through the exercise of will has a parallel in the view put forward by some academics that we live in a society in which the individual has become a key site of political change. One representative of this view is the sociologist Anthony Giddens. In his recent writings (1991, 1992), Giddens has located the significance of the notion of identity in contemporary society in relation to a movement away from *emancipatory politics* to *life politics*. Emancipatory politics in its various forms is seen by Giddens to have been concerned with releasing people from the constraints of traditional social positions – of class, gender, race and age – by breaking down hierarchies. Clearly, as the final section of this chapter indicates, consumer culture is seen by some as an important process in this breakdown, or at least in the refiguring of these hierarchies, through the resources it offers for a more flexible relationship between the individual and self-identity.

Life politics, in contrast to emancipatory politics, is said to be a politics of self-determination. The protests, campaigns, strikes and rallies associated with emancipatory politics were an attempt to reveal the invasion of people's everyday lives by social and political forces of domination and exploitation. Life politics is said to work at a different level. It concerns a *reflexive* relation to the self in which the individual is less concerned with protesting about the actions of others than with taking control (that phrase again) of the shape of his or her own life through the negotiation of self-identity. Giddens writes that life politics 'is a politics of self-actualisation in a reflexively organised environment, where that reflexivity links self and body to systems of global scope' (1991: 214). As it has become possible for the individual to construct personal identities in a reflexively organized environment, so identity has become a social issue, a topic for public debate, and a site of political change.

Prominent examples of this life politics are the emergence of the so-called green consumer in the late 1980s (Simmons 1994) and the lesbian, gay and queer subcultures that have recently emerged in response to the recognition of the buying power of the so-called pink pound (Hamer and Budge 1994). So, for instance, Simmons describes the emergence of the green consumer in terms of a reflexive process, in which a variety of different actors and intermediaries within the green consumer field of action, including environmental groups, retailers, product manufacturers, market researchers, consumer groups and government departments, are brought together, each of them representing the green consumer and the nature of green consumer action in different ways. (See figure 8.1.)

Giddens argues that consumer culture has contributed to a reflexive understanding of identity, in so far as it provides many of the resources with which individuals fashion their own personal and political identities. He and other writers (see Beck, Giddens and Lash 1994) have pointed out that the aestheticization of everyday life that is part of consumer culture can be seen as an important part of such an altered world, as an enhancement of the material environment in such a way as simultaneously to numb and excite the senses. Indeed, the process of aestheticization is sometimes held to have culminated in 'total environments', such as theme parks, holiday worlds or tourist bubbles, small, enclosed, self-contained worlds which overload the senses (see 'Nike town'). For Giddens, the mod-

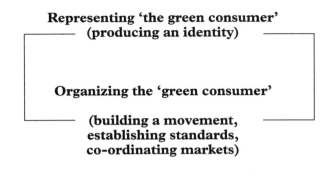

**Representing 'the green consumer'
(producing an identity)**

Organizing the 'green consumer'

**(building a movement,
establishing standards,
co-ordinating markets)**

Figure 8.1 The reflexive construction of the green consumer
Source: Simmons 1995.

ern condition entails both opportunities and dangers for the individual. The material conditions within which and in response to which we form our identities are not always benign. They both afford possibilities for personal development and they threaten that development – increased freedoms go hand in hand with increased responsibilities. But is this reflexive relation the same for all individuals? Do we all have access to the same freedoms and suffer from the same responsibilities? Is consumer culture an adventure playground for everyone?

There are a number of arguments which suggest that it is not. First, there is the fact that a significant proportion of the populations of Euro-American societies live in poverty. While, as chapter 1 pointed out, economic deprivation does not necessarily mean that an individual will not participate in consumer culture, it clearly sets some limits on the nature of that participation.

From Adlands ideal home (Mont-Blanc pen, Braun calculator, Tizio lamp) to Sainsbury's fresh food counter (why buy Radicchio rather than Iceberg? Kos it says much more about you than ordinary lettuce can) . . . Design is everything and everything is design. Designer death on your television screen; designer water in your fridge; designer labels in your wardrobe; designer condoms between your sheets. The designer lifestyle can be yours – if the price is right. (*The Face* 1988: 154)

In addition, as chapters 4, 5, 6 and 7 have suggested, the capacity to exercise consumer choice is shaped by the uneven history of the development of consumer culture and is, in part, a matter of how aesthetic knowledge and cultural resources are distributed within the art-culture system. Moreover, these chapters suggest that while the enjoyment of the capacity for calculated decontrol – playfulness – may be characteristic of the new middle classes, it is not the only way in which the movement between the oppositions of being in control and out of control is negotiated in the context of consumer culture. They show that the negotiation of the dimension of identity in terms of being in or out of control is not understood by everyone in terms of the calculated decontrol of emotions, of enjoyment or play. It is not necessarily a project of heroization; nor do the practices of masquerade, imitation and putting-identity-into-process necessarily conceal the paradox identified by Dittmar; rather, they may serve to highlight this paradox, contributing to the tensions which disturb the legitimacy of the lifestyle promoted by the new middle classes.

In chapter 5, for example, it was argued that men and women do not have the same relation to the performance of their personal identities, in paid work, at home or in leisure activities. The chapter suggested that, because understandings of femininity are closely tied to the idea of masquerade, women, on the whole, do not have the same capacity to claim ownership of the identities they perform as men. This was seen to be a consequence of the relative lack of control that women have in relation to the definition of their own self-identity, which is typically set in relation to masculine demands and expectations. As the saying goes, 'beauty is in the eye of the beholder'. It was suggested that women's relationship to personal identity is therefore not only or not best described as reflexivity, strategic experimentation or the calculated decontrol that Featherstone describes as typical of the new middle classes, but as an enforced decontrol, in which women's claims to self-possession are often on shaky ground.

The political implications for women of being unable to lay claim to self-possession, of not being able to exercise calculated decontrol, have been understood in a number of different ways. On the one hand, it is argued that it is (middle-class) men who have been most duped by consumer culture, since their typical mode of participation suggests that they are under the misapprehension that, as individuals, they are sufficiently in control to be able to enjoy losing it, temporarily at least. This can be seen as a fantasy, blinding these

Nike Town, Chicago's sporting pantheon
Ruth Shurman

When Midwestern children persuade their parents to visit Chicago, they don't want to eat deep-pan pizza atop the world's tallest building, or tour the haunts of Al Capone. They want to visit a shoe shop.

This is something more than your average shoe shop. More, even, than a shoe emporium. It is Nike Town, a temple dedicated to a trademark. Nike Town is the biggest pull on Michigan Avenue's Magnificent Mile. Every day, thousands of people make the pilgrimage to revel in the prowess of the corporation and the sportsmen it endorses.

In the grey-marbled entrance hall, an array of framed *Sports Illustrated* covers portrays the Nike team, from Andre Agassi to Charles Barkley. Ambient music echoes through the lobby as you pause to read the reverent paean to athleticism: 'To be a professional athlete is to be a member of one of the most exclusive groups in the world... Among the great, a few become recognised as the best.'

In Chicago, the best is unequivocally Michael Jordan, who led the Chicago Bulls to a three-peat (three consecutive National Basketball Association championships). A lifesize white plaster cast of M.J. in mid-flight, mesh shorts aflutter, dangles behind a glass panel inscribed, 'A Good Guy Who Plays Great Ball'. A toddler in green dungarees points at the cast, chuckles and shouts the Pepsi slogan, 'I'd like to be like Mike'.

Around the corner, the showcasing of products begins in earnest. A genealogy of the sports shoe progresses abruptly from 8000BC (the sage brush woven slipper) to the morning in 1971 when Nike founder, Bill

Bowerman, shrieked 'Eureka?' at the breakfast table, poured latex into a waffle iron and produced the first Nike track sole. Exhibits are organised for each sport, with a shoe and clothing collection alongside. The basic design – matt black metalwork and curving bare brick walls – is decorated accordingly. Benches in the tennis area are a discreet All-England green, while the women's fitness room has pink and orange vinyl seating. The current Nike slogan ('Just Do It') is omnipresent, on the walls, on T-shirts, posters and TV monitors. Although the shop clears about $100,000 of shoes and clothing every day, the place manages to avoid exuding a shopping atmosphere.

Over in the basketball department, people flock to the altar to Michael Jordan. No male seems able to resist practising his wrist action and slam-dunk shooting style as he steps on to the mini basketball court. Hidden speakers play the sound of crowds cheering and $150 sneakers squeaking over a wooden court. A 30-foot tall photograph of M.J. leaping through ethereal, swirling clouds hangs behind the hoop. Underneath, there is a quote from William Blake about soaring birds.

Further along, the sound of twittering birdsong and footsteps on gravel and twigs announces your arrival in the cross-country running department. Round the back, the cycling gear attracts a sniggering couple who toy with the cycling shorts designed to make man's day in the saddle a little more comfortable. 'Hey, honey,' says the girl, pouting at her partner, 'I bet you need the extra padding.'

On the top floor, everyone clusters to get a good look at the exhibits in the T-shirt gallery. The shirts are mounted and framed. You flip through them like posters in an art shop, to see if you prefer the Nike hip-hop T-shirt, the Nike Rasta T-shirt, the Nike Fifties T-shirt or the classic Nike swoop logo T-shirt. In an adjoining room, a wide, concave video screen continually plays Nike commercials. Nobody mistakes this for a marketing device; it is, of course, a chance to see your favourite Nike moments once again.

A murmur of nostalgia greets the start of the black-and-white ad with a woman springing forth from a bath tub and sprinting away with a determined grimace on her face. The voiceover intones, 'You are born. And oh, how you wailed'. The Eighties ads seem very dated, targeting the executive who likes to work out between arbitrage sessions. The crop of '93 looks more like it was filmed on a gang-controlled housing project, a trend that could stimulate the proliferation of lethal sartorially-related shootings.

Past the baseball, the (American) football, the wrestling and the golf, there is a display devoted to Nike Town itself, with an annotated replica of the building. Beside it is the Nike Town clothing line, designed so you can dress up as Nike Town sales assistants when you get home and be part of the narcissistic dream. When a company gets this big, it scarcely needs to sponsor athletes and events any more. Nike Town is the event, the number one sight to see in this city. Like they say, 'Just Do It'.

The Observer Magazine

men to their manipulation by the workings of either the commodity-form or the sign-form. From this point of view women, at least, do not suffer under this illusion. On the other hand, it is argued that women should seek to assert their rights to self-possession and consumer culture. In this view, women's mobilization of femininity as a mask or masquerade and their expertise in consuming provides them with a valuable resource in the struggles over authenticity that are part of consumer culture, albeit a resource that is double-edged since it is a relation to the self in which the claims of self-possession are contingent and never secure.

The picture is different again, once race is recognized as an important aspect of the development of consumer culture. It was argued in chapter 6 that the participation of black people in consumer culture has been simultaneously rendered invisible and appropriated as a source of authenticity in many white lifestyles. So, for example, reference was made to how the imperialist phenomenon of cultural cross-dressing – what Gail Ching-Liang Low (1989) describes as 'the fantasy of the white man disguised as native' – has been adopted and adapted in the contemporary invitation to white consumers to change races. At the same time, however, the value of imitation or mimicry was also identified as a technique by which black people have come to inhabit the unstable terrain of contemporary culture. While this technique may result in a much less secure position in consumer culture than that available to many white people, it is one which allows for a flexible, responsive constantly mutating relation to identity as a matter of political strategy. Moreover, given the continuing intensification of commodity production on a global scale, and its apparently insatiable appetite for novelty, it may be that the cultural practices of diasporas are becoming more likely to serve as the basis for the creation of black identities in processes of unsettling, recombination, hybridization and cut-and-mix.

The instability of identity is seen to be even greater in relation to age. In chapter 7 the argument that time is increasingly disengaged from age or generation in consumer culture was presented; as a consequence, it was suggested that, in the time of post-subcultural pop, anyone can buy youth(fulness) as a commodity in the global hypermarket. For some writers this is seen to have dislocated young people, while for others, such as Redhead, this does not necessarily represent a move *back* to the future, but can offer a move *forward* to the past.

These chapters thus suggest both that the negotiation of self-control is not always playful, and that this lack of playfulness is a consequence of the fact that not all individuals are in a position to exercise the capacity of calculated decontrol in the same way: members of different social groups have different relationships to this dimension of their self-identities. Reflexivity may thus be too general a term to describe relations between individuals and their personal identities, obscuring the multiple and sometimes contradictory relations between the individual reflection upon and performance of personal identity carried out by people who are members of different social groups. While our environment might be increasingly organized to facilitate reflexivity, we are not able, nor do we all choose, to respond to it in the same way.

Moreover, some writers would suggest that there has recently been an increase in the public expression of anxieties in relation to the idealism– materialism paradox with the consequence that the playfulness identified by Featherstone as characteristic of the new middle classes has become less and less realizable as cultural capital. These anxieties feed on the disturbing ambiguity of the use of phrases such as 'making up your mind' to describe the process of making a decision. Rachel Bowlby (1993) identifies a number of different ways in which the phrase 'making up your mind' is understood; they include:

1   supply a lack, as in phrases such as 'make up the difference' or 'make up for lost time';
2   add something, with a positive connotation of enhancement or adornment, ending in a situation in which someone is 'made up' (in contrast to the first meaning, which merely involves the avoidance of something negative);
3   putting together pieces;
4   to invent, with a buried connotation of fictionality.

The multiplicity of these meanings illustrates the complexity of the processes by which decisions are made or choices taken; all attest to the difficulties and uncertainties involved in making choices. Is making up one's mind an arbitrary process, part of the artificial making up of an imaginary whole person out of bits and pieces? Or is it the decisive, rational, goal-oriented act of the sovereign individual? That these processes are being made ever yet more fraught, so Eve Sedgwick (1994) suggests, is a consequence of the ways in which *sites of volition*, or sites for the exercise of the will, are being multiplied in contemporary consumer culture.

Sedgwick suggests that there has been a multiplication of sites in the fields of exercise, health, therapy, diet, love and sexuality as well as the art-culture system, and that this has led to a widespread anxiety in society about the exercise of individual will. This anxiety is expressed in the fear that we are all living in the shadow of the threat of becoming addicts of some kind or another. (In Lunt and Livingstone's discussion groups, a common topic was the pressure to consume, a pressure which people felt was recent and growing (1992: 29–33)). In the past, the concept of addiction – of losing the capacity to exercise one's will and being under a compulsion to act – was defined in relation to a special category of substances, so-called foreign or noxious substances, alcohol or drugs. Certain substances were believed to be dangerous because they were seen to break down the individual's 'natural' capacity to regulate his or her consumption reasonably. The danger was attributed to the substance. But now, it seems, addiction can be applied to consumption of almost any kind of substance.

Food, for example, is a substance to which, it is believed by some, one can now be addicted; and you can also be addicted to activities – to exercise, to keep-fit, to relationships, to sex and, of course, to shopping. Moreover, one can be addicted not only to too much of a substance such as food – in which case, you might be invited to attend an Overeaters Anonymous self-help group, but also to its refusal – as anorexics are said to be, or its controlled, intermittent ingestion – as in the case of bulimics. As the number of activities to which one can be addicted grows, it seems even trying to control addiction can be addictive. As Sedgwick wryly notes,

> Within the last year, there has even been a spate of journalism on the theme that the self-help groups and books that have popularized this radical critique of addiction, and that promote themselves as the only way out of it, may themselves be addictive. (1994:133)

She suggests that, since it is no longer the substance that is identified as the locus of danger, then it must be the relation between the individual and the substance or the activity, *the individual exercise of will itself*, that is being identified as dangerous in contemporary society. She concludes that the pervasiveness of the vocabulary of addiction to describe almost any activity is an indication that the assertion of will – making up one's mind – has become increasingly problematic in contemporary Euro-American societies. All of us,

she suggests, are caught between the 'twin hurricanes' of 'Just Do It' and 'Just Say No'.

What is important about Sedgwick's argument, then, is that it points to the fact that while the notion of consumer choice is sometimes interpreted positively, as in the celebration of the skills of the calculating, risk-taking, playful consumer who enjoys the swing from being in control to being out of control and back again, it is also interpreted negatively as in the figure of the addict, who is out of control. Indeed, one interpretation of Sedgwick's analysis is that the dominance of consumer culture itself may be threatened by the spread of anxieties concerning the potential harmfulness of the spread of calculated decontrol. It may be that as economic conditions have worsened in the current recession, the magical solution of the playful creation of self in the lifestyle of the new middle classes has been revealed to be illusory – the bubble has burst – and that consumer culture is facing a deep crisis. Evidence for this view is to be found not only in anxieties about addiction, but also in the emergence of an ethos of anti-materialism and the ecological critique of non-sustainable growth.

G is for Greed

Greed was an Eighties motivating force, diluting the human in an unflinching quest for selfish success. The Me Generation stomped adamantly through a self-created world of material gratification, single minded careerism and constant paranoia. 'Greed is good', intoned *Wall Street's* Gordon Gekko in a speech which summed up the Eighties rationale with terrifying accuracy, but as with most of the decade's trends, it's rapidly being superceded by general disillusionment. Live Aid gave impetus to a growing sense of global charity and, while bringing with it a certain dull tokenism, its offshoots (Save the Rainforests, Ferry Aid, Comic Relief) suggested a universal rejection of self-serving avarice. Too much greed has left us, inevitably, with gut ache. (Mathur 1989:61)

However, it is important to recognize here that while there may be some evidence to suggest that the lifestyle adopted by the new middle classes in the 1980s is falling out of favour, this does not mean that the significance of consumer culture itself is fading. Whether positively or negatively valued, it is still some interpretation of the capacity to exercise consumer choice that is deemed to be central to the idea of personal or self-identity in contemporary society. From this point of view, it is interesting to note that some aspects of both the contemporary ethos of anti-materialism and green politics are explicitly intertwined with a politics of consumption. How one exercises the will to choose – either by choosing to purchase one good rather than another, or by choosing not to purchase certain goods at all – is still taken as an indication of who one is.

In other words, 'consumer choice' is still the means by which our society thinks about individual agency and autonomy and makes judgements (good or bad) about personal identity. The significance of consumer culture is thus to be found in the fact that the individual is no longer judged by him or herself or by society in terms of how well they carry out their duty or responsibility in relation to some wider collective or external morality ('the family', 'the community', 'the greater good of all' or 'God's will'), but in terms of how well they exercise their capacity to make a (consumer) choice.

The individual, consumer culture and social life

A further theme that has been addressed in this book is whether consumer culture has contributed to the decline in significance of modes of belonging to class, gender, race and age and whether membership of any of these groups is increasingly to be seen as *elective* rather than ascribed, that is, whether it is a matter of choice, rather than imposed. So, for example, Featherstone asks:

> What does it mean to suggest that long-held fashion-codes have been violated, that there is a war against uniformity, a surfeit of difference which results in a loss of meaning? The implication is that we are moving towards a society without fixed status groups in which the adoption of styles of life (manifest in choice of clothes, leisure activities, consumer goods, bodily dispositions) which are fixed to specific groups have been surpassed. (1991: 83)

As he goes on to point out, if this inference is correct, then we would be moving towards a society in which previously existing social divisions and forms of social inequality are coming to be irrelevant, where the social is losing its significance as a reference point of identity, and where collective solidarity (or what is sometimes called collectivism) is disappearing. This is what Baudrillard (1988) has described as the implosion of the social, its collapse from within as art (or, rather, artifice) triumphs over reality.

However, Featherstone himself suggests that what we are witnessing in the claim for a movement beyond fashion is in fact a move *within*, not *beyond*, the social. For Featherstone, this disturbance to the social field can be understood as a consequence of the strategies of the new middle classes who are redefining the terms of exchange between cultural and economic capital, but are not undermining the field as such. It has been argued here, however, that these disturbances should not just be understood in relation to the actions of class groups, but also to those based on gender, race and age.

One approach to the reworking of the social focuses on the emergence of what is called *neo-tribalism*. This is an approach that has been proposed by a number of writers including Maffesoli (1991; 1993) and Bauman (1990; 1992a; 1992b), although, in these two cases, with rather different political conclusions. Both adopt the concept *neo*-tribalism to describe the groupings arising in contemporary society as a variant of the tribal life described by 'classical' anthropologists.

What makes the 'tribes' one joins by purchasing their symbols superficially similar to the real tribes is that both set themselves apart from other groups and make a lot of fuss about underlining their separate identity and avoiding confusion; both cede their own identity to their members – define them by proxy. But here the similarity ends and a decisive difference begins: the 'tribes' (let us call them henceforth **neo-tribes** to prevent misunderstanding) could not care less about who proclaim themselves members. They have no councils of elders or boards or admission committees to decide who has the right to be in and who ought to be kept out. They employ no gatekeepers and no border guards. They have no institution of authority, no supreme court which may pronounce on the correctness of members' behaviour. (Maffesoli 1991: 206–7)

Whether excluded or included, membership of the pre-modern tribe was seldom a matter of individual choice; in contrast, neo-tribes are formed by a multitude of individual acts of self-identification. Maffesoli claims:

Overall, within massification, processes of condensation are constantly occurring through which more or less ephemeral tribal groupings are organized which cohere on the basis of their own minor values, and which attract and collide with each other in an endless dance, forming themselves into a constellation whose vague boundaries are perfectly fluid. (1991: 12)

Neo-tribes are marked by their fluidity: they are locally condensed and dispersed, periodically assembled and scattered. They are momentary condensations in the flux of everyday consumer life; however, while they are fragile, ephemeral and unstable, they command intense emotional or affectual involvement from their fickle members. Maffesoli writes:

it is no longer possible to say that any aspect of social life, not cookery, nor attention to appearance, nor small celebrations, nor relaxing walks, is frivolous or insignificant. In so far as such activities may provide a focus for collective emotions, they constitute real underground movements, demands for life which have to be analysed. 'Banal' forms of existence may, from a utilitarian or rationalist perspective, serve no purpose but they are full of meaning, even if it tends to get worn away in practice. (1991: 8)

The inner organization, aims and aspirations of neo-tribes are unimportant, argues Maffesoli; their existence is the only purpose they need. Membership does not require an admission procedure; neo-tribes exist solely by virtue of individual decisions to sport the insignia of tribal allegiance. They persevere only thanks to their continuing seductive capacity; they cannot outlive their power of attraction.

Maffesoli further argues that the existing sociological categories of class, gender, race and age are no longer adequate to describe these groups, which are short-lived and 'transversal', operating *across* existing categories and *along* fluctuating and short-lived networks of affinity, interest and neighbourhood. Individuals move between these groupings incessantly, modifying their behaviour, outlook and identity as they move. However, the individual is not isolated, but is part and parcel of an emotional geography of places – sports stadia, concert halls, shopping malls – which are invested with the emotion that previously characterized sacred sites. Furthermore, neo-tribes are to be understood in terms of aesthetics, a recognition, Maffesoli suggests, that points to 'the importance of the "immaterial" in the very heart of the "material"' (1991: 11).

The role of aesthetics, Maffesoli argues, is visible in the practices of self-fashioning adopted in contemporary tribes, practices in which the individual fashions or creates his or her own self-identity as if it were an artwork. So, for example,

> Whether trendy exercises in sensory isolation, or various forms of body-building, or jogging, or Eastern techniques of one sort or another, the body is being constructed as a value, even to the extent of its epiphany. . . . Note, however, that even in its most private aspects, the body is being constructed only in order to be seen; it is theatralized [*sic*] to the highest degree. Within advertising, fashion, dance, the body is adorned only to be made into a spectacle. (1991: 18–19)

However, it is important to note that, for Maffesoli, these practices of self-fashioning do not result in greater individuation or privatization but, rather, the 'functions of aggregation and reinforcement which I call *sociality*' (1991: 19).

In contrast to Maffesoli, Bauman sees the phenomenon of neo-tribalism, which he describes in superficially very similar terms to Maffesoli, to have very different political implications, tending to argue for the 'unambiguously individualistic impact of the neo-tribal phenomenon' (1992b: 25). Bauman argues that the individual – increasingly detached from his or her membership of the social categories of class, gender, race and age – is engaged in the tribal scene in a privatized relationship of fluctuating freedom and dependence in a desperate search for community. While membership of neo-tribes appears to be a matter of choice, the way of life they offer is, in fact, prescribed: 'If the neo-tribes themselves do not care to guard their entry, there is someone else who does: *the market*' (1991: 207).

Rather than being a source of new forms of sociality, of collective belonging and association, Bauman believes that neo-tribes are an adaptive response to the disaggregation of sociality and the resulting confusion this creates for the increasingly isolated individual faced with contradictory advice from a bewildering array of experts on how to care for the self: 'Tribes are simultaneously refuges for those trying in vain to escape the loneliness of privatized survival, and the stuff from which private policies of survival, and thus the identity of the survivor are self-assembled' (1992b: 25). He argues that not only do 'fear campaigns' promote specific products of expert knowledge (in the form of diets, exercise programmes, fashion and beauty advice, psychological profiling, and so on), but the contemporary cult of specialists diffuses feelings of helplessness and incompetence which produce a need for the continual assistance of 'people in the know'. He writes:

Neo-tribalism is an indispensable complement of a habitat in which private survivals are serviced by the variegated and often contradictory advice of experts. . . . The choice, however, is a daunting task, as the hierarchies of relevance suggested by the experts servicing different problem areas are hardly ever compatible. It is in this difficult yet indispensable matter of choice that tribes perform a crucial function, as they sanction global *lifestyles*, each offering its own structure of relevances. . . . For the individual, joining a tribe means adopting a peculiar lifestyle; or, rather, the road to a coherent lifestyle leads through the adoption of tribally sanctioned structure of relevances complete with a kit of totemic symbols. (1992b: 25)

For Bauman, neo-tribalism thus encourages a process of individualization by supporting an ethos of survivalism; this is an ethos which 'can be put to socially destructive as much as to socially creative uses. More often than not, it is put to uses that are both destructive and constructive' (1992b: 12). Bauman suggests that the lifestyle of survivalism is one in which the individual is encouraged to take responsibility for him or herself *as* an individual. The resources of self-identity – health, beauty and taste – are managed for individual profit. This view is in contrast to that adopted by Maffesoli, for whom the opposition between the individual and the social is being *fused* in 'the confusional societal' of neo-tribalism (1993: 4). For Maffesoli, individuals no longer have functions accruing from their social position, but roles acquired through the reversible practices of self-fashioning, roles which enable the feeling of participating in a general representation or spectacle, and thus 'privilege the grasping of the whole' (1993: 4).

She has been called a fashion guru, a psychic, a prophet, even a sorceress. She is Li Edelkoort, a 43-year-old Dutch woman who probably has more influence on the way we dress and live than any designer.

Edelkoort is Europe's leading trends forecaster. From the loft of a converted factory in Paris's arrondissement, she tells the future with the confidence of a fairground crystal-ball gazer . . .

Her big new theory is that the era of the individual is fading.

'This individualism has made us very alone. Not everyone can be like Madonna, with the energy to create a new self every day. People are regrouping themselves together, even if it's just to dance the tango or cook together. There could be a political follow-up to this. Groups are wanting to take things into their hands – and politicians are not aware of this, or are pretending not to be aware. (Tredre 1993)

Complaints about apathy and depoliticisation are as old as politics itself. They are the stock-in-trade of activists who celebrate the golden age of political culture in some earlier moment – 1945, 1968 or whenever. But the past decade has witnessed a massive loss of confidence in what many held to be the bedrock of formal democracy. Faith in government, in the credibility of politicians, in the power of governments to do anything, has hit an all time low . . .

Is there really nowhere to go but the shops ? . . .

What needs saying at this stage is that our conception of politics must be prised open. . . . Today's consumer culture straddles public and private space, creating blurred areas in between. Privatised car culture, with its collective red nose days and stickers for lead-free petrol; cosmetics as the quintessential expression of consumer choice now carry anxieties over eco-politics. These are the localised points where consumption meshes with social demands and aspirations. So the above cannot be about individualism *versus* collectivism, but about articulating the two in a new relation that can form the basis for a future common sense. (Mort 1989: 40–1)

In many ways, the notion of neo-tribalism describes well the outcome for social life of the processes described here as consumer culture (although the use of the term 'neo-tribalism' can be criticized
for the similarity between its reliance upon racialized notions of 'the
primitive' or 'animalism' and those techniques for the appropriation
of a racialized authenticity described in chapter 6. It can thus be
seen as the academic equivalent of the painted faces – black and
white – employed by Benetton to sell its jumpers.) Indeed, the
aspect of the refiguring of the social field which has been given most
attention here has been the way in which consumer culture has provided the resources for an increasingly stylized relation between an
individual and his or her self-identity. However, as noted above, it
has been argued that this stylization is not brought into play in the
same way for all individuals.

This argument has particular implications for the question of
whether consumer culture is undermining the basis of group
belonging in contemporary society. As noted above, Featherstone
suggests that the individualizing potential offered to people in consumer culture to fashion themselves is sometimes assumed to be
undercutting any sense of belonging to social groups, and some
interpretations of Maffesoli and Bauman's description of neo-tribalism would suggest that they both support this view. However, other
writers hold that this view is wrong. Alan Warde, for example,
asserts the continuing importance of group solidaristic considera-
tions in the choice and development of lifestyles:

> Though necessarily aware of the styles associated with neo-tribes, the
> consumer chooses the group as much as, and probably more than the
> style; and membership of the group commands a certain path through
> the enormous number of commodities on sale. Belonging comes before
> identity. (1994: 70)

He thus suggests that group belonging still precedes and shapes participation in lifestyles. However, it may be that it is neither that
belonging comes before self-identity nor that self-identity comes
before belonging, but that belonging and self-identity are done
together, simultaneously, although not always in the same way.

In general terms, the analyses discussed in this book have suggested that what it is to be middle- or working-class, to be a man or
a woman, to be black or white, to be young or old is not simply a
matter of social positioning, but is also in part defined by the individual's relation to self-identity, a relation closely linked to notions

of authenticity. Or, to put this another way, what it is to belong to a social group is, in part, a particular kind of relation to self. (This is not to argue that individual self-assembly is the same as self-determination; merely that an individual's mode of self-assembly is one way in which social belonging is done: it is both shaped by and is able to shape the ties of social belonging.) In the course of this book it has been argued that this relation has been and is being transformed or reorganized by contemporary consumer culture: that it is the different kinds of stylized relation enabled by consumer culture that are helping to shape the *specific* kinds of belonging to the social groupings of class, gender, race and age that are characteristic of contemporary society. In other words, consumer culture provides an important context for the development of novel relationships of individual self-assembly *and* group membership.

However, these relationships do not function in the same way for everyone and, consequently, they do not enable everyone to understand themselves as individuals in possession of themselves. In this sense, social groupings, rather than being displaced, are being reworked in the diverse processes of stylization characteristic of contemporary consumer culture. This suggests that questions of difference, struggle and inequality will not disappear, but will surface in struggles between social groupings in different ways, including the politics of identity. As the processes of self-assembly are transformed in the practices of consumer culture, the co-ordinates of the social field are transformed: not flattened but redrawn.

Bibliography

Abercrombie, N. 1991: The privilege of the producer. In R. Keat and N. Abercrombie (eds), *Enterprise Culture*, London: Routledge, 171–86.

—— 1994: Authority and consumer society. In R. Keat, N. Whiteley and N. Abercrombie (eds), *The Authority of the Consumer*, London: Routledge, 43–57.

—— 1996: *Television and Society*. Cambridge: Polity.

—— Hill, S. and Turner, B. 1986: *Sovereign Individuals of Capitalism*. London: Allen and Unwin.

—— and Warde, A. 1988: *Contemporary British Society: A New Introduction to Sociology*. Cambridge: Polity.

Abrams, M. 1961: *Teenage Consumer Spending in 1959: Middle Class Boys and Girls*. London: London Press Exchange.

Adkins, L. 1995: *Gendered Work: Sexuality, Family and the Labour Market*. Buckingham and Bristol: Open University Press.

Adorno, T. 1974: *Minima Moralia: Reflections on a Damaged Life*. London: NLB.

—— and Horkheimer, M. 1979: *Dialectic of Enlightenment*. London: Allen Lane.

Amin, A. and Goddard, J. (eds) 1986: *Technological Change, Industrial Restructuring and Regional Development*. London: Allen and Unwin.

—— and Thrift, N. (eds) 1994: *Globalization, Institutional and Regional Development in Europe*. Oxford: Oxford University Press.

Anderson, M., Bechhofer, F. and Gershuny, J. 1994 (eds): *The Social Economy of the Household*. Oxford: Oxford University Press.

Ang, I. 1991: *Desperately Seeking the Audience*. London: Routledge.

Appadurai, A. 1986 (ed.): *The Social Life of Things*. Cambridge: Cambridge University Press.

—— 1993: Disjuncture and difference in the global cultural economy. In B. Robbins (ed.), *The Phantom Public Sphere*, Minneapolis: University of Minnesota Press, 269–97.

Back, L. and Quaade, V. 1993: Dream utopias, nightmare realities: Imaging race and culture within the world of Benetton advertising. *Third Text*, 22, 65–80.

Baudrillard, J. 1983: *Simulations*, trans. P. Foss, P. Patton and P. Beitchman. New York: Semiotext(e).

—— 1988: *Selected Writings* ed. M. Poster. Cambridge: Polity.

Bauman, Z. 1987: *Legislators and Interpreters: On Modernity, Postmodernity and Intellectuals*. Cambridge: Polity.

—— 1990: *Thinking Sociologically*. Oxford: Blackwell.

—— 1992a: *Intimations of Postmodernity*, London: Routledge.

—— 1992b: Survival as a social construct. *Theory, Culture and Society*, 9, 1–36.

Beck, U., Giddens, A. and Lash, S. 1994: *Reflexive Modernization*. Cambridge: Polity.

Bennett, O. 1991: Selective memory. *Creative Review*, November, 55–6.

Benson, R. and Armstrong, S. 1994: These people know what you want. *The Face*, July, 54–6.

Benson, S. P. 1986: *Counter Cultures: Saleswomen, Managers and Customers in American Department Stores*. Urbana and Chicago: University of Illinois Press.

Berger, J. 1972: *Ways of Seeing*. London: BBC Books.

Berland, J. 1992: Angels dancing: cultural technologies and the production of space. In L. Grossberg, C. Nelson and P. Treichler (eds), *Cultural Studies*, New York and London: Routledge, 38–50.

Bhabha, H. 1990 (ed.): *Nation and Narration*. London: Routledge.

—— 1994: *The Location of Culture*. London: Routledge.

Bourdieu, P. 1977: *Outline of a Theory of Practice*, trans. R. Nice. Cambridge: Cambridge University Press.

—— 1984: *Distinction: A Social Critique of the Judgement of Taste*. London: Routledge and Kegan Paul.

Bowlby, R. 1985: *Just Looking: Consumer Culture in Dreiser, Gissing and Zola*. New York and London: Methuen.

—— 1993: *Shopping with Freud*. London: Routledge.

Braverman, H. 1974: *Labour and Monopoly Capital*. London: Monthly Review Press.

Brooker, E. 1993: Ticking over. *Guardian Weekend*, 9 October, 36–8.

Campbell, C. 1989: *The Romantic Ethic and the Spirit of Modern Consumerism*. London: Blackwell.

Cannon, D. 1994: The desire for the new: its nature and social location as presented in theories of fashion and modern consumerism. In R. Silverstone and E. Hirsch (eds), *Consuming Technologies: Media and Information in Domestic Spaces*, London: Routledge, 48–67.

—— 1994: *Generation X and the New Work Ethic*. London: Demos.

Castells, M. 1977: *The Urban Question: A Marxist Approach*. London: Edward Arnold.

Chambers, E. 1992: Blackness as a cultural ikon. *Ten-8*, 2:3, 122–7.

Chua, B. Huat 1992: Shopping for women's fashion in Singapore. In R. Shields (ed.), *Lifestyle Shopping*, London and New York: Routledge.

Clifford, J. 1988: *The Predicament of Culture*. Cambridge and London: Harvard University Press.

Cohen, S. 1972: *Folk Devils and Moral Panics: The Creation of the Mods and Rockers*. London: McGibbon and Kee.

Coupland, D. 1992: *Generation X*. London: Abacus.

—— 1993: *Shampoo Planet*. London: Simon and Schuster.

Cowan, R. 1983: *More Work for Mother: The Ironies of Household Technology from the Open Hearth to the Microwave*. New York: Basic Books.

Cowe, R. (1994): The high street fights back. *Finance Guardian*, 24 December, 32.

de Certeau, M. 1988: *The Practice of Everyday Life*. Berkeley and Los Angeles and London: University of California Press.

Debord, G. 1977: *Society of the Spectacle*. Detroit: Black and Red.

Delphy, C. 1984: *Close to Home*. Cambridge: Hutchinson.

—— and Leonard, D. 1992: *Familiar Exploitation: A New Analysis of Marriage in Contemporary Western Societies*. Cambridge: Polity.

Dittmar, H. 1992: *The Social Psychology of Material Possessions*. Hemel Hempstead: Harvester Wheatsheaf.

Douglas, M. and Isherwood, B. 1979: *The World of Goods*. London: Allen Lane.

Dowling, R. 1993: Femininity, place and commodities: a retail case study. *Antipode*, 25: 4, 295–319.

Ducille, A. 1994: Dyes and dolls: multicultural Barbie and the merchandising of difference. *differences*, 6: 1, 46–68.

Eco, U. 1984: A guide to the neo-television of the 80s. *Framework*, 25, 18–27.

Elliott, R. 1994: Addictive consumption: function and fragmentation in post-modernity. *Journal of Consumer Policy*, 17, 159–79.

Enninful, E. 1994: On the street: the future of fashion discussed by the creative upstarts who are influencing its cutting edge. *i-D*, October, 36–40.

Evans, C. and Thornton, M. 1989: *Women and Fashion: A New Look*. London and New York: Quartet Books.

Ewen, S. 1976: *Captains of Consciousness: Advertising and the Social Roots of the Consumer Culture*. New York: McGraw Hill.

—— 1988: *All Consuming Images: The Politics of Style in Contemporary Culture*. New York: Basic Books.

—— and Ewen, E. 1982: *Channels of Desire*. New York: McGraw-Hill.

The Face, 1988: Designer everything, September, 154.

Featherstone, M. 1991: *Consumer Culture and Postmodernism*, London: Sage.

Fernando, S. 1992: 'Blackened images'. *Ten-8*, 2:3, 140–7.

Fine, B. and Leopold, E. 1993: *The World of Consumption*. London: Routledge.

Forty, A. 1986: *Objects of Desire*. London: Thames and Hudson.

Friedan, B. 1965: *The Feminine Mystique*. Harmondsworth: Penguin.

Friedman, J. 1991: Consuming desires: strategies of selfhood and appropriation. *Cultural Anthropology*, 6: 2, 154–64.

—— 1994: Introduction. In J. Friedman (ed.), *Consumption and Identity*, Chur: Harwood Academic Publishers, 1–23.

Frith, S. 1993: Youth/music/television. In S. Frith, A. Goodwin and L. Grossberg (eds), *Sound and Vision: The Music Video Reader*, London and New York Routledge, 67–85.

Fuller, M. 1982: Young, female and black. In E. Cashmore and B. Troyna (eds), *Black Youth in Crisis*, London: Allen and Unwin, 142–58.

Gaines, J. 1988: White privilege and looking relations – race and gender in feminist film theory. *Screen*, 29:4, 12–27.

Game, A. and Pringle, R. 1984: *Gender at Work*. London: Pluto Press.

Garnham, N. 1990: *Capitalism and Communication: Global Culture and the Economics of Information*. London: Sage.

Gates, H. J. Jr. 1992: The black man's burden. In G. Dent (ed.), *Black Popular Culture*, Seattle: Bay Press.

Gershuny, J. 1978: *After Industrial Society*. London: Macmillan.

—— 1983: *Social Innovation and the Division of Labour*. Oxford: Oxford University Press.

Giddens, A. 1991: *Modernity and Self-Identity*. Cambridge: Polity.

—— 1992: *The Transformation of Intimacy*. Cambridge: Polity.

Gilbert, S. M. and Gubar, S. 1988: *No Man's Land: The Place of the Woman Writer in the Twentieth Century*. New Haven: Yale University Press.

Gilroy, P. 1987: *There Ain't No Black in the Union Jack*. London: Unwin Hyman.

—— 1992: Wearing your art on your sleeve. *Ten-8*, 2: 3, 128–39.

—— 1993: *The Black Atlantic: Modernity and Double Consciousness*. London: Verso.

Habitat 1994: autumn/winter catalogue. London.

Hall, S. 1992: What is this 'Black' in Black popular culture? In G. Dent (ed.), *Black Popular Culture*, Seattle: Bay Press, 21–37.

Hamer, D. and Budge, B. 1994: *The Good, the Bad, and the Gorgeous: Popular Culture's Romance with Lesbianism*. London: Pandora.

Harvey, D. 1989: *The Condition of Postmodernity*. Oxford: Blackwell.

Haug, W. F. 1986: *Critique of Commodity Aesthetics*. Cambridge: Polity Press.

Hebdige, D. 1979: *Subculture: The Meaning of Style*. London: Methuen.

—— 1987: *Cut'n'Mix: Culture, Identity and Caribbean Music*. London: Methuen.

—— 1988: *Hiding in the Light: On Images and Things*. London: Routledge.

Hewitt, R. 1986: *White Talk – Black Talk: Inter-racial Friendship and Communication amongst Adolescents* Cambridge: Cambridge University Press.

Hirsch, F. 1977: *The Social Limits of Growth*. London: Routledge.

Hirschman, E. C. 1992: The consciousness of addiction: toward a general theory of compulsive consumption. *Journal of Consumer Research*, 19, September, 155–79.

Hoggart, R. 1994: A walk along the sceptred aisles. *The Independent*, 4 November, 21.

Huyssen, A. 1986: *After the Great Divide: Modernism, Mass Culture and Postmodernism*. London: Macmillan.

Jameson, F. 1991: *Postmodernism, or, the Cultural Logic of Late Capitalism*. London: Verso.

Jefferson, T. and Hall, S. 1976 (eds): *Resistance Through Rituals: Youth Subcultures in Post-war Britain*. London: Hutchinson.

Jhally, S. 1987: *The Codes of Advertising*. New York: Frances Pinter.

—— 1989: Advertising as religion: the dialectic of technology and magic. In I. Angus and S. Jhally (eds), *Cultural Politics in Contemporary America*, New York: Routledge, 23–47.

Keegan, R. 1992: Distilling the essence. *Ten-8*, 2: 3, 148–9.

Kellner, D. 1983: Critical theory, commodities and the consumer society. *Theory, Culture and Society*, 3, 66–84.

King, B. 1989: The burden of Max Headroom. *Screen*, 30: 1 and 2, 122–38.

Kohn, M. 1988a: The cash dispenser. In *The Face*, September, 180.

—— 1988b: The pink pound. *The Face*, September, 132.

Kopytoff, I. 1986: The cultural biography of things: commoditization as process. In Appadurai, A. (ed.), *The Social Life of Things*, Cambridge: Cambridge University Press.

Lamont, M. 1992: *Money, Morals and Manners: The Culture of the French and the American Upper-Middle Class*. Chicago: University of Chicago Press.

Lash, S. 1990: *The Sociology of Postmodernism*. London: Routledge.

—— and Urry, J. 1987: *The End of Organized Capitalism*. Cambridge: Polity.

—— 1994: *Economies of Signs and Spaces*. London: Sage.

Lee, M. 1993: *Consumer Culture Reborn: The Cultural Politics of Consumption*. London: Routledge.

Leiss, W. 1976: *The Limits of Satisfaction*. Toronto: Toronto University Press.

—— Kline, S. and Jhally, S. 1986: *Social Communication as Advertising: Persons, Products and Images of Well-being*. New York: Macmillan.

Lévi-Strauss, C. 196: *Totemism* trans. R. Needham. London: Merlin Press.

Lipsitz, G. 1994: We know what time it is: race, class and youth culture in the nineties. In A. Ross and T. Rose (eds), *Microphone Fiends: Youth Music and Youth Culture*, London and New York: Routledge, 17–28.

Low, G. Ching-Liang 1989: White skins/black masks: the pleasures and politics of imperialism. *New Formations*, 9, winter, 83–103.

Lunt, P. and Livingstone, S. 1992: *Mass Consumption and Personal Identity: Everyday Economic Experience*. Buckingham and Bristol: Open University Press.

Lury, A. 1994: Advertising: moving beyond the stereotypes. In R. Keat, N. Whiteley and N. Abercrombie (eds.), *The Authority of the Consumer*, London: Routledge, 91–102.

Lury, C. 1993: *Cultural Rights: Technology, Legality and Personality*. London: Routledge.

Lury, K. 1995: Inscribing and describing performers: youth, gender and media technologies. *Young: Nordic Journal of Youth Research*, 3: 1, February, 39–50.

Mac an Ghaill, M. 1989: *Young, Gifted and Black*. London: Routledge.

MacAlister Hall, M. 1992: A nation of shoppers. *Observer Magazine*, 13 December, 16–29.

Mack, J. and Lansley, S. 1985: *Poor Britain*. London: George Allen and Unwin.

Mackinnon, C. 1983: Feminism, Marxism, method and the state: an agenda for theory. In E. Abel and E. K. Abel (eds), *The Signs Reader: Women, Gender and Scholarship*, Chicago and London: University of Chicago Press, 227–57.

Macpherson, C. B. 1962: *The Political Theory of Possessive Individualism: Hobbes to Locke*. London: Clarendon Press.

Maffesoli, M. 1991: The ethic of aesthetics. *Theory, Culture and Society*, 8, 7–20.

—— 1993: *The Shadow of Dionysus: A Contribution to the Sociology of the Orgy*. Albany: State University of New York Press.

Marcuse, H. 1968: *One Dimensional Man*. London: Sphere.

Martin, B. 1981: *A Sociology of Contemporary Cultural Change*. Oxford: Blackwell.

Mathur, P. 1989: An eighties alphabet. *Blitz: A Magazine of the Nineties*, December, 56–67.

Mauss, M. 1954, reprinted 1990: *The Gift: The Form and Reason for Exchange in Archaic Societies*. London: Routledge.

McClintock, A. 1994: Soft-soaping empire: commodity racism and imperial advertising. In G. Robertson et al. (eds), *Travellers' Tales: Narratives of Home and Displacement*, London: Routledge, 131–55.

McCracken, G. 1988: *Culture and Consumption: New Approaches to the Symbolic Character of Consumer Goods and Activities*. Bloomington and Indianopolis: Indiana University Press.

McKendrick, N., Brewer, J. and Plumb, J. H. 1982: *The Birth of a Consumer Society*. London: Europa.

McRobbie, A. 1991: *Feminism and Youth Culture: From 'Jackie' to 'Just Seventeen'*. Basingstoke and London: Macmillan.

—— 1994: *Postmodernism and Popular Culture*. London: Routledge.

—— and Nava, M. (eds) 1984: *Gender and Generation*. London: Macmillan.

Mercer, K. 1994: *Welcome to the Jungle: New Positions in Black Cultural Studies*. New York and London: Routledge.

Miller, D. 1987: *Material Culture and Mass Consumption*. Oxford: Blackwell.

Moi, T. 1991: Appropriating Bourdieu: feminist theory and Pierre Bourdieu's sociology of culture. *New Literary History*, 22: 1017–49.

Mort, F. 1989: The writing on the wall. *New Statesman and Society*, 12 May, 40–1.

Mulhern, F. 1974: *The Moment of 'Scrutiny'*. London: New Left Books.

Mulvey, L. 1975: Visual pleasure and narrative cinema. *Screen*, 16: 3, 6–18.

Myers, K. 1986: *Understains: The Sense and Seduction of Advertising*. London: Pandora.

Naughton, J. 1992: Personal services. *Observer Magazine*, 13 December, 68–9.

Nava, M. 1992: *Changing Cultures: Feminism, Youth and Consumerism*. London: Sage.

Nicholson-Lord, D. 1992: In the consumer's cathedral. *The Independent on Sunday*, 13 December, 3.

Oakley, A. 1976: *Housewife*. Harmondsworth: Penguin.

Partington, A. 1991: Melodrama's gendered audience. In S. Franklin, C. Lury and J. Stacey (eds), *Off-Centre: Feminism and Cultural Studies*, London: Harper Collins, 49–68.

Pateman, C. 1988: *The Sexual Contract*. Cambridge: Polity.

Piore, M. J. and Sabel, C. 1984: *The Second Industrial Divide: Possibilities for Prosperity*, New York: Basic Books.

Polan, B. 1989: Buying and selling a new decade. *The Weekend Guardian*, 11 November, 9.

Pope, P. 1995: The premier league. *Melody Maker*, 14 January: 10–11.

Preteceille, E. and Terrail, J. -P. 1985: *Capitalism, Consumption and Needs*. Oxford: Basil Blackwell.

Radner, H. 1995: *Shopping Around: Feminist Culture and the Pursuit of Pleasure*. New York: Routledge.

Rai, A. 1994: An American Raj in Filmistan: images of Elvis in Indian films. *Screen*, 35: 1, 51–77.

Ramamurthy, A. 1991: *Black Markets: Images of Black People in Advertising and Packaging (1980–1990)*. London: Cornerhouse and Arts Council.

Redhead, S. 1990: *The End-of-the-Century Party: Youth and Pop Towards 2000*. Manchester and New York: Manchester University Press.

Rheingold, H. 1994: *The Virtual Community: Finding Connection in a Computerized World*. London: Secker and Warburg.

Rich, A. 1981: *Compulsory Heterosexuality and Lesbian Existence*. London: Onlywomen Press.

Ross, A. 1989: *No Respect: Intellectuals and Popular Culture*. New York and London: Routledge.

Sahlins, M. 1974: *Stone Age Economics*. London: Tavistock.

—— 1976: *Culture and Practical Reason*. Chicago: Chicago University Press.

Saunders, P. 1990: *A Nation of Home Owners*. London: Unwin Hyman.

—— and Harris, C. 1994: *Privatization and Popular Capitalism*. Milton Keynes: Open University Press.

Savage, J. and Frith, S. 1993: *Pearls and Swine: The Intellectuals and the Mass Media*. Manchester: Working Papers in Popular Cultural Studies, Manchester Institute for Popular Culture.

Savage, M. et al. 1992: *Property, Bureaucracy and Culture: Middle Class Formation in Contemporary Britain*. London: Routledge.

Scott, H. 1995: The new Chelsea girls. *Elle*, May, 27–8.

Sedgwick, E. Kosofsky 1994: *Tendencies*. London: Routledge.

Seger, L. 1990: *Creating Unforgettable Characters*. New York: Henry Holt.

Seltzer, M. 1993: Serial killers (1). *Differences: A Journal of Feminist Cultural Studies*, 5: 1, 92–128.

Simmons, P. 1994: Constructions of the green consumer: rhetoric, agency and organization. Unpublished paper.

Skeggs, B. (forthcoming): *Becoming Respectable: An Ethnography of White, Working-class Women*. London: Sage.

Stacey, J. 1994: *Stargazing: Hollywood Cinema and Female Spectatorship*. London and New York: Routledge.

Steedman, C. 1986: *Landscape for a Good Woman: A Story of Two Lives*. London: Virago.

Strathern, M. 1994: Foreword: the mirror of technology. In R. Silverstone and E. Hirsch (eds), *Consuming Technologies: Media and Information in Domestic Spaces*, London: Routledge, pp. vii–xiv.

Thomas, T. 1993: Slimming eats into new man's soul. *The European*, 12–18 November.

Thompson, J. 1990: *Ideology and Modern Culture: Critical Social Theory in the Era of Mass Communication*. Cambridge: Polity.

Thornton, S. 1994: Moral panic, the media and British rave culture. In A. Ross and T. Rose (eds), *Microphone Fiends: Youth Music and Youth Culture*, London and New York: Routledge, 176–92.

Tredre, R. 1993: Future chic. *The Observer Life*, 10 October, 14.

Turkle, S. 1986: *The Second Self: Computers and the Human Spirit*. New York: Simon and Schuster.

Tyler, C. -A. 1991: Boys will be girls: the politics of gay drag. In D. Fuss (ed.), *Inside/Out: Lesbian Theories, Gay Theories*, New York and London: Routledge, 32–70.

Veblen, T. 1925: *The Theory of the Leisure Class: An Economic Study of Institutions*. London: Allen and Unwin.

Warde, A. 1992: Notes on the relationship between production and consumption. In R. Burrows and C. Marsh (eds), *Consumption and Class: Divisions and Change*, London: Macmillan, 15–31.

—— 1994: Consumers, identity and belonging: reflections on some themes of Zygmunt Bauman. In R. Keat, N. Whiteley and N. Abercrombie (eds), *The Authority of the Consumer*, London: Routledge, 58–74.

Weber, M. 1930: *The Protestant Ethic and the Spirit of Capitalism*, trans. T. Parsons. London: Allen and Unwin.

Weedon, C. and Jordan, G. 1995: *Cultural Politics: Class, Gender, Race and the Postmodern World*. Oxford: Blackwell.

Wernick, A. 1991: *Promotional Culture: Advertising, Ideology and Symbolic Expression*. London: Sage.

West, C. 1990: The new cultural politics of difference. In R. Ferguson, M. Gever, Trinh T. Min-ha and C. West (eds), *Out There: Marginalization and Contemporary Cultures*, Boston: MIT/New Museum.

—— 1992: Nihilism in Black America. In G. Dent (ed.), *Black Popular Culture*, Seattle: Bay Press, 37–47.

Whiteley, N. 1994: High art and the high street: the 'commerce-and-culture' debate. In R. Keat, N. Whiteley and N. Abercrombie (eds), *The Authority of the Consumer*, London: Routledge, 119–38.

Williams, P. J. 1993: *The Alchemy of Race and Rights*. London: Virago.

Williams, R. 1974: *Television: Technology and Cultural Form*. London: Fontana.

—— 1980: Advertising: the magic system. In id., *Problems in Materialism and Culture*, London: Verso.

—— 1983: *Keywords: A Vocabulary of Culture and Society*. London: Fontana.

Williamson, J. 1986: Woman is an island: femininity and colonization. In

T. Modleski (ed.), *Studies in Entertainment: Critical Approaches to Mass Culture*, Bloomington and Indianopolis: Indiana University Press, 99–119.

Willis, P. 1982: The motor-bike and motor-bike culture. In B. Waites et al. (eds), *Popular Culture: Past and Present*, London: Croom Helm, 284–94.

—— 1990: *Common Culture*. Milton Keynes: Open University Press.

Willis, S. 1990: I want the Black one: is there a place for Afro-American culture in commodity culture? *New Formations*, 10, spring, 77–97.

—— 1993: Disney World: public use/private state. *The South Atlantic Quarterly*, 92: 1, 119–37.

Willmott, P. and Young, M. 1973: *The Symmetrical Family: A Study of Work and Leisure in the London Region*. London: Routledge and Kegan Paul.

Winship, J. 1983: '*Options* – For the way you want to live now', or a magazine for superwoman. *Theory, Culture and Society*, 1:3, 44–65.

—— 1987: *Inside Women's Magazines*. London: Pandora.

Winward, J. 1994: The organized consumer and consumer information co-operatives. In R. Keat et al. (eds), *The Authority of the Consumer*, London: Routledge, 75–90.

Wynne, D. and O'Connor, J. 1992: Tourists, hamburgers and street musicians. In R. Reichardt and G. Muskens (eds), *Post-Communism, the Market and the Arts*, Frankfurt: Peter Lang, 101–27.

York, P. 1980: *Style Wars*. London: Sidgwick and Jackson.

—— 1994: The dead beat of the street. *The Independent on Sunday*, 24 November, 24.

Young, M. and Wilmott, P. 1957: *Family and Kinship in East London*. London: Routledge and Kegan Paul.

Zukin, S. 1988: *Loftliving: Culture and Capital in Urban Change*. London: Radius.

—— 1991: *Landscapes of Power*. Berkeley and Los Angeles: University of California Press.

—— 1992: Postmodern urban landscapes: mapping culture and power. In S. Lash and J. Friedman (eds), *Modernity and Identity*, Oxford: Blackwell, 221–48.

Index